Robert Frost

SELECT POEMS

Robert Frost

SELECT POEMS

[Edited with Introduction, Author's Information, Complete Text, Summary and Analysis and Study Questions]

Aditya Nandwani
B.A. English (Hons), Delhi University;
M.A. (English), IGNOU; Print Journalism (English) YMCA

ANMOL PUBLICATIONS PVT. LTD.
NEW DELHI - 110 002 (INDIA)

ANMOL PUBLICATIONS PVT. LTD.

H.O.: 4374/4B, Ansari Road, Darya Ganj,
New Delhi-110 002 (India)
Ph.: 23278000, 23261597

B.O.: No. 1015, Ist Main Road, BSK IIIrd Stage
IIIrd Phase, IIIrd Block
Bangalore - 560 085 (India)
Visit us at: www.anmolpublications.com

Select Poems

First Published, 2009

PRINTED IN INDIA

Printed at Mehra Offset Press, Delhi.

Contents

Preface

Robert Frost (26 Mar. 1874-29 Jan. 1963), was one of the well known American poets and also regarded as one of the finest of rural New England's 20th century pastoral poets. Most of his works were made familiar in classrooms and lecture platforms. Interestingly, Frost was awarded the Pulitzer Prize four times. He always considered Nature and rural surroundings as a source for insights "from delight to wisdom", or as he also said: "Literature begins with geography."

This legendary poet was born in San Francisco, California. His father William Prescott Frost Jr. was a journalist and an ardent Democrat. Unfortunately, his father died when Frost was about eleven years old. To earn livelihood, Frost's Scottish mother, the former Isabelle Moody, started working as a schoolteacher. In 1892, Frost graduated from high school and attended Darthmouth College for a few months. Over the next ten years he held a number of jobs, such as textile mill and taught Latin at his mother's school in Methuen, Massachusetts. In 1894 the New York Independent published Frost's poem 'My Butterfly', earning him $15. He had also five poems privately printed.

Author

Chapter 1

Introduction

Robert (Lee) Frost (1874-1963)

American poet, one of the finest of rural New England's 20th century pastoral poets. Frost published his first books in Great Britain in the 1910s, but he soon became in his own country the most read and constantly anthologized poet, whose work was made familiar in classrooms and lecture platforms. Frost was awarded the Pulitzer Prize four times. Nature and Frost's rural surroundings were for him a source for insights "from delight to wisdom", or as he also said: "Literature begins with geography."

FIRE AND ICE

Some say the world will end in fire,
Some say in ice.
From what I've tasted of desire
I hold with those who favour fire.
But if it had to perish twice,
I think I know enough of hate
To say that for destruction ice
Is also great
And would suffice.

Robert Frost was born in San Francisco, California. His father William Prescott Frost Jr., a journalist and an ardent Democrat, died when Frost was about eleven years old. To support her family, Frost's Scottish mother, the former Isabelle Moody, resumed her career as a schoolteacher. They moved to Lawrence, Massachusetts, where Frost's paternal grandfather, William Prescott Frost, gave his grandson a good schooling.

After graduating from a high school in 1892, Frost attended Darthmouth College for a few months. Over the next ten years he held a number of jobs. Frost worked among others in a textile mill and taught Latin at his mother's school in Methuen, Massachusetts. In 1894 the New York Independent published Frost's poem 'My Butterfly', earning him $15. He had also five poems privately printed. While working as a teacher Frost continued to write and publish his poems in magazines. In 1895 he married a former schoolmate, Elinor Miriam White; they had six children.

From 1897 to 1899 Frost studied at Harvard, but left without receiving a degree due family problems and poor health. He moved to Derry, New Hampshire, working there as a cobbler, farmer, and teacher at Pinkerton Academy - he held the post for five years - and at the state normal school in Plymouth. When he sent his poems to The Atlantic Monthly they were returned with this note: "We regret that The Atlantic has no place for your vigorous verse."

In 1912 Frost sold the Derry farm and took his wife and four young children to England. There he published his first collection of poems, A BOY'S WILL, at the age of 39. It was followed by NORTH BOSTON (1914), which gained international reputation. The collection contains some of Frost's best-known poems: 'Mending Wall,' 'The Death of the Hired Man,' 'Home Burial,' 'A Servant to Servants,' 'After Apple-Picking,' and 'The Wood-Pile.' The poems, written with blank verse or looser free verse of dialogue, were drawn from his own life, recurrent losses, everyday tasks, and his loneliness. "This is one of the most revolutionary books of modern times," wrote the British poet and essayist Edward Thomas (1878-1917), Frost's friend, in his review in the Daily News, "but one of the quietest and least aggressive. It speaks, and it is poetry."

While in England Frost became acquainted with the F.S. Flint, Edward Thomas, and Ezra Pound, who called Frost's poems "modern georgics", and the Georgian Poets Wilfred Gibson and Lascelles Abercrombie. In 1915 he returned to the US in 1915 with his family and bought a farm near Franconia,

New Hampshire. When the editor of The Atlantic Monthly asked for poems, he gave the very ones that had previously been rejected. Frost taught later at Amherst College (1916-38) and Michigan universities. In 1916 he was made a member of the National Institute of Arts and Letters. On the same year appeared his third collection of verse, MOUNTAIN INTERVAL, which contained such poems as 'The Road Not Taken,' 'The Oven Bird,' 'Birches,' and 'The Hill Wife.'

Frost's poems show deep appreciation of natural world and sensibility about the human aspirations. His images - woods, stars, houses, brooks - are usually taken from everyday life. With his down-to-earth approach to his subjects, readers found it is easy to follow the poet into deeper truths, without being burdened with pedantry. Often Frost used the rhythms and vocabulary of ordinary speech or even the looser free verse of dialogue.

In 1920 Frost purchased a farm in South Shaftsbury, Vermont, near Middlebury College, where he cofounded the Bread Loaf School and Conference of English. His wife died in 1938 and he lost four of his children. Two of his daughters suffered mental breakdowns, and his son Carol, a frustrated poet and farmer, committed suicide in 1940 with a deer hunter rifle. Frost also suffered from depression and the continual self-doubt led him to cling to the desire to be awarded the Nobel Prize for literature. He had been told in 1950, that he was among candidates nominated by the Swedish committee.

After the death of his wife, Frost became strongly attracted to Kathleen (Kay) Morrison, married to Theodore Morrison. Frost employed her from 1938 as his secretary and adviser, but she probably became also his lover. Frost also composed for her one of his finest love poems, 'A Witness Tree.' The only son of the Morrisons was killed in a car accident in 1955.

With his future biographer, Lawrance Thompson, Frost travelled in 1957 to England, and to Israel and Greece in 1961. He participated in the inauguration of President John Kennedy in 1961 by reciting two of his poems. When the sun and the wind prevented him from reading his new poem, 'The Preface', Frost recited his old poem, 'The Gift Outright', from memory.

In 1962 Frost travelled in the Soviet Union as a member of a goodwill group. He had a long talk with Premier Nikita Khrushchev, whom he described admiringly as "no fathead"; as smart, big and "not a coward." Frost also reported that Khrushchev had said the United States was "too liberal to fight," it caused a considerable stir in Washington. Among the honors and rewards Frost received were tributes from the U.S.

Senate (1950), the American Academy of Poets (1953), New York University (1956), the Huntington Hartford Foundation (1958), the Congressional Gold Medal (1962), the Edward MacDowell Medal (1962). In 1930 he was elected to the American Academy of Arts and Letters, Amherst College appointed him Saimpson Lecturer for Life (1949), and in 1958 he was made poetry consultant for the Library of Congress.

At the time of his death on January 29, 1963, Frost was considered a kind of unofficial poet laureate of the US. "I would have written of me on my stone: I had a lover's quarrel with the world," Frost once said. Frost depicted the fields and farms of his surroundings, observing the details of rural life, which hide universal meaning. A Masque of Reason (1945) and A Masque of Mercy (1947), which used the Old Testament characters of Job and Jonah, examined the complex relationship between man and God. However, Frost developed a suspicion for religious mysticism. His half humorous view of the world produced such remarks as "I never take my side in a quarrel", or "I'm never serious except when I'm fooling."

Although Frost's works were generally praised, the lack of seriousness concerning social and economic problems of the 1930s, and his hostility toward the policies of the New Deal annoyed some more socially orientated critics. "Political freedom is nothing to me. I bestow it right and left," Frost stated in 'The Figure a Poem Makes', first published in 1939 as the preface to an edition of his Collected Poems. Later biographers have created a complex and contradictory portrait of the poet. In Lawrance Thompson's three-volume official biography (1966-1976) Frost was presented as a misanthrope, anti-intellectual, cruel, and angry man, but in Jay Parini's work (1999) he was again viewed with sympathy: "He was a loner who liked company; a poet of isolation who sought a mass audience; a rebel who sought to fit in. Although a family man to the core, he frequently felt alienated from his wife and children and withdrew into reveries. While preferring to stay at home, he traveled more than any poet of his generation to give lectures and readings, even though he remained terrified of public speaking to the end." Frost's personal notebooks, characterized as his "intellectual autobiography", were published in 2007. Because the handwriting of the poet was difficult to read - the notebooks were written for his own personal use - a dispute soon arose over the exact wording.

Chapter 2

Biography

Robert Frost (1874-1963), four-time Pulitzer Prize winning American poet, teacher and lecturer wrote many popular and oft-quoted poems including "After Apple-Picking", "The Road Not Taken", "Home Burial" and "Mending Wall";

I let my neighbour know beyond the hill;
And on a day we meet to walk the line
And set the wall between us once again.
We keep the wall between us as we go.
To each the boulders that have fallen to each.
And some are loaves and some so nearly balls
We have to use a spell to make them balance:
"Stay where you are until our backs are turned!"
We wear our fingers rough with handling them.
Oh, just another kind of out-door game,
One on a side. It comes to little more:
There where it is we do not need the wall:
He is all pine and I am apple orchard.
My apple trees will never get across
And eat the cones under his pines, I tell him.
He only says, "Good fences make good neighbours."

At times bittersweet, sometimes ironic, or simply marveling at his surroundings, one can also see autobiographical details in Frost's works; he suffered devastating losses in his life including the untimely deaths of his sister, two of his children and his wife. He knew the soul's depths of psychic despair but was also capable of delighting in birch trees 'loaded with ice a sunny winter morning'. While memorialising the rural landscape, vernacular, culture and people of New England in his traditional verse style, his poems also transcend the boundaries of time and place with metaphysical significance and modern exploration of human nature in all her beauty and contradictions. Though not without his critics, millions of readers the world over have found comfort and profound meaning in his poetry and he has influenced numerous other authors, poets, musicians, and playwrights into the 21st Century.

Robert Lee Frost (named after Southern General Robert E. Lee) was born on 26 March 1874 in San Francisco, California to Isabelle Moodie (1844-1900) teacher, and William Prescott Frost Jr. (1850-1885), teacher and journalist. San Francisco was a lively city full of citizens of Pioneering spirit, including Will who had ventured there from New Hampshire to seek his fortune as a journalist.

He also started gambling and drinking, habits which left his family in dire financial straits when he died in 1885 after contracting tuberculosis. Honouring his last wishes to be buried in Lawrence, Massachusetts where he was born, Isabelle, Robert and his sister Jeanie Florence (1876-1929) made the long train journey across the country to the New England town. Isabelle took up teaching again to support her children.

With both parents as teachers, young Robert was early on exposed to the world of books and reading, studying such works as those by William Shakespeare and poets Robert Burns and William Wordsworth. He also formed a life-long love of nature, the great outdoors and rural countryside. After enrolling in Lawrence High School he was soon writing his own poems including "La Noche Triste" (1890) which was published in the school's paper. He excelled in many subjects including history, botany, Latin and Greek, and played football, graduating at the head of his class.

In 1892 he entered Dartmouth, the Ivy League College in Hanover, New Hampshire, but soon became disenchanted with the atmosphere of campus life. He then took on a series of jobs including teaching and working in a mill, all the while continuing to write poetry.

Frost got his first break as a poet in 1894 when the New

York magazine Independent published "My Butterfly: An Elegy" for a stipend of $15. A year later a wish he had had for some time came true; on 19 December 1895 he married Elinor Miriam White (1872-1938), his co-valedictorian and sweetheart from school. They had gone separate ways upon graduation to attend college, and while Frost had left early, Elinor wanted to wait until she was finished before getting married. They would have six children together; sons Elliott (b.1896-1900) and Carol (1902-1940) and daughters Lesley (b.1899), Irma (b.1903), Marjorie (b.1905-1934), and Elinor Bettina (1907-1907).

The newlyweds continued to teach, which Frost always enjoyed, but the demanding schedule interfered with his writing. In 1897 he entered Harvard University in Cambridge, Massachusetts, though illness caused him to leave in 1899 before finishing his degree. Despite that, it was one of many institutions that would award him an honorary degree later on. The next ten years, the 'Derry years', were trying times for Frost with a growing family to support. In 1900 they moved to a farm bought by his paternal grandfather in Derry, New Hampshire to try poultry farming.

The same year his son Elliot died of cholera. Frost suffered greatly from grief and guilt, and compounding this was the loss of his mother to cancer the same year. In 1907 Elinor Bettina died just one day after birth. But the farm was a peaceful and secluded setting and Frost enjoyed farming, tending to his orchard trees, chickens and various other chores. This period inspired such poems as "The Mending Wall" (written in England in 1913) and "Hyla Brook" (1906). The house built in the typical New England clapboard style is now a restored State Historical Landmark.

But it was soon time for a change. In 1911 he sold the farm and the Frosts set sail for England. Elinor was enthusiastic about traveling, even with four children, and they moved into a cottage in Beaconsfield, just outside of London. Then finally it happened; after writing poetry and trying to get noticed by publishers for over twenty years, Frost's first collection of poetry A Boy's Will was published in England in 1913 by a small London printer, David Nutt. American publisher Henry

Holt printed it in 1915. Frost's work was well-received and fellow poets Edward Thomas and Ezra Pound became friends, supporters, and helped promote his work. North of Boston (1914) followed. When World War I started the Frosts were back in New Hampshire, settling at their newly bought farm in Franconia in 1915. A year later Robert began teaching English at Amherst College. Mountain Interval was published in 1916 which contained many poems written at Franconia. He was also starting lecture tours for his ever-growing audience of avid readers.

In 1920, Frost bought 'Stone House' (now a museum) in South Shaftsbury, Vermont. There he wrote many of the poems contained in his fourth collection of poetry New Hampshire (1923) which won him the Pulitzer Prize for Poetry in 1923. It includes "Stopping By Woods On A Snowy Evening";

The woods are lovely, dark and deep.
But I have promises to keep,
And miles to go before I sleep,
And miles to go before I sleep.

While he also farmed on the idyllic property with its breathtaking views of mountains and valleys, another project Frost undertook was the founding of the Bread Loaf School of English at Middlebury College in Ripton, Vermont. After his son Carol married Lillian LaBatt (1905-1995) and his grandson Prescott arrived, he gave them Stone House to live in where Carol planted his thousand apple trees. Frost bought a second farm in Shaftsbury, "The Gulley". At the height of his career, his next collection of poems West-running Brook (1928) was published just one year before another great loss of a loved one hit him; his sister Jeanie died.

By now Frost was a popular speaker and had a demanding schedule of which Elinor, acting as his secretary, organised for him, so he spent a fair bit of time traveling, though still maintaining an impressive output of poetry. He was awarded the Pulitzer Prize for Poetry a second time in 1931 for his Collected Poems (1930), and also in 1937 for A Further Range (1936), and yet again in 1943 for his collection A Witness Tree (1942). All his children were married and he spent much time with them and his grandchildren, though it was not long before the heavy blows of loss struck again; his beloved daughter Marjorie died in 1934 after the birth of her first child, and in 1938 Elinor died of a heart attack. In 1940 Carol committed suicide.

Leaving the Stone House and The Gulley behind, in 1939 Frost bought the Homer Noble Farm in Ripton, Vermont for his summer residence, located near the Bread Loaf School. He occupied the cabin on the property 'Than smoke and mist who better could appraise, The kindred spirit of an inner haze?' ("A Cabin in the Clearing") while his friends and colleagues the Morrisons stayed in the main house. Collected Poems (1939) was followed by A Masque of Reason (play, 1945), Steeple Bush (1947), A Masque of Mercy (play, 1947), Complete Poems (1949), and In the Clearing (1962). At the Inauguration of American President John F. Kennedy on 20 January 1961, Frost recited his poem "The Gift Outright" (1942).

Robert Frost died on the 29th of January 1963 in Boston, Massachusetts. 'Safe!, Now let the night be dark for all of me. Let the night be too dark for me to see, Into the future. Let what will be, be.' ("Acceptance") He lies buried in the family plot in the Old Bennington Cemetery behind the Old First Congregational Church near Shaftsbury, Vermont. His gravestone reads 'I Had A Lover's Quarrel With The World'.

Just nine months after Frost's death, Kennedy gave a speech at Amherst College, singing Frosts' praises and speaking on the importance of the Arts in America. Later he said;

"The death of Robert Frost leaves a vacancy in the American spirit.His death impoverishes us all; but he has bequeathed his Nation a body of imperishable verse from which Americans will forever gain joy and understanding."

Life and Career

Frost was born in San Francisco, where he spent his first eleven years. After the death of his father, a journalist, he moved with his mother and sister to eastern Massachusetts near his paternal grandparents. He wrote his first poems while a student at Lawrence High School, from which he graduated as co-valedictorian with the woman he was to marry, Elinor Miriam White. He entered Dartmouth College in the fall of 1892 but stayed for less than a term, returning home to teach school and to work at various jobs, including factory-hand and newspaperman.

In 1894 he sold his first poem, 'My Butterfly: An Elegy', to a New York magazine, The Independent. That same year, unable to persuade Elinor to marry him (she wanted to finish college first), he headed south on a reckless journey into Virginia's Dismal Swamp. After emerging unscathed he came home to Lawrence where he and Elinor were married in December 1895.

Both husband and wife taught school for a time, then in 1897 Frost entered Harvard College as a special student, remaining there just short of two years. He performed well at Harvard, but his health was uncertain and he rejoined his wife in Lawrence, where she was about to bear a second child. In October of 1900 he settled with his family on a farm just over the Massachusetts line in New Hampshire, purchased for him by his grandfather. There, over the next nine years, he wrote many of the poems that would make up his first published volumes. But his attempt at poultry farming was none too successful, and by 1906 he had begun teaching English at Pinkerton Academy, a secondary school in New Hampshire.

That same year two of his most accomplished early poems, 'The Tuft of Flowers' and 'The Trial by Existence', were published. Meanwhile he and Elinor produced six children, two of whom died in infancy. After a year spent teaching at the State Normal School in Plymouth, New Hampshire, he sold the Derry farm and in the fall of 1912 sailed with his family from Boston to Glasgow, then settled outside London in Beaconsfield.

Within two months of his arrival in England, Frost placed his first book of poems, A Boy's Will (1913) with a small London publisher, David Nutt. He also made acquaintances in the literary world, such as the poet F. S. Flint, who introduced him to Ezra Pound, who in turn reviewed both A

Boy's Will and North of Boston, which followed it the next year. He became friends with members of the Georgian school of poets—particularly with Wilfred Gibson and Lascelles Abercrombie—and in 1914, on their urgings, he moved to Gloucestershire to be nearer them and to experience English country living. The most important friend he made in England was Edward Thomas, whom Frost encouraged to write poetry and who wrote sharply intelligent reviews of Frost's first two books.

While many reviewers were content to speak of the American poet's 'simplicity' and artlessness, Thomas recognized the originality and success of Frost's experiments with the cadences of vernacular speech—with what Frost called 'the sound of sense'. His best early poems, such as 'Mowin,' 'Mending Wall,' and 'Home Burial,' were composed under the assumption that, in Frost's formulation from one of his letters, 'the ear does it. The ear is the only true writer and the only true reader.' The best part of a poet's work, he insisted, was to be found in the sentence-sounds poems made, as of people talking. Like Wordsworth (as Edward Thomas pointed out in one of his reviews of North of Boston), Frost boldly employed 'ordinary' words and cadences ('I have sunk to a diction even Wordsworth kept above', he said in another letter) yet contrived to throw over them—in Wordsworth's formulation from his preface to the Lyrical Ballads—'a certain colouring of imagination'.

England's entry into the First World War hastened Frost's return to America early in 1915. By the time he landed in New York City, his American publisher, Henry Holt, had brought out North of Boston (Holt would continue to publish Frost throughout his life). He was fêted by editors and critics in the literary worlds of both New York and Boston, and he continued shrewdly to publicize himself, providing anthologists and interviewers with a vocabulary to describe his poetic aims. A third volume of verse, Mountain Interval, published in 1916 but still drawing on poems he had written in England and before, showed no falling off from his previous standard. In fact such poems as 'The Road Not Taken,' 'An

Old Man's Winter Night,' 'The Oven Bird,' 'Birches,' 'Putting in the Seed,' and 'Out, Out—' were among the best he had written or was to write. Like the somewhat late-coming and even drab oven bird of his poem, Frost knew in 'singing not to sing,' and a century after the ecstatic flights of romantic poets like Keats and Shelley, Frost's bird remained earthbound (the oven bird, in fact, builds its nests on the ground) and, like the poet who created him, sang about the things of this world.

Soon after he re-established himself in America, Frost purchased a farm in Franconia, New Hampshire (he would purchase a number of farms over the course of his life) and then, at the behest of President Alexander Meiklejohn, joined the faculty of Amherst College in Massachusetts. Frost was later to teach at the University of Michigan and at Dartmouth College, but his relationship to Amherst (sometimes a troubled one) was the most significant educational alliance he formed. Meanwhile he had begun the practice of reading his poems aloud— rather, 'saying' them, as he liked to put it public gatherings.

These occasions, which continued throughout his life, were often intensive ones in which he would read, comment on, and reflect largely about his poems and about the world in general. Particularly at colleges and universities he commanded the ears and often hearts of generations of students, and he received so many honorary degrees from the academy that he eventually had the hoods made into a quilt.

Frost won the first of four Pulitzer Prizes in 1924 for his fourth book, New Hampshire, and followed it with West-Running Brook (1928) and A Further Range (1936), which also won a Pulitzer. Yet the latter volume occasioned, from critics on the left, the first really harsh criticism Frost's poetry had received. One of those critics, Rolfe Humphries, complained in New Masses (his review was titled 'A Further Shrinking') that Frost no longer showed either a dramatic or a sympathetic attitude toward his New England characters; that in setting himself against systematic political and social reforms (especially, Franklin Roosevelt's New Deal), he had become querulous and sarcastic, all too personally present in his quarrel with the way things were going. It is true that, for one reason or another, Frost no longer wrote poems like the dramatic monologues and dialogues in North Of Boston, and that poems from A Further Range, such as 'Two Tramps in Mud Time' or 'Provide, Provide', were argumentative and at times didactic in their thrust.

But he had become expert at composing poems that had affinities with light verse and that consisted of a pointed, witty treatment of issues and ideas. Such a treatment purchased its surface brilliance at the cost of deeper sympathies and explorations.

Those deeper concerns were to make themselves felt once again, however, in what was to be Frost's last truly significant book of verse, A Witness Tree (1942). During the 1930s, as he became ever more honoured and revered, Frost endured a terrible series of family disasters. In 1934 his youngest and best-loved child, Marjorie, died a slow death from the puerperal fever contracted after giving birth to her first child; in 1938 his wife Elinor died suddenly of a heart attack, then, when he seemed to be pulling things together once more, his son Carol committed suicide in 1940.

Another daughter, Irma, suffered—as did Frost's sister Jeannie—from mental disorders and was finally institutionalized. A number of poems in A Witness Tree undoubtedly derived their dark tone from the family tragedies suffered over the decade; but at any rate lyrics such as 'The Silken Tent', 'I Could Give All to Time', 'Never Again Would Birds' Song Be the Same', and 'The Most of It' stand in the top rank of Frost's work (he himself thought that some of his best poetry was contained in this book). In words from his prose essay 'The Figure a Poem Makes', they exhibit both 'how a poem can have wildness and at the same time a subject that shall be fulfilled.'

Except for the publishing of a major poem, 'Directive', in his 1947 volume, Steeple Bush, Frost's poetry after the Second World War was mainly occasional, a relaxation from earlier intensities. He made a triumphant return to England in 1957 to receive honorary degrees from Oxford and Cambridge; he expended his efforts to have Pound released from St Elizabeth's Hospital; and under the Kennedy administration he made a somewhat less-than-satisfactory visit to Russia, in which he attempted, in conversation with Premier Khrushchev, to mediate between the superpowers. His last reading was given to a large audience in Boston in December 1962; the following day he went into hospital for a prostate operation and suffered a severe heart attack while convalescing, then a series of embolisms, one of which killed him in January of 1963.

Frost once wrote about Edwin Arlington Robinson that 'his life was a revel in the felicities of language', and surely the claim could be made, even more appropriately, of Frost himself. While standing apart from the modernist work of his famous contemporaries—Eliot, Pound, Stevens—his own poetry, in its complication of tone and its delicate balancing of gravity and wit ('I am never more serious than when joking,' he said more than once), asks for constant vigilance on the reader's part: a listening ear for the special postures of speech and the dramatic effects of silences. Like the works of his great predecessor, Emerson, Frost's poetry has never been sufficiently appreciated in England, the country which gave him his start.

This neglect may be in part a reaction to the rather promiscuous admiration he inspired from so many different sorts of American readers (and non-readers), many of whom would have no time for Eliot or Stevens. But if, for some Americans, the homely nature of Frost's materials—cows, apples, and snow-covered woods—predisposes them to like his poetry, such readers are no more narrow than the 'cosmopolitan' ones who accept mythical allusions in Eliot or Pound but disdain stone walls as a fit vehicle for serious poetry. Frost's own formulation to an American friend in 1914 is helpful in thinking about his achievement: he told the friend, Sidney Cox, that the true poet's pleasure lay in making 'his own words as he goes' rather than depending upon words whose meanings were fixed: 'We write of things we see and we write in accents we hear. Thus we gather both our material and our technique with the imagination from life; and our technique becomes as much material as material itself.' It was this principle that Pound saluted in Frost when, in his review of North of Boston, he remarked conclusively: 'I know more of farm life than I did before I had read his poems. That means I know more of "Life".'

Frost, Robert (26 Mar. 1874-29 Jan. 1963), poet, was born Robert Lee Frost in San Francisco to Isabelle Moodie, of Scottish birth, and William Prescott Frost, Jr., a descendant of a Devonshire Frost who had sailed to New Hampshire in 1634. The father was a former teacher turned newspaper man, a hard drinker, a gambler, and a harsh disciplinarian, who fought to succeed in politics for as long as his health allowed. In the wake of his death (as a consumptive) in his thirty-sixth year, his impoverished widow, with the help of funds from her father-in-law, moved east.

She resumed her teaching career in the fall of 1885 in Salem, New Hampshire, where Robert and his younger sister were enrolled in the fifth-grade class. Soon he was playing baseball, trapping animals, climbing birches. And his mother, who had filled his early years with Shakespeare, Bible stories, and myths, was reading aloud from Tom Brown's School Days, Burns, Ralph Waldo Emerson, Wordsworth, and Percy's Reliques. Before long he was memorizing poetry and reading books on his own.

Frost's high school years in Lawrence, Massachusetts, marked a further change. Greek and Latin delighted him; at the end of the first year he was head of his class. An older student, Carl Burell, introduced him to botany and astronomy. More important, Frost became a promising writer: his poem "La Noche Triste," inspired by William H. Prescott's History of the Conquest of Mexico (1843), appeared in the April 1890 issue of the high school Bulletin, of which he was soon made editor. He joined the debating society, played on the football team, and again was head of his class. At the beginning of his senior year he fell in love with Elinor White, who had also published poetry in the Bulletin. On commencement day (1892) they shared valedictory honors and, before summer ended, pledged themselves to each other in a secret ritual.

In the fall they went their separate ways: Elinor to St. Lawrence University in Canton, New York, Frost to Dartmouth on a scholarship and with his grandfather's aid. Though he relished his courses in Latin and Greek and his own wide reading of English verse, in particular Francis Turner Palgrave's Golden Treasury of the Best Songs and Lyrical Poems in the English Language, the campus life dismayed him. Isolated and restless, he quit at the end of December, being needed, he said, to take over his mother's unruly eighth-grade class. He was nursing the hope that Elinor might give up school to marry him, but when she returned in April his attempts to persuade her failed.

After working for months as a trimmer of lamps in a woolen mill in Lawrence, Frost turned to teaching in grade school, while also writing poetry. At the end of the term, startling news greeted him: the New York Independent had accepted "My Butterfly: An Elegy," with a stipend of $15. His first professionally published poem would appear in November—he could earn his living as a writer! Once again he implored Elinor to marry him; once again she refused. Convinced there was now another suitor, he engaged a printer to make two leather-bound, gold-stamped copies of Twilight, each containing five of his poems.

He took the train to Canton, knocked at her door, and handed her his gift. The inimically cool reception hurled him into despair. Pained and distraught, he destroyed his copy and went home. Still distraught, on 6 November he set out for the Dismal Swamp in Virginia—to throw his life away? punish Elinor? make her relent? On 30 November 1894, frightened and worn, he was back in Lawrence. Before long he became a reporter, then returned to teaching. Elinor, having finished college, also taught in his mother's private school. Then at long last, on 19 December 1895, they were married by a Swedenborgian pastor. Nine months later, Elliot, a son, was born.

They both kept working as teachers, and Frost kept publishing poems. In the fall of 1897, thanks to his grandfather's loan, Frost, at age twenty-three, entered Harvard in the hope of becoming a high school teacher of Latin and Greek. Certain courses proved meaningful, most of all in the classics and geology, but also in philosophy with Hugo Münsterberg, who assigned Psychology: Briefer Course by William James, Frost's "greatest inspiration," then absent on leave. In March 1899, however, severe chest and stomach pains combined with worries about his ailing mother and pregnant wife forced him to leave Harvard.

Medical warnings—the threat of tuberculosis—drove Frost from the indoor life of teaching. In May 1900, with his grandfather's help, he rented a poultry farm in Methuen. Two months later, Elliot, the Frosts' three-year-old, became gravely ill with cholera infantum; on 8 July he died. Frost flailed himself for not having summoned a doctor in time, believing that God was punishing him by taking his child away. Elinor, silent for days, at last let fly at him for his "self-centered senselessness" in believing that any such thing as a god's benevolent concern for human affairs could exist; life was hateful and the world evil, but with a fourteen-month-old daughter,

Lesley, to care for, they would have to go on. And when their landlord ordered them to leave by fall, Elinor took matters in hand. She persuaded Grandfather Frost to buy for their use the thirty-acre farm that her mother had found in Derry, New Hampshire, and to arrange, in addition, for Carl Burell, Frost's high school friend, to move in to help with the chores.

The "Derry Years" (1900-1911) were especially creative ones, bringing forth—complete or in draft—nearly all of A Boy's Will (1913), much, if not most, of North of Boston (1914), many poems of Mountain Interval (1916), as well as some that appeared in each of his later books. Yet at times in the first two years he was deeply depressed: in November 1900 his mother died; in July 1901, his other firm supporter, Grandfather Frost. But the latter's will bequeathed to his grandson an immediate annuity of $500 and after ten years an annuity of $800 and the deed to the Derry property.

Frost continued to write at night: poems and articles for poultry journals. He enjoyed working the farm by day and learning about the countryside and the lives of its people. By 1906, though fairly well off compared to his neighbors, yet with four children under seven, he was pressed for money. With the aid of a pastor-friend and a school trustee who admired his poems, he obtained a position at the nearby Pinkerton Academy, which he held with outstanding success. A pedagogic original, he introduced a conversational classroom style.

He directed students in plays he adapted from Marlowe, Milton, Sheridan, and Yeats. He revised the English curriculum. And besides teaching seven classes a day, he helped with athletics, the student paper, and the debating team. At the end of five years, utterly exhausted, he resigned.

In the fall of 1911 he was teaching again, part time in the Plymouth, New Hampshire, Normal School. But in December he announced to his editor-friend at the Independent, Susan Ward, that "the long deferred forward movement you have been living in wait for is to begin next year." In July 1912 he started making plans for a radical change of scene. When he suggested England to Elinor as "the place to be poor and to write poems, 'Yes,' she cried, 'let's go over and live under thatch.' "

On 2 September 1912 the Frosts arrived in London. They stayed there briefly before moving into "The Bungalow" in Beaconsfield, where they would live for eighteen months. Elinor, charmed by the "dear little cottage" and its long grassy yard, strolled the countryside with the children; Frost traveled at will to London—forty minutes by train—roaming the streets, the bookshops, "everywhere." Before long he was finishing the manuscript of A Boy's Will that he had brought to England and adding a few new poems. In October the book was accepted by David Nutt for publication the following March.

Through the next few months Frost was seized by a powerful surge of creativity, producing twelve or more lengthy poems, each strikingly different from the brooding narratives of A Boy's Will: dialog-narratives in a style of "living" speech new to the language, exploring the inward lives of ordinary people in the New England countryside. By April 1913, most of (if not all) the poems that would constitute North of Boston had been written.

At the January 1913 opening of Monro's Poetry Bookshop Frost was urged by the poet Frank Flint to call on Ezra Pound (whom he had never heard of), a reviewer for various journals. Frost waited until 13 March, about a week before A Boy's Will was to appear. At Pound's insistence, they walked to the publisher's office for a copy. On their return, Pound started reading at once, then told his guest to "run along home" so he could write his review for Poetry, a new American monthly. In the next few weeks, thanks to Pound and Flint, Frost came to meet some of the best-known writers then living in England, including Yeats, H.D. (Hilda Doolittle), Richard Aldington, and Ford Madox Ford.

A Boy's Will, finally issued on 1 April 1913, elicited favorable but qualified reviews. Chronicling the growth of a youth from self-centered idealism to maturity and acceptance of loss, the thirty-two lyrics offered few hints of the masterful volumes to come, except for those in "Mowing," "Storm Fear," and scattered passages.

Yeats pronounced the poetry "the best written in America for some time," leading Elinor to "hope"—in vain—that "he would say so publicly." Happily, in the fall, on his return from a family vacation in Scotland, Frost was greeted by two extraordinary tributes in the Nation and the Chicago Dial and a superb review in the Academy.

During the next few months, Frost came to know the writers Robert Bridges, Walter de la Mare, W. H. Davies, and Ralph Hodgson; the Georgian poets Rupert Brooke, Wilfred Gibson, Lascelles Abercrombie; and the essayist and poet Edward Thomas, who would become his bosom friend. With Flint and T. E. Hulme he discussed poetics, having spoken in letters to his Pinkerton friends John Bartlett and Sidney Cox of "the sounds of sense with all their irregularity of accent across the regular beat of the metre" and "the sentence sound

[that] often says more than the words." He also wrote that he wanted not "a success with the critical few" but "to get outside to the general reader who buys books by the thousands."

In April, badly strained for funds, Frost moved his family 100 miles northwest of London to an ancient cottage, not far from Abercrombie's and Gibson's, in the rolling Gloucestershire farmland near Dymock. On 15 May North of Boston appeared, to be hailed in June by important reviews, particularly those by Abercrombie ("there will never be," said Frost, "any other just like it"), Ford Madox Ford ("an achievement much finer than Whitman's"), Richard Aldington ("it would be very difficult to overpraise it"), and Edward Thomas ("Only at the end of the best pieces, such as 'The Death of the Hired Man,' 'Home Burial,' 'The Black Cottage,' and 'The Wood-pile,' do we realise that they are masterpieces of a deep and mysterious tenderness").

By August, Frost's reputation as a leading poet had been firmly established in England, and Henry Holt of New York had agreed to publish his books in America. By the end of 1914, however, financial need forced him to leave Britain.

When Frost and his family returned to the United States in February, he was hailed as a leading voice of the "new poetry" movement. Holt's editor introduced him to the staff of the New Republic, which had just published a favorable review of North of Boston, and Tufts College invited him to be its Phi Beta Kappa poet. Before the year's end, he had met with Edwin Arlington Robinson, William Dean Howells, Louis Untermeyer (who would become his intimate friend), Ellery Sedgwick of the Atlantic Monthly, and other literary figures.

In the following year he was made Phi Beta Kappa poet at Harvard and elected to the National Institute of Arts and Letters. Mountain Interval, which appeared in November 1916, offered readers some of his finest poems, such as "Birches," "Out, Out—," "The Hill Wife," and "An Old Man's Winter Night."

Frost's move to Amherst in 1917 launched him on the twofold career he would lead for the rest of his life: teaching whatever "subjects" he pleased at a congenial college

(Amherst, 1917-1963, with interruptions; the University of Michigan, 1921-1923, 1925-1926; Harvard, 1939-1943; Dartmouth, 1943-1949) and "barding around," his term for "saying" poems in a conversational performance.

Audiences flocked to listen to the "gentle farmer-poet" whose platform manner concealed the ever-troubled, agitated private man who sought through each of his poems "a momentary stay against confusion." In the great short lyrics of New Hampshire (1923) and West-Running Brook (1928)—such as "Fire and Ice," "Stopping by Woods on a Snowy Evening," and the title poem of the latter book—a bleak outlook on life persuasively emerges from the combination of dramatic tension and nature imagery freighted with ambiguity. Only the will to create form, the poet in effect says, can stave off the nothingness that confronts us as mortal beings.

In 1930 Frost won a second Pulitzer Prize for Collected Poems—the first had been won by New Hampshire—and in the next few years, other prizes and honors, including the Charles Eliot Norton Professorship of Poetry at Harvard. However, when A Further Range appeared in 1936, several influential leftist critics, unaware that Frost had "twice been approached" by the New Masses "to be their proletarian poet," attacked him for his conservative political views, ignoring the bitter meanings in "Provide, Provide" and such master poems as "Desert Places," "Design," and "Neither Out Far nor In Deep." A Further Range earned him a third Pulitzer Prize in May 1937.

Ten months later, on 26 March 1938, Elinor died and his world collapsed. Four years before, in the wake of their daughter Marjorie's death, they had helped each other bear the grief. Alone now, wracked in misery and guilty over his sometimes insensitive behaviour toward Elinor, he hoped to find calm through his children, but Lesley's ragings only deepened his pain. For some time he continued to teach, then resigned his position, sold his Amherst house, and returned to his farm. In July Theodore Morrison invited him to speak at the Breadloaf Writers' Conference in August. Frost's lectures enthralled his listeners, but at times his erratic public behaviour drew worried attention. To the great relief of his friends, Kathleen Morrison, the director's wife, stepped in to offer him help with his affairs. He accepted at once and made her his official secretary-manager.

Weeks before, however, Kathleen had called at his farm to invite him to visit her at a nearby summer house. Before long he proposed marriage, but she insisted on secrecy, on maintaining appearances. "We wanted to marry," he told Stanley Burnshaw, his editor in the 1960s. "It was all decided. But you know how matters seem at times—others to think of. It was thought best," he repeated, "It was thought best"—marriage without benefit of clergy, an altered way of life. He continued to bard around and to teach, residing from January through March at "Pencil Pines," his newly built Miami retreat; at his Cambridge house until late May; then in Ripton, near Breadloaf, for the summer; and in Cambridge again through December.

During the 1940s Frost published four new books: A Witness Tree (1942), inscribed "To K.M.For Her Part in It," containing some of his finest poems, among them "The Most of It" and "The Silken Tent," and for which he received his fourth Pulitzer Prize; two deceptively playful blank verse dialogs, A Masque of Reason (1945) and A Masque of Mercy (1947), on the relationship between God and man, to be "taken" in light of his statements on "irony. a kind of guardedness" and "style. the way the man takes himself. If it is with outer humor, it must be with inner seriousness"; and fourth, Steeple Bush (1947), his weakest volume, although it included "Directive," one of Frost's major poems. None but his intimates knew of the decade's griefs: his son Carol's suicide in 1940, his daughter Irma's placement in a mental hospital in 1947.

In the last fourteen years of his life Frost was the most highly esteemed American poet of the twentieth century, having received forty-four honorary degrees and a host of government tributes, including birthday greetings from the Senate, a congressional medal, an appointment as honorary consultant to the Library of Congress, and an invitation from

John F. Kennedy to recite a poem at his presidential inauguration. Thrice, at the State Department's request, he traveled on good-will missions: to Brazil (1954), to Britain (1957), and to Greece (1961, on his return from Israel, where he had lectured at the Hebrew University).

More important for Frost as an artist and for his readers were the changed perceptions of his works, which began with Randall Jarrell's 1947 essay "The Other Frost." Jarrell saw him as "the subtlest and saddest of poets" whose "extraordinary strange poems express an attitude that, at its most extreme, makes pessimism a hopeful evasion." Twelve years later Lionel Trilling hailed Frost at his eighty-fifth birthday dinner for his "representation of the terrible actualities of life in a new way," for though "the manifest America of [his] poems may be pastoral, the actual America is tragic." And two years earlier, in London at the English-Speaking Union, T. S. Eliot (who in 1922 had dismissed Frost's verse as "unreadable") toasted him as "perhaps the most eminent, the most distinguished Anglo-American poet now living," whose "kind of local feeling in poetry. can go without universality: the relation of Dante to Florence,. of Robert Frost to New England."

In the Clearing, Frost's ninth and last collection of poems, appeared on 26 March 1962, the date of his eighty-eighth birthday dinner in Washington, attended by some 200 guests who heard Justices Earl Warren and Felix Frankfurter, Adlai Stevenson, Mark Van Doren, and Robert Penn Warren speak in his honour. Five months later, at the president's request, Frost made a twelve-day trip to the USSR, where he met with fellow writers and with Premier Nikita Khrushchev. On his return, "bone tired" and exhausted after eighteen sleepless hours, he made some ill-considered public remark, which was taken as a slur on both Khrushchev and President Kennedy. To Frost's deep dismay, the president did not receive him.

On 2 December at the Ford Forum Hall in Boston Frost made his last address and, though admitting he felt a bit tired, he stayed the evening through. In the morning he felt much too ill to keep his doctor's appointment. After considerable wrangling, he agreed to enter a hospital "for observation and tests." He remained in its care until his death in the early hours of 29 January 1963. Tributes poured in from all over the land and from abroad.

A small private service on the 31st at Harvard's Memorial Church for family members and friends was followed by a public one on 17 February at the Amherst College Chapel, where 700 guests listened to Mark Van Doren's recital of eleven Frost poems he had chosen for the occasion. Eight months later, at the October dedication of the Robert Frost Library at Amherst, President Kennedy paid tribute to the poetry, to "its tide that lifts all spirits," and to the poet "whose sense of the human tragedy fortified him against self-deception and easy consolation."

Within a decade, however, the poet's public image was shattered by the appearance of the second volume of Lawrance Thompson's authorized biography, Robert Frost: The Years of Triumph, 1915-1937 (1970), which reviewers took at face value to be an accurate account of a man whom Helen Vendler deemed a "monster of egotism" (New York Times Book Review, 9 Aug. 1970). Although Frost later came to have grave misgivings about his choice, he had designated Thompson his official biographer in 1939.

For whatever reason, the poet felt unable to renounce that decision despite his awareness of Thompson's frequently unsympathetic, even hostile constructions of his attitudes and conduct. Although reviewers perceived in Thompson, as Vendler put it, "an affectation of fairness," they tended to subscribe, nevertheless, to the "monster-myth" that poisoned Frost's reputation. Evidence that he was not a wrecker of others' lives was soon at hand in the form of The Family Letters of Robert and Elinor Frost, edited by Arnold Grade (1972). More than a decade would pass before the tide was turned: first by W. H. Pritchard's Frost: A Literary Life Reconsidered (1984) and then by Stanley Burnshaw's Robert Frost Himself (1986), which enabled Publishers' Weekly to state that "the unfortunately influential 'monster-myth' stands here convincingly corrected."

Chapter 3

Chronology of Frost's Life

1874 Born on March 26 in San Francisco, first child of Isabelle Moodie and William Prescott Frost Jr. Named after Confederate General Robert E. Lee.

1875 Father becomes city editor of the San Francisco Daily Evening Post.

1876 Travels east with his mother, who is expecting another child, and is upset with father's drinking and gambling. His sister, Jeanie Florence, is born in Lawrence, Mass June 25. Returns back to SF in fall. Father is diagnosed as consumptive.

1879 Attends kindergarten, but goes home after one day suffering from nervous stomach pain and does not return.

1880 Father is elected as delegate to the Democratic National Convention in Cincinnati. Frost attends first grade, but soon drops out again.

1881 Frost enters second grade. Baptized in mother's Sweden-borgian church.

1882 Drops out of school and is educated at home.

1883 Frost hears voices when left alone and is told by mother that he shares her gift for "second hearing" and "second sight." Father continues to drink as his health deteriorates.

1885 Father dies of tuberculosis on May 5, leaving family with only $8 after expenses are paid. Family moves to Lawrence, Mass. to live with grandparents. Robert and Jeanie dislike grandparents' sternness and rigorous discipline.

Enters third grade after testing, while younger sister enters fourth grade.

1886 Moves to Salem Depot, New Hampshire, where mother begins teaching the fifth to eighth grades. Frost and Jeanie enter the fifth grade.

1888 Passes entrance examinations for Lawrence High School in June. Enrolls in "classical" (college prep) programme. Mother resigns from the Salem Depot district school.

1889 Finishes school year at head of his class.

1890 First published poem, "La Noche Triste," based on episode in Prescott's Conquest of Mexico, appears in thē Lawrence High School Bulletin in April; a second poem, "The Song of the Wave," appears in the Bulletin in May.

1891 Passes preliminary entrance examinations for Harvard College. Elected chief editor of the Bulletin for the 1891-92 school year. Meets and falls in love with fellow student Elinor Miriam White (b. 1872) during fall.

1892 Becomes engaged to Elinor. Dependent upon grandparents for financial support, enters Dartmouth College instead of Harvard because it is cheaper, and because grandparents blame Harvard for his father's bad habits. Bored by college life and restless, leaves Dartmouth at the end of December.

1893 Briefly teaches unruly eighth-grade class in Methuen for several weeks. Frost tries to convince Elinor to marry him before returning to St. lawrence University in canton, New York, but fails.

1894 Returns to teaching grades one through six in Salem. In March, he learns The Independent will publish his poem "My Butterfly: An Elegy" and will pay him $15. Tries to convince Elinor to marry him at once. Gets printer to make him two copies of collection of his poems, called Twilight.

Goes to visit Elinor to present her with a copy, but is thrown into despair by her cool reception; destroys his own copy and returns home. Depressed, he decides to go the Dismal Swamp on the Virginia-North Carolina border. Leaves Lawrence on November 6 and travels by train and boat to Norfolk, Virginia, then follows wagon road and walks for miles into the swamp at night. Meets a pat of boatmen at canal lock who agree to take him though swamp to Elizabeth City, North Carolina. Stays with boat as it crosses Albemarle Sound to Mags Head on the Atlantic coast. Begins return journey by hopping freight cars from Elizabeth City to Baltimore. Exhausted and frightened, writes mother for return fare and arrives in Lawrence on November 30.

1895 Works as reporter in Lawrence for Daily American and Sentinel. Frost teaches at Salem district school Marries Elinor White in Lawrence on December 19 in ceremony conducted by Swedenborgian pastor.

1896 Son Elliott is born on September 25.

1897 Passes Harvard College entrance examinations, borrows money from grandfather and enters Harvard as a freshman.

1899 Withdraws from Harvard on march 31. Daughter Lesley born on April 28. Insists his mother see a doctor, and learns that she has advanced cancer.

1900 Son Elliott dies of cholera on July 8 and is buried in Lawrence. Elinor suffers sever depression. Frost's heath declines. Mother enters sanatorium in Penacook, NH. Mother dies of cancer on November 2 and is buried in Lawrence.

1901 Reads Thoreau's Walden for the first time. Grandfather William Prescott Frost dies on July 10; his will gives Frost a $500 annuity and use of the Derry farm for ten years, after which the annuity is to be increased to $800 and Frost is to be given ownership of the farm.

1902 Son Carol is born May 27.

1903 Publishes short story "Trap nests" in The Eastern Poultryman in February (will be published 11 times in the Poultryman and in Farm-Poultry between 1903 and 1905). Daughter Irma is born on June 27.

1905 Daughter Marjorie is born on March 28. 1906 - Starts part-time position teaching English literature at Pinkerton Academy in Derry. Publishes poem "The Tuft of Flowers" in the Derry Enterprise. Eventually assumes full-time teaching post at Pinkerton Academy.

1907 Daughter Elinor Bettina is born on June 18, and dies on June 21.

1909 Frost impresses the New Hampshire superintendent of public instruction, and lectures about his teaching methods before several conventions of New Hampshire teachers. Poem "Into Mine Own" appears in New England Magazine in May. Sells all of the poultry and moves family to apartment in nearby Derry village.

1910 Revises English curriculum for the Pinkerton Academy and develops programme emphasizing an informal, conversational teaching style. He writes in the school catalog: "The general aim of the course in English is twofold: to bring our students under the influence of the great books, and to teach them the satisfactions of superior speech." Father-in-law dies May 26.

1911 Accepts offer to teach at State Normal School and moves family to Plymouth. Teaches courses in education and psychology. Sells the Derry farm.

1912 Decides to live in England for a few years and devote himself to writing full time. Sails with family on August 23. Stays in London briefly before renting a cottage in Beaconsfield, Buckinghamshire, 20 miles north of London. Submits A Boy's Will in October to London firm of David Nutt and Company, which accepts it for publication.

1913 A Boy's Will is published April 1. Meets numerous literary figures, including Ezra Pound, Hilda Doolittle, Form Hermann Hueffer (Ford Madox Ford), Ernest Rhys, and William Butler Yeats (who tells Pound that A Boy's Will is "the best poetry written in America for a long time"). Friendship with Pound becomes strained ("He says I must write something much more like vers libre or he will let me perish by neglect. He really threatens"). Forms close friendship with Edward Thomas.

1914 Moves near Dymock, Gloucestershire. North of Boston is published on May 15 and is favorably reviewed in The Nation, The Outlook, The Times Literary Supplement, Pall Mall Gazette, The English Review, The Bookman, and The Daily News. Encourages Thomas to write poetry. Amused by local concern that he may be a spy when war breaks out in August. Learns that Henry Holt and Company will publish his books in the US. Decides to return to America. Concerned that review by Pound may cause Americans to consider him to be one of Pound's "party of American literary refugees."

1915 Arrives in New York February 23. North of Boston was published in America on February 20. Meets with a number of editors in New York. A Boy's Will is published in April. Buys farm in Franconia, New Hampshire. Meets Edwin Arlington Robinson and Louis Untermeyer. Wife Elinor suffers miscarriage.

1916 Gives talks and readings in throughout New England. Elected to the National Institute of Arts and Letters. Mountain Interval published November 27. Accepts offer from Alexander Meiklejohn, president of Amherst College, to teach for one semester at a salary of $2,000.

1917 Moves to Amherst in January. A Way Out, a one act play, is published. Deeply grieved by the death of Edward Thomas (E.T.), killed during the battle of Arras. Teaching position at Amherst is extended. Lesley enters Wellesley College.

1918 Meets Vachel Lindsay, Sara Teasdale, and James Oppenheim. Pleased when Lesley leaves college after her freshman year to do war work in an aircraft factory. During national epidemic, Frost suffers severe case of influenza that lasts for months.

1920 Resigns position at Amherst in February over disagreements with Meiklejohn, whom Frost considers too morally permissive, and to devote more time to writing. Sister Jeanie was arrested in Portland, Maine, or March 25 for disturbing the peace, and was pronounced instance by an attending physician. Frost commits Jeanie to the state mental hospital at Augusta, Maine. Begins serving as consulting editor for Henry Holt and company at a salary of $100 per month.

1921 gives talks and readings, receiving at least 4100 plus expenses for each. Spends one week in march as "poet in residence" at Queens University in Kingston, Ontario. Begins long association with Bread Loaf School of English in Ripton, Vermont. Move to Ann Arbor, Michigan after accepting a $5,000 fellowship at University of Michigan. Does not teach, but advises students and gives talks.

1922 Helps arrange poets' lecture series which includes Carl Sandburg, Louis Untermeyer, and Amy Lowell. Fellowship at Michigan is renewed for another year.

1923 Select Poems is published by Henry Holt in March. Awarded LHD by the University of Vermont. Accepts appointment as professor of English at Amherst College after Mieklejohn is dismissed. Discusses quantum theory with physicist Neils Bohr during a visit to Amherst in October. New Hampshire published by Henry Holt November 15.

1924 Awarded Pulitzer Prize for New Hampshire in May. Receives Honorary Litt.D. degrees from Middlebury College and Yale University. Grandson William Prescott Frost, son of Carol, is born on October 15. Gives notice to Amherst of his acceptance of lifetime appointment at University of Michigan as Fellow in Letters, with no teaching obligations to begin next autumn.

1925 Friends throw Frost a "Fiftieth Birthday Dinner" because Frost believes he was born in 1875, not 1874. Writes obituary tribute to Amy Lowell for The Christian Science Monitor in May. Works in Ann Arbor, while Elinor and family stay home. Daughter Marjorie is hospitalized in December suffering from pneumonia, a peri-cardiac infection, chronic appendicitis and nervous exhaustion.

1926 Family joins him in Ann Arbor in Spring. After visit from Amherst president Daniel Olds, Frost accepts offer to rejoin college as a part-time professor of English for $5,000 a year and no obligation to teach formal classes. Participates in inaugural session of the Bread Loaf Writers' Conference.

1927 Moves to Amherst in January where he teaches for ten weeks. Marjorie enters Johns Hopkins Hospital for ten weeks of treatment.

1928 Signs new contract with Holt providing for royalty increase from 15 to 20 percent at 5,000 copies of a book are sold, as well as a $2,000 advance and monthly payments of $250 for the next five years. Sails for France with Elinor and Marjorie in August. Travels through England and Scotland with Elinor, who is suffering from depression. Meets T.S. Eliot for the first time. Returns to America in November. Learns that daughter Lesley, who married in September, is unhappy and contemplating divorce. West-running Brook is published by Holt, which also publishes and expanded edition of Selected Poems.

1929 Permits Marjorie to begin nursing school. Sister Jeanie dies in state mental hospital in August, Maine in early September. Frost and Elinor move into farm they purchased in South Shaftsbury.

1930 Collected Poem published in November. Elected in the American Academy of Arts and Letters. Visits Marjorie who has been hospitalized in Baltimore with tuberculosis.

1931 Decides with doctors that Marjorie should enter sanatorium in boulder, Colorado. Awarded Pulitzer Prize for Collected Poems in June. Lesley's second daughter is born, and her divorce becomes final soon after. Receives Russell Loines Poetry Prize from the National Institute of Arts and Letters.

1932 Moves into new house in Amherst. Meets Marjorie's fianc‰ in Boulder. Attends Olympic Games in Los Angeles. Is displeased with T.S. Eliot's slighting remarks concerning Robert Burns and other Scottish poets.

1933 Continues heavy lecture schedule to earn extra money for his children's expenses. Due to exhaustion, unable to attend Marjorie's wedding in Billings, Montana.

1934 Marjorie develops puerperal fever after daughter is born in March, dies May 2 and is buried in Billings.Daughter is taken care of by Carol and his wife Lillian. Elinor suffers severe attach of angina pectoris in November. Under doctor orders, Frost and Elinor go to Key West in December.

1935 Meets Wallace Stevens in Key West. Gives lecture at University of Miami. Returns north with Elinor in March. Writes preface to Edwin Arlington Robinson's last book, King Jasper. With Elinor, rents house in Coconut Grove, Florida.

1936 Privately publishes a small volume of Marjorie's poems, Franconia. Begins appointment as Charles Eliot Norton Professor of Poetry at Harvard University. A Further Range, published by Holt in May, is made a selection of the Book-of-the-Month Club.

1937 Wins Pulitzer Prize for A Further Range. elected to membership in the American Philosophical Society. Elinor undergoes surgery for breast cancer in early October.

1938 Elinor dies of heart failure in Gainesville, Florida March 20. Frost collapses and is unable to attend cremation. Resigns position at Amherst College and returns to South Shaftsbury. Asks Kathleen Morrison to marry him; she refuses. His continuing emotional instability draws attention. Morrison agrees to work for him as a paid secretary and take care of arranging lecture appearances (and will do so for the rest of Frost's life). After threatening to leave Henry Holt, the firm offers him a contract which guarantees a 20 percent royalty on all books sold and raises his monthly payment to $300.

1939 Awarded the Gold Medal by the national Institute of Arts and Letters in New York. Frost takes first plane trip, flying to Cuba with Paul and May Engle for short stay. Enlarged edition of Collected Poems is published by Holt in February. Accepts two-year appointment as

Ralph Waldo Emerson Fellow in Poetry at Harvard in May. Designates Lawrence Thompson as his "official" biographer on condition that the biography only appear after his death. Suffers painful attack of acidosis in December.

1940 Undergoes surgery for hemorrhoids. Health improves and purchases five acres of land in South Miami. Tries to talk his son, whose long-standing depression and suspiciousness have become more acute since Elinor's death, out of his suicidal thoughts. Returns to Boston thinking crisis is over and is horrified when Carol commits suicide with a deer-hunting rifle on October 9. Returns to South Shaftsbury immediately to make funeral arrangements and to be with Carol's son Prescott, who had discovered the body. Frost writes to Untermeyer: "I took the wrong way with him. I tried many ways and every single on of them was wrong."

1941 Moves in March to Cambridge (will continue to live there for the remainder of his life, spending summers at Noble Farm, and winters in South Miami).

1942 A Winter Tree, dedicated to Kathleen Morrison is published by Holt in April; sales reach 10,000 copies within two months.

1943 Awarded Pulitzer Prize for A Witness Tree, becoming the first person to receive the Prize four times. Accepts appointment at Dartmouth College as George Ticknor Fellow in Humanities, with $2,500 stipend and $500 for expenses. Hospitalized in December with serious case of pneumonia.

1945 A Masque of Reason is published by Holt in March.

1946 Daughter Irma's mental condition deteriorates.

1947 Receives his 17th honorary degree in March, from Berkeley. Steeple Bush published by Holt in May.

Suffers pains in his and arms after reading critical review in Time. Frost has Irma, whose condition has deteriorated, to the state mental hospital in Concord, New Hampshire. A Masque of Mercy is published by Holt in September.

1948 Despite enjoying work at Dartmouth, feels close to Amherst and accepts offer to return there as Simpson Lecturer in Literature with a salary of $3,500, a position he will hold until his death).

1949 Angered by award of Bollingen Prize to Ezra Pound, now confined to a mental hospital and under indictment for treason for his radio broadcasts from Italy during WW II. Complete Poems of Robert Frost 1949 is published in May.

1950 US Senate adopts resolution honoring Frost on his 75th birthday (actually his 76th). Begins friendship with Connery Lathem, who will become a posthumous editor of Frost's work.

1951 Due to worsening eyesight, now often recites poems from memory. Has cancerous lesion removed from upper right side of his face.

1953 Awarded the Fellowship of the Academy of American Poets, with a stipend of $5,000 in march. Undergoes surgery in late December for a recurrence of facial skin cancer.

1954 Invited to the White House by his friend Sherman Adams, who is now serving as chief of staff to President Eisenhower. Having learned he was born in 1874, celebrates his 80th birthday. Holt publishes Aforesaid, a new selection of his poems, in a limited edition of 650 copies. Serves as a delegate to the World Congress of Writers held in Sao, Paulo, August 4-19.

1955-66 Vermont state legislature names mountain in Ripton after Frost. Has patchwork quilts made from 26 academic hoods he has received along with honorary degrees.

1957 Frost, T.S. Eliot and Ernest Hemingway sign

letter, drafted by Archibald MacLeish, asking Attorney General Herbert Brownell to drop the treason indictment against Ezra Pound. Becomes on the third American to receive honorary Litt.D. Degrees by Oxford and Cambridge. While touring England, meets W.H. Auden, E.M. Forster, and Graham Greene. Becomes actively involved in effort to free Ezra Pound.

1958 Invited by President Eisenhower to the White House in February. Drafts statement in support of Pound's release for use at court hearing in April that ends with the dismissal of the indictment (Pound is discharged from federal mental hospital in May). Frost is appointed that same month to be Consultant in Poetry to the Library of Congress. Receives Emerson-Thoreau Medal of the American Academy of Arts and Sciences; delivers address "On Emerson."

1959 Predicts in March that John F. Kennedy will win the 1960 presidential election. Appointed to three-year term as Honorary Consultant in the Humanities at the Library of Congress.

1960 Testifies before Senate subcommittee in favour of a bill to establish a National Academy of Culture. Congress passes bill awarding Frost a gold medal in recognition of his poetry. Pleased when Kennedy invites him to take part in inaugural ceremonies.

1961 Writes new poem for inauguration, but is unable to read it in glare of bright sunlight and recites only "The Gift Outright." Travels to Israel and Greece to lecture. Vermont state legislature names Frost "Poet Laureate of Vermont."

1962 Fall seriously ill with pneumonia and is hospitalized in South Miami in February. In the Clearing published by Holt in March. In late August, travels to the Soviet Union as a part of a cultural exchange programme at the invitation of President Kennedy. exhausted and ill, Frost is too weak to leave his guest house and Soviet Premier Nikita Khrushchev comes to visit him; they talk for 90 minutes. Returns to America, still suffering from exhaustion and tells press on arrival that Khrushchev "said we were too liberal to fight," causing a controversy that strains friendship with Kennedy. Learns that an anonymous donor has given $3.5 million for construction of The Robert Frost Library at Amherst. Admits in October, during Cuban Missile crisis that Khrushchev had not said the words he had attributed to him. Undergoes prostrate operation in December. Doctors find cancer in his prostate and bladder. Suffers pulmonary embolism on December 23.

1963 Awarded the Bollingen Prize for Poetry. Suffers another embolism on January 7. Dies shortly after midnight on January 29. Private memorial service for friends and family is held in Appleton Chapel in Harvard yard, and public service is held at Johnson Chapel, Amherst College. Ashes are interred in the Frost family plot in Old Bennington, Vermont.

Chapter 4

Major Works

Poetry

A Boy's Will
North of Boston
Mountain Interval
Selected Poems
New Hampshire
Several Short Poems
Selected Poems
West-Running Brook
The Lovely Shall Be Choosers
Collected Poems of Robert Frost
The Lone Striker
Selected Poems: Third Edition
Three Poems
The Gold Hesperidee
From Snow to Snow
A Further Range
Collected Poems of Robert Frost
A Witness Tree
Steeple Bush
Complete Poems of Robert Frost, 1949
Hard Not To Be King
Aforesaid
A Remembrance Collection of New Poems
You Come Too
In the Clearing
The Poetry of Robert Frost

Plays

A Way Out: A One Act Play.
The Cow's in the Corn: A One Act Irish Play in Rhyme.
A Masque of Reason.
A Masque of Mercy.

Prose

The Letters of Robert Frost to Louis Untermeyer.
Robert Frost and John Bartlett: The Record of a Friendship, by Margaret Bartlett Anderson.
Selected Letters of Robert Frost.
Interviews with Robert Frost.
Family Letters of Robert and Elinor Frost.
Robert Frost and Sidney Cox: Forty Years of Friendship.

Chapter 5

Popular Quotes by Robert Frost

Robert Frost is recognized as an important "nature poet" in American literature, famous for his depiction of the New England landscape. Some of his most famous works include: "The Road Not Taken," "Mending Wall," "After Apple-Picking," and "Home Burial." Here are a few quotes from Robert Frost.

"The kind of Unitarian
Who having by elimination got
From many gods to Three, and Three to One,
Thinks why not taper off to none at all."
- Robert Frost, "A Masque of Mercy"
"The artist in me cries out for design."
- Robert Frost, "A Masque of Reason"
"And of course there must be something wrong
In wanting to silence any song."
- Robert Frost, "A Minor Bird"
"The birch begins to crack its outer sheath
Of baby green and show the white beneath."
- Robert Frost, "A Young Birch"
"Where my imaginary line
Bends square in woods, an iron spine
And pile of real rocks have been founded."
- Robert Frost, "Beech"
"For Thought has a pair of dauntless wings."
- Robert Frost, "Bond and Free"
"They must have seen ahead what now appears:
They would bring empires down about our ears
And by the example of our Declaration

Make everybody want to be a nation."
- Robert Frost, "For John F. Kennedy His Inauguration"
"I dwell in a lonely house I know
That vanished many a summer ago."
- Robert Frost, "Ghost House"
"All those who try to go it sole alone,
Too proud to be beholden for relief,
Are absolutely sure to come to grief."
- Robert Frost, "Haec Fabula Docet"
"A brush had left a crooked stroke
Of what was either cloud or smoke
From north to south across the blue;
A piercing little star was through."
- Robert Frost, "Looking for a Sunset Bird in Winter"
"You linger your little hour and are gone,
And still the woods sweep leafily on."
- Robert Frost, "On Going Unnoticed"
"Life is not so sinister-grave.
Matter of fact has made them brave.
He is husband, she is wife.
She fears not him, they fear not life."
- Robert Frost, "On the Heart's
Beginning to Cloud the Mind"
"But with one step backward taken
I saved myself from going.
A world torn loose went by me."
- Robert Frost, "One Step Backward Taken"
"They listened at his heart.
Little—less—nothing!—and that ended it.
No more to build on there. And they, since they
Were not the one dead, turned to their affairs."
- Robert Frost, "Out, Out"
"By measure. It was word and note,
The wind the wind had meant to be
A little through the lips and throat.
The aim was song the wind could see."
- Robert Frost, "The Aim Was Song"
"Before I built a wall I'd ask to know

What I was walling in or walling out,
And to whom I was like to give offense.
Something there is that doesn't love a wall,
That wants it down.'"
- Robert Frost, "The Mending Wall"
"They are that that talks of going
But never gets away;
And that talks no less for knowing,
As it grows wiser and older,
That now it means to stay."
- Robert Frost, "The Sound of the Trees"

Chapter 6

Complete Text of Selected Poems by Robert Frost

Acquainted with the Night

I have been one acquainted with the night.
I have walked out in rain—and back in rain.
I have outwalked the furthest city light.
I have looked down the saddest city lane.
I have passed by the watchman on his beat
And dropped my eyes, unwilling to explain.
I have stood still and stopped the sound of feet
When far away an interrupted cry
Came over houses from another street,
But not to call me back or say good-by;
And further still at an unearthly height
One luminary clock against the sky
Proclaimed the time was neither wrong nor right.
I have been one acquainted with the night.

After Apple Picking

My long two-pointed ladder's sticking through a tree
Toward heaven still.
And there's a barrel that I didn't fill
Beside it, and there may be two or three
Apples I didn't pick upon some bough.
But I am done with apple-picking now.
Essence of winter sleep is on the night,
The scent of apples; I am drowsing off.

I cannot shake the shimmer from my sight
I got from looking through a pane of glass
I skimmed this morning from the water-trough,
And held against the world of hoary grass.
It melted, and I let it fall and break.
But I was well
Upon my way to sleep before it fell,
And I could tell
What form my dreaming was about to take.
Magnified apples appear and reappear,
Stem end and blossom end,
And every fleck of russet showing clear.
My instep arch not only keeps the ache,
It keeps the pressure of a ladder-round.
And I keep hearing from the cellar-bin
That rumbling sound
Of load on load of apples coming in.
For I have had too much
Of apple-picking; I am overtired
Of the great harvest I myself desired.
There were ten thousand thousand fruit to touch,
Cherish in hand, lift down, and not let fall,
For all
That struck the earth,
No matter if not bruised, or spiked with stubble,
Went surely to the cider-apple heap
As of no worth.
One can see what will trouble
This sleep of mine, whatever sleep it is.
Were he not gone,
The woodchuck could say whether it's like his
Long sleep, as I describe its coming on,
Or just some human sleep.

Birches

When I see birches bend to left and right
Across the lines of straighter darker trees,
I like to think some boy's been swinging them.

But swinging doesn't bend them down to stay.
Ice-storms do that. Often you must have seen them
Loaded with ice a sunny winter morning
After a rain. They click upon themselves
As the breeze rises, and turn many-colored
As the stir cracks and crazes their enamel.
Soon the sun's warmth makes them shed crystal shells
Shattering and avalanching on the snow-crust-
Such heaps of broken glass to sweep away
You'd think the inner dome of heaven had fallen.
They are dragged to the withered bracken by the load,
And they seem not to break; though once they are bowed
So low for long, they never right themselves:
You may see their trunks arching in the woods
Years afterwards, trailing their leaves on the ground
Like girls on hands and knees that throw their hair
Before them over their heads to dry in the sun.
But I was going to say when Truth broke in
With all her matter-of-fact about the ice-storm
(Now am I free to be poetical?)
I should prefer to have some boy bend them
As he went out and in to fetch the cows-
Some boy too far from town to learn baseball,
Whose only play was what he found himself,
Summer or winter, and could play alone.
One by one he subdued his father's trees
By riding them down over and over again
Until he took the stiffness out of them,
And not one but hung limp, not one was left
For him to conquer. He learned all there was
To learn about not launching out too soon
And so not carrying the tree away
Clear to the ground. He always kept his poise
To the top branches, climbing carefully
With the same pains you use to fill a cup
Up to the brim, and even above the brim.
Then he flung outward, feet first, with a swish,
Kicking his way down through the air to the ground.

So was I once myself a swinger of birches.
And so I dream of going back to be.
It's when I'm weary of considerations,
And life is too much like a pathless wood
Where your face burns and tickles with the cobwebs
Broken across it, and one eye is weeping
From a twig's having lashed across it open.
I'd like to get away from earth awhile
And then come back to it and begin over.
May no fate willfully misunderstand me
And half grant what I wish and snatch me away
Not to return. Earth's the right place for love:
I don't know where it's likely to go better.
I'd like to go by climbing a birch tree,
And climb black branches up a snow-white trunk
Toward heaven, till the tree could bear no more,
But dipped its top and set me down again.
That would be good both going and coming back.
One could do worse than be a swinger of birches.

Come In

As I came to the edge of the woods,
Thrush music — hark!
Now if it was dusk outside,
Inside it was dark.
To dark in the woods for a bird
By sleight of wing
To better its perch for the night,
Though it still could sing.
The last of the light of the sun
That had died in the west
Still lived for one song more
In a thrush's breast.
Far in the pillared dark
Thrush music went —
Almost like a call to come in
To the dark and lament.
But no, I was out for stars;

I would not come in.
I meant not even if asked;
And I hadn't been.

Desert Places

Snow falling and night falling fast, oh, fast
In a field I looked into going past,
And the ground almost covered smooth in snow,
But a few weeds and stubble showing last.
The woods around it have it—it is theirs.
All animals are smothered in their lairs.
I am too absent-spirited to count;
The loneliness includes me unawares.
And lonely as it is that loneliness
Will be more lonely ere it be less—
A blanker whiteness of benighted snow
With no expression, nothing to express.
They cannot scare me with their empty spaces
Between stars—on stars where no human race is.
I have it in me so much nearer home
To scare myself with my own desert places.

Design

I found a dimpled spider, fat and white,
On a white heal-all, holding up a moth
Like a white piece of rigid satin cloth—
Assorted characters of death and blight
Mixed ready to begin the morning right,
Like the ingredients of a witches' broth—
A snow-drop spider, a flower like a froth,
And dead wings carried like a paper kite.
What had that flower to do with being white,
The wayside blue and innocent heal-all?
What brought the kindred spider to that height,
Then steered the white moth thither in the night?
What but design of darkness to appall?—
If design govern in a thing so small.

Dust of Snow

The way a crow
Shook down on me
The dust of snow
From a hemlock tree
Has given my heart
A change of mood
And saved some part
Of a day I had rued.

To Earthward

Love at the lips was touch
As sweet as I could bear;
And once that seemed too much;
I lived on air
That crossed me from sweet things,
The flow of - was it musk
From hidden grapevine springs
Down hill at dusk?
I had the swirl and ache
From sprays of honeysuckle
That when they're gathered shake
Dew on the knuckle.
I craved strong sweets, but those
Seemed strong when I was young;
The petal of the rose
It was that stung.
Now no joy but lacks salt
That is not dashed with pain
And weariness and fault;
I crave the stain
Of tears, the aftermark
Of almost too much love,
The sweet of bitter bark
And burning clove.
When stiff and sore and scarred
I take away my hand

From leaning on it hard
In grass and sand,
The hurt is not enough:
I long for weight and strength
To feel the earth as rough
To all my length.

Fire and Ice

Some say the world will end in fire,
Some say in ice.
From what I've tasted of desire
I hold with those who favour fire.
But if it had to perish twice,
I think I know enough of hate
To know that for destruction ice
Is also great
And would suffice.
{Sh] Mending Wall
Something there is that doesn't love a wall,
That sends the frozen-ground-swell under it,
And spills the upper boulders in the sun,
And makes gaps even two can pass abreast.
The work of hunters is another thing:
I have come after them and made repair
Where they have left not one stone on a stone,
But they would have the rabbit out of hiding,
To please the yelping dogs. The gaps I mean,
No one has seen them made or heard them made,
But at spring mending-time we find them there.
I let my neighbort know beyond the hill;
And on a day we meet to walk the line
And set the wall between us once again.
We keep the wall between us as we go.
To each the boulders that have fallen to each.
And some are loaves and some so nearly balls
We have to use a spell to make them balance:
'Stay where you are until our backs are turned!'
We wear our fingers rough with handling them.

Oh, just another kind of out-door game,
One on a side. It comes to little more:
There where it is we do not need the wall:
He is all pine and I am apple orchard.
My apple trees will never get across
And eat the cones under his pines, I tell him.
He only says, 'Good fences make good neighbours'.
Spring is the mischief in me, and I wonder
If I could put a notion in his head:
'Why do they make good neighbours? Isn't it
Where there are cows?
But here there are no cows.
Before I built a wall I'd ask to know
What I was walling in or walling out,
And to whom I was like to give offence.
Something there is that doesn't love a wall,
That wants it down.' I could say '.Elves' to him,
But it's not elves exactly, and I'd rather
He said it for himself. I see him there
Bringing a stone grasped firmly by the top
In each hand, like an old-stone savage armed.
He moves in darkness as it seems to me —
Not of woods only and the shade of trees.
He will not go behind his father's saying,
And he likes having thought of it so well
He says again, Good fences make good neighbours.

Mowing

There was never a sound beside the wood but one,
And that was my long scythe whispering to the ground.
What was it it whispered? I knew not well myself;
Perhaps it was something about the heat of the sun,
Something, perhaps, about the lack of sound—
And that was why it whispered and did not speak.
It was no dream of the gift of idle hours,
Or easy gold at the hand of fay or elf:
Anything more than the truth would have
seemed too weak

To the earnest love that laid the swale in rows,
Not without feeble-pointed spikes of flowers
(Pale orchises), and scared a bright green snake.
The fact is the sweetest dream that labour knows.
My long scythe whispered and left the hay to make.

The Need of Being Versed in Country Things

The house had gone to bring again
To the midnight sky a sunset glow.
Now the chimney was all of the house that stood,
Like a pistil after the petals go.
The barn opposed across the way,
That would have joined the house in flame
Had it been the will of the wind, was left
To bear forsaken the place's name.
No more it opened with all one end
For teams that came by the stony road
To drum on the floor with scurrying hoofs
And brush the mow with the summer load.
The birds that came to it through the air
At broken windows flew out and in,
Their murmur more like the sigh we sigh
From too much dwelling on what has been.
Yet for them the lilac renewed its leaf,
And the aged elm, though touched with fire;
And the dry pump flung up an awkward arm;
And the fence post carried a strand of wire.
For them there was really nothing sad.
But though they rejoiced in the nest they kept,
One had to be versed in country things
Not to believe the phoebes wept.

Not to Keep

They sent him back to her. The letter came
Saying. and she could have him. And before
She could be sure there was no hidden ill
Under the formal writing, he was in her sight —
Living. — They gave him back to her alive —

How else? They are not known to send the dead —
And not disfigured visibly. His face? —
His hands? She had to look — to ask,
"What was it, dear?" And she had given all
And still she had all — they had — they the lucky!
Wasn't she glad now? Everything seemed won,
And all the rest for them permissable ease.
She had to ask, "What was it, dear?"
"Enough,
Yet not enough. A bullet through and through,
High in the breast. Nothing but what good care
And medicine and rest — and you a week,
Can cure me of to go again." The same
Grim giving to do over for them both.
She dared no more than ask him with her eyes
How was it with him for a second trial.
And with his eyes he asked her not to ask.
They had given him back to her, but not to keep.

Nothing Gold can Stay

Nature's first green is gold,
Her hardest hue to hold.
Her early leaf's a flower;
But only so an hour.
Then leaf subsides to leaf.
So Eden sank to grief,
So dawn goes down to day.
Nothing gold can stay.

An Old Man's Winter Night

All out of doors looked darkly in at him
Through the thin frost, almost in separate stars,
That gathers on the pane in empty rooms.
What kept his eyes from giving back the gaze
Was the lamp tilted near them in his hand.
What kept him from remembering what it was
That brought him to that creaking room was age.
He stood with barrels round him - at a loss.

And having scared the cellar under him
In clomping there, he scared it once again
In clomping off; - and scared the outer night,
Which has its sounds, familiar, like the roar
Of trees and crack of branches, common things,
But nothing so like beating on a box.
A light he was to no one but himself
Where now he sat, concerned with he knew what,
A quiet light, and then not even that.
He consigned to the moon, such as she was,
So late-arising, to the broken moon
As better than the sun in any case
For such a charge, his snow upon the roof,
His icicles along the wall to keep;
And slept. The log that shifted with a jolt
Once in the stove, disturbed him and he shifted,
And eased his heavy breathing, but still slept.
One aged man - one man - can't keep a house,
A farm, a countryside, or if he can,
It's thus he does it of a winter night.

On Looking Up by Chance at the Constellations

You'll wait a long, long time for anything much
To happen in heaven beyond the floats of cloud
And the Northern Lights that run like tingling nerves.
The sun and moon get crossed, but they never touch,
Nor strike out fire from each other nor crash out loud.
The planets seem to interfere in their curves —
But nothing ever happens, no harm is done.
We may as well go patiently on with our life,
And look elsewhere than to stars and moon and sun
For the shocks and changes we need to keep us sane.
It is true the longest drout will end in rain,
The longest peace in China will end in strife.
Still it wouldn't reward the watcher to stay awake
In hopes of seeing the calm of heaven break
On his particular time and personal sight.
That calm seems certainly safe to last to-night.

Once by the Pacific

The shattered water made a misty din.
Great waves looked over others coming in,
And thought of doing something to the shore
That water never did to land before.
The clouds were low and hairy in the skies,
Like locks blown forward in the gleam of eyes.
You could not tell, and yet it looked as if
The shore was lucky in being backed by cliff,
The cliff in being backed by continent;
It looked as if a night of dark intent
Was coming, and not only a night, an age.
Someone had better be prepared for rage.
There would be more than ocean-water broken
Before God's last Put out the Light was spoken.

"Out,

The buzz-saw snarled and rattled in the yard
And made dust and dropped stove-length sticks of wood,
Sweet-scented stuff when the breeze drew across it.
And from there those that lifted eyes could count
Five mountain ranges one behind the other
Under the sunset far into Vermont.
And the saw snarled and rattled, snarled and rattled,
As it ran light, or had to bear a load.
And nothing happened: day was all but done.
Call it a day, I wish they might have said
To please the boy by giving him the half hour
That a boy counts so much when saved from work.
His sister stood beside them in her apron
To tell them 'Supper'. At the word, the saw,
As if to prove saws knew what supper meant,
Leaped out at the boy's hand, or seemed to leap—
He must have given the hand. However it was,
Neither refused the meeting. But the hand!
The boy's first outcry was a rueful laugh.
As he swung toward them holding up the hand
Half in appeal, but half as if to keep

The life from spilling. Then the boy saw all—
Since he was old enough to know, big boy
Doing a man's work, though a child at heart—
He saw all spoiled. 'Don't let him cut my hand off
The doctor, when he comes. Don't let him, sister!'
So. But the hand was gone already.
The doctor put him in the dark of ether.
He lay and puffed his lips out with his breath.
And then — the watcher at his pulse took fright.
No one believed. They listened at his heart.
Little — less — nothing! — and that ended it.
No more to build on there. And they, since they
Were not the one dead, turned to their affairs.

The Oven Bird

There is a singer everyone has heard,
Loud, a mid-summer and a mid-wood bird,
Who makes the solid tree trunks sound again.
He says that leaves are old and that for flowers
Mid-summer is to spring as one to ten.
He says the early petal-fall is past
When pear and cherry bloom went down in showers
On sunny days a moment overcast;
And comes that other fall we name the fall.
He says the highway dust is over all.
The bird would cease and be as other birds
But that he knows in singing not to sing.
The question that he frames in all but words
Is what to make of a diminished thing.

Reluctance

Out through the fields and the woods
And over the walls I have wended;
I have climbed the hills of view
And looked at the world, and descended;
I have come by the highway home,
And lo, it is ended.
The leaves are all dead on the ground,

Save those that the oak is keeping
To ravel them one by one
And let them go scraping and creeping
Out over the crusted snow,
When others are sleeping.
And the dead leaves lie huddled and still,
No longer blown hither and thither;
The last lone aster is gone;
The flowers of the witch-hazel wither;
The heart is still aching to seek,
But the feet question 'Whither?'
Ah, when to the heart of man
Was it ever less than a treason
To go with the drift of things,
To yield with a grace to reason,
And bow and accept the end
Of a love or a season?

The Road not Taken

Two roads diverged in a yellow wood,
And sorry I could not travel both
And be one traveller, long I stood
And looked down one as far as I could
To where it bent in the undergrowth;
Then took the other, as just as fair,
And having perhaps the better claim,
Because it was grassy and wanted wear;
Though as for that the passing there
Had worn them really about the same,
And both that morning equally lay
In leaves no step had trodden black.
Oh, I kept the first for another day!
Yet knowing how way leads on to way,
I doubted if I should ever come back.
I shall be telling this with a sigh
Somewhere ages and ages hence:
Two roads diverged in a wood, and I—
I took the one less traveled by,

And that has made all the difference.

The Soldier

He is that fallen lance that lies as hurled,
That lies unlifted now, come dew, come rust,
But still lies pointed as it ploughed the dust.
If we who sight along it round the world,
See nothing worthy to have been its mark,
It is because like men we look too near,
Forgetting that as fitted to the sphere,
Our missiles always make too short an arc.
They fall, they rip the grass, they intersect
The curve of earth, and striking, break their own;
They make us cringe for metal-point on stone.
But this we know, the obstacle that checked
And tripped the body, shot the spirit on
Further than target ever showed or shone.

[SH]The Sound of the Trees

I WONDER about the trees.
Why do we wish to bear
Forever the noise of these
More than another noise
So close to our dwelling place?
We suffer them by the day
Till we lose all measure of pace,
And fixity in our joys,
And acquire a listening air.
They are that that talks of going
But never gets away;
And that talks no less for knowing,
As it grows wiser and older,
That now it means to stay.
My feet tug at the floor
And my head sways to my shoulder
Sometimes when I watch trees sway,
From the window or the door.
I shall set forth for somewhere,

I shall make the reckless choice
Some day when they are in voice
And tossing so as to scare
The white clouds over them on.
I shall have less to say, But I shall be gone.

Spring Pools

These pools that, though in forests, still reflect
The total sky almost without defect,
And like the flowers beside them, chill and shiver,
Will like the flowers beside them, soon be gone,
And yet not out by any brook or river,
But up by roots to bring dark foliage on.
The trees that have it in their pent-up buds
To darken nature and be summer woods—
Let them think twice before they use their powers
To blot out and drink up and sweep away
These flowery waters and these watery flowers
From snow that melted only yesterday.

Stopping By Woods on a Snowy Evening

Whose woods these are I think I know
His house is in the village though;
He will not see me stopping here
To watch his woods fill up with snow.
My little horse must think it queer
To stop without a farmhouse near
Between the woods and frozen lake
The darkest evening of the year.
He gives his harness bells a shake
To ask if there is some mistake.
The only other sound's the sweep
Of easy wind and downy flake.
The woods are lovely, dark and deep.
But I have promises to keep,
And miles to go before I sleep.
And miles to go before I sleep.

A Time To Talk

When a friend calls to me from the road
And slows his horse to a meaning walk,
I don't stand still and look around
On all the hills I haven't hoed,
And shout from where I am, What is it?
No, not as there is a time to talk.
I thrust my hoe in the mellow ground,
Blade-end up and five feet tall,
And plod: I go up to the stone wall
For a friendly visit.

The Tuft of Flowers

I went to turn the grass once after one
Who mowed it in the dew before the sun.
The dew was gone that made his blade so keen
Before I came to view the leveled scene.
I looked for him behind an isle of trees;
I listened for his whetstone on the breeze.
But he had gone his way, the grass all mown,
And I must be, as he had been,—alone,
'As all must be,' I said within my heart,
'Whether they work together or apart.'
But as I said it, swift there passed me by
On noiseless wing a 'wildered butterfly,
Seeking with memories grown dim o'er night
Some resting flowei of yesterday's delight.
And once I marked his flight go round and round,
As where some flower lay withering on the ground.
And then he flew as far as eye could see,
And then on tremulous wing came back to me.
I thought of questions that have no reply,
And would have turned to toss the grass to dry;
But he turned first, and led my eye to look
At a tall tuft of flowers beside a brook,
A leaping tongue of bloom the scythe had spared
Beside a reedy brook the scythe had bared.

I left my place to know them by their name,
Finding them butterfly weed when I came.
The mower in the dew had loved them thus,
By leaving them to flourish, not for us,
Nor yet to draw one thought of ours to him.
But from sheer morning gladness at the brim.
The butterfly and I had lit upon,
Nevertheless, a message from the dawn,
That made me hear the wakening birds around,
And hear his long scythe whispering to the ground,
And feel a spirit kindred to my own;
So that henceforth I worked no more alone;
But glad with him, I worked as with his aid,
And weary, sought at noon with him the shade;
And dreaming, as it were, held brotherly speech
With one whose thought I had not hoped to reach.
'Men work together,' I told him from the heart,
'Whether they work together or apart.'
And would suffice.

Wild Grapes

What tree may not the fig be gathered from?
The grape may not be gathered from the birch?
It's all you know the grape, or know the birch.
As a girl gathered from the birch myself
Equally with my weight in grapes, one autumn,
I ought to know what tree the grape is fruit of.
I was born, I suppose, like anyone,
And grew to be a little boyish girl
My brother could not always leave at home.
But that beginning was wiped out in fear
The day I swung suspended with the grapes,
And was come after like Eurydice
And brought down safely from the upper regions;
And the life I live now's an extra life
I can waste as I please on whom I please.
So if you see me celebrate two birthdays,
And give myself out of two different ages,

One of them five years younger than I look—
One day my brother led me to a glade
Where a white birch he knew of stood alone,
Wearing a thin head-dress of pointed leaves,
And heavy on her heavy hair behind,
Against her neck, an ornament of grapes.
Grapes, I knew grapes from having seen them last year.
One bunch of them, and there began to be
Bunches all round me growing in white birches,
The way they grew round Leif the Lucky's German;
Mostly as much beyond my lifted hands, though,
As the moon used to seem when I was younger,
And only freely to be had for climbing.
My brother did the climbing; and at first
Threw me down grapes to miss and scatter
And have to hunt for in sweet fern and hardhack;
Which gave him some time to himself to eat,
But not so much, perhaps, as a boy needed.
So then, to make me wholly self-supporting,
He climbed still higher and bent the tree to earth
And put it in my hands to pick my own grapes.
"Here, take a tree-top, I'll get down another.
Hold on with all your might when I let go."
I said I had the tree. It wasn't true.
The opposite was true. The tree had me.
The minute it was left with me alone
It caught me up as if I were the fish
And it the fishpole. So I was translated
To loud cries from my brother of "Let go!
Don't you know anything, you girl? Let go!"
But I, with something of the baby grip
Acquired ancestrally in just such trees
When wilder mothers than our wildest now
Hung babies out on branches by the hands
To dry or wash or tan, I don't know which,
(You'll have to ask an evolutionist)—
I held on uncomplainingly for life.
My brother tried to make me laugh to help me.

"What are you doing up there in those grapes?
Don't be afraid. A few of them won't hurt you.
I mean, they won't pick you if you don't them."
Much danger of my picking anything!
By that time I was pretty well reduced
To a philosophy of hang-and-let-hang.
"Now you know how it feels," my brother said,
"To be a bunch of fox-grapes, as they call them,
That when it thinks it has escaped the fox
By growing where it shouldn't—on a birch,
Where a fox wouldn't think to look for it—
And if he looked and found it, couldn't reach it—
Just then come you and I to gather it.
Only you have the advantage of the grapes
In one way: you have one more stem to cling by,
And promise more resistance to the picker."
One by one I lost off my hat and shoes,
And still I clung. I let my head fall back,
And shut my eyes against the sun, my ears
Against my brother's nonsense; "Drop," he said,
"I'll catch you in my arms. It isn't far."
(Stated in lengths of him it might not be.)
"Drop or I'll shake the tree and shake you down."
Grim silence on my part as I sank lower,
My small wrists stretching till they
showed the banjo strings.
"Why, if she isn't serious about it!
Hold tight awhile till I think what to do.
I'll bend the tree down and let you down by it."
I don't know much about the letting down;
But once I felt ground with my stocking feet
And the world came revolving back to me,
I know I looked long at my curled-up fingers,
Before I straightened them and brushed the bark off.
My brother said: "Don't you weigh anything?
Try to weigh something next time, so you won't
Be run off with by birch trees into space."
It wasn't my not weighing anything

So much as my not knowing anything—
My brother had been nearer right before.
I had not taken the first step in knowledge;
I had not learned to let go with the hands,
As still I have not learned to with the heart,
And have no wish to with the heart—nor need,
That I can see. The mind—is not the heart.
I may yet live, as I know others live,
To wish in vain to let go with the mind—
Of cares, at night, to sleep; but nothing tells me
That I need learn to let go with the heart.

The Wood-Pile

Out walking in the frozen swamp one gray day
I paused and said, 'I will turn back from here.
No, I will go on farther - and we shall see'.
The hard snow held me, save where now and then
One foot went through. The view was all in lines
Straight up and down of tall slim trees
Too much alike to mark or name a place by
So as to say for certain I was here
Or somewhere else: I was just far from home.
A small bird flew before me. He was careful
To put a tree between us when he lighted,
And say no word to tell me who he was
Who was so foolish as to think what he thought.
He thought that I was after him for a feather—
The white one in his tail; like one who takes
Everything said as personal to himself.
One flight out sideways would have undeceived him.
And then there was a pile of wood for which
I forgot him and let his little fear
Carry him off the way I might have gone,
Without so much as wishing him good-night.
He went behind it to make his last stand.
It was a cord of maple, cut and split
And piled and measured, four by four by eight.
And not another like it could I see.

No runner tracks in this year's snow looped near it.
And it was older sure than this year's cutting,
Or even last year's or the year's before.
The wood was gray and the bark warping off it
And the pile somewhat sunken. Clematis
Had wound strings round and round it like a bundle.
What held it though on one side was a tree
Still growing, and on one a stake and prop,
These latter about to fall. I thought that only
Someone who lived in turning to fresh tasks
Could so forget his handiwork on which
He spent himself the labour of his axe,
And leave it there far from a useful fireplace
To warm the frozen swamp as best it could
With the slow smokeless burning of decay.
Robert Frost (1874 - 1963)

Chapter 7

Critical Commentaries on Works by Robert Frost

On "Mending Wall"

George Montiero

"Who are bad neighbors? " asked H. D. Thoreau, for the sole purpose of answering his own question. "They who suffer their neighbors' cattle to go at large because they don't want their ill will,—are afraid to anger them. They are abettors of the ill-doers." Thoreau could have as readily asked, "Who are good neighbors?" Whereupon, following his reasoning, one could answer, "Those who build and maintain walls which keep out their neighbors' cattle."

How, and indeed whether, the good will of one's neighbour is fostered by boundaries, however, was a general question that would engage Thoreau's latter-day disciple, Robert Frost. Were walls and fences instrumental in the retention and renewal of human relationships Is a question central to "Mending Wall." The answers the poem presents us with are somewhat less than clear- cut. This is so, at least partly, because Frost has purposely and purposefully left out of his poem a piece of important information. One key to the poet's omission lies in the final lines of the poem.

I see him there,
Bringing a stone grasped firmly by the top
In each hand, like an old-stone savage armed.
He moves in darkness as it seems to me,

Not of woods only and the shade of trees.
He will not go behind his father's saying,
And he likes having thought of it so well
He says again, "Good fences make good neighbors."

In these lines the poet moves back through time, beyond his own earlier questioning of the possible reasons for continuing the annual repair of those now apparently useless boundaries, to an earlier, darker age. Indeed, his neighbour seems to be moving in a "darkness" that is, suggestively, "not of woods only and the shade of trees." To the poet he is now "like an old-stone savage armed." Even on New England farms in this century the ways of the savage continue, it would seem, no matter how transformed, no matter how radically attenuated.

Indeed, Frost shrewdly, and characteristic ally, stopped his poem just short of the mythological link toward which the poem is moving. That Frost and his neighbour engage in what is tantamount to a vestigial ritual and that further, prodded by the poet, the neighbour would defend his father's idea (proverbially expressed) that "Good fences make good neighbors" relates this poem to traditions and rituals antedating the Romans. The god of boundaries they named Terminus was not invented by the Romans, but he became one of their important household gods. Annually Terminus was honored in a ritual which not only reaffirmed boundaries but which also provided the occasion for predetermined traditional festivities among neighbors.

The festival of the Terminalia was celebrated in Rome and in the country on the 23rd of February.The neighbours on either side of any boundary gathered around the landmark [the stones which marked boundaries], with their wives, children, and servants; and crowned it, each on his own side, with garlands, and offered cakes and, bloodless sacrifices. In later times, however, a lamb, or sucking pig, was sometimes slain, and the stone sprinkled with the blood. Lastly, the whole neighbourhood joined in a general feast.

If his neighbour does not know that this annual ritual of walking the boundaries to repair their common wall has its obscure source in the all-but-totally lost mysteries of ancient man, that information could not possibly have been unknown to the serious student of the Classics who wrote the poem. What impresses itself upon the poet is that, for whatever reasons, men continue to need marked boundaries, even when they find it difficult to justify their existence.

In conclusion, it should be noted that Frost's decision—a characteristic and revealing decision—not to link explicitly his view of his farmers' ritualistic occupation to the myth and ritual from which it probably derives distinguishes his poetic method from that of the Modernists, who were then predominant. By contrast, a similar mythic parallel in a representative poem by a T. S. Eliot or an Ezra Pound, for example, would have been made, less subtly, either through direct statement or by pointed allusion.

Frank Lentricchia

The mass of men lead lives of quiet deperation. There is no play in them, for this comes after work. (Thoreau) "Mending Wall"' is the opening poem of Frost's second volume, North of Boston. One of the dominating moods of this volume, forcefully established in such important poems as "The Death of the Hired Man," "Home Burial, " "The Black Cottage," and "A Servant to Servants," and carried through some of the minor pieces, flows from the tension of having to maintain balance at the precipitous edge of hysteria. With "The Mountain" and with "A Hundred Collars," "Mending Wall" stands opposed to such visions of human existence; more precisely put, to existences that are fashioned by the neurotic visions of central characters like the wife in "Home Burial," the servant in "A Servant to Servants." "Mending Wall" dramatizes the redemptive imagination in its playful phase, guided surely and confidently by a man who has his world under full control, who in his serenity is riding his realities, not being shocked by them into traumatic response.

The place of "Mending Wall" in the structure of North of Boston suggests, in its sharp contrasts to the dark tones of some of the major poems in the volume, the psychological necessities of sustaining supreme fictions.

The opening lines evoke the coy posture of the shrewd imaginative man who understands the words of the farmer in 'The Mountain": "All the fun's in how you say a thing,"

Something there is that doesn't love a wall,
That sends a frozen-ground-swell under it
And spills the upper boulders in the sun,
And makes gaps even two can pass abreast.

It does not take more than one reading of the poem to understand that the speaker is not a country primitive who is easily spooked by the normal processes of nature. He knows very well what it is "that doesn't love a wall" (frost, of course). His fun lies in not naming it. And in not naming the scientific truth he is able to manipulate intransigent fact into the world of the mind where all things are pliable. The artful vagueness of the phrase "Something there is" is enchanting and magical, suggesting even the bushed tones of reverence before mystery in nature. And the speaker (who is not at all reverent toward nature) consciously works at deepening that sense of mystery:

The work of hunters is another thing:
I have come after them and made repair
Where they would have left not one stone on a stone,
But they would have the rabbit out of hiding,
To please the yelping dogs. The gaps I mean,
No one has seen them made or heard them made,
But at spring mending-time we find them there.

The play of the mature, imaginative man is grounded in ironic awareness—and must be. Even as he excludes verifiable realities from his fictive world the unmistakable tone of scorn for the hunters comes seeping through. He may step into a fictive world but not before glancing back briefly at the brutality that attends upon the play of others. Having paid for his imaginaive excursions by establishing his complex awareness, he is free to close the magic circle cast out by his playful energies, and close out the world reported by the senses ("No one has seen them made or heard them made"). In knowing how to say a thing in and through adroit linguistic manipulation, the fiction of the "something" that doesn't love a wall is created; the imagined reality stands formed before him, ready to be entered.

Like the selves dramatized in "Going For Water" and "The Tuft of Flowers," this persona would prefer not to be alone in his imaginative journey:

I let my neighbour know beyond the hill;
And on a day we meet to walk the line
And set the wall between us once again.
We keep the wall between us as we go.
To each the boulders that have fallen to each.
And some are loaves and some so nearly balls
We have to use a spell to make them balance:
"Stay where you are until our backs are turned!"
We wear our fingers rough with handling them.
Oh, just another kind of outdoor game,
One on a side. It comes to little more:
There where it is we do not need the wall:
He is all pine and I am apple orchard.
My apple trees will never get across
And eat the cones under his pines, I tell him.
He only says, "Good fences make good neighbors."

If the fact of a broken wall is excuse enough to make a fiction about why it got that way, then that same fact may be the occasion for two together to take a journey in the mind. For those still tempted to read "Mending Wall" as political allegory (the narrator standing for a broad-minded liberal internationalism, the thick-headed second speaker representing a selfish super-patriot) they must first face the line "I let my neighbour know beyond the hill." "Mending Wall" has nothing to do with one-world political ideals, with good or bad neighbour policies: on this point the title of the poem is helpful. It is a poem that celebrates a process, not the thing itself.

It is a poem, furthermore, that distinguishes between two kinds of people: one who seizes the particular occasion of mending as fuel for the imagination and as a release from the dull ritual of work each spring an one who is trapped by work and by the New England past as it comes down to him in the form of his father's cliché. Tied as he is to his father's words that "Good fences make good neighbors," the neighbour beyond the hill is committed to an end, the fence's completion. His participation in the process of rebuilding is sheer work—he never plays the outdoor game.

The narrator, however, is not committed to ends, but to the process itself which he sees as having non-utilitarian value: "There where it is we do not need the wall." The process itself is the matrix of the play that redeems work by transforming it into the pleasure of an outdoor game in which you need to cast spells to make rocks balance. Overt magic-making is acceptable in the world of this poem because we are governed by the narrator's perspective; we are in the fictive world where all things are possible, where walls go tumbling for mysterious reasons.

Kant's theory that work and the aesthetic activity are antagonistic, polar activities of man is, in effect, disproven, as the narrator makes work take on the aesthetic dimension. The real differences between the two people in the poem is that one moves in a world of freedom; aware of the resources of the mind, he nurtures the latent imaginative power within himself and makes it a factor in everyday living; while the other, unaware of the value of imagination, must live his unliberated life without it. And this difference makes a difference in the quality of the life lived.

The narrator of "Mending Wall" does not give up easily: he tries again to tempt his neighbour to enter into the fictive world with him and to share his experience of play:

Spring is the mischief in me, and I wonder
If I could put a notion in his head:
"Why do they make good neighbors? Isn't it
Where there are cows? But here there are no cows.
Before I built a wall I'd ask to know
What I was walling in or walling out,
And to whom I was like to give offense.
Something there is that doesn't love a wall,
That wants it down." I could say "Elves" to him,
But it's not elves exactly, and I'd rather
He said it for himself.

All to no avail: the outrageously appropriate pun on "offense"—a linguistic emblem of the poem's spirit of play and freedom—falls on deaf ears. The neighbour won't say "elves," those little folk who don't love a wall; he will not enter the play world of imagination. He moves in "darkness," our narrator concludes, "like an old-stone savage armed." The characterization is philosophically precise in the logic of post-Kantian aesthetics; the recalcitrant and plodding neighbour is a slave to the rituals of the quotidian, a primitive whose spirit has not been freed by the artistic consciousness that lies dormant within. It is the play spirit of imagination, as Schiller suggests, which distinguishes the civilized man from his cave-dwelling ancestor—that "old-stone savage" who moved in "darkness."

John C. Kemp

The conflict in "Mending Wall" develops as the speaker reveals more and more of himself while portraying a native Yankee and responding to the regional spirit he embodies. The opposition between observer and observed—and the tension produced by the observer's awareness of the difference—is crucial to the poem. Ultimately, the very knowledge of this opposition becomes itself a kind of barrier behind which the persona, for all his dislike of walls, finds himself confined.

But at the beginning, the Yankee farmer is not present, and the persona introduces himself in a reflective, offhanded way, musing about walls:

Something there is that doesn't love a wall,
That sends the frozen-ground-swell under it
And spills the upper boulders in the sun,
And makes gaps even two can pass abreast.

Clearly, he is a casual sort. He broaches no difficult subjects, nor does he insist on talking about himself; yet Frost is at his best in a sentence like this. Through the language and rhythm of the lines we gain a faint but unmistakable sense of the poem's conflict. Like the "frozen-ground-swell," it gathers strength while lying buried beneath the denotative surface of the poem. From the start, we suspect that the speaker has more sympathy than he admits for whatever it is "that doesn't love a wall."

Frost establishes at the outset his speaker's discursive indirection. He combines the indefinite pronoun "something" with the loose expletive construction "there is" to evoke a ruminative vagueness even before raising the central subject of walls. A more straightforward character (like the Yankee farmer) might condense this opening line to three direct words: "Something dislikes walls." But Frost employs informal, indulgently convoluted language to provide a linguistic texture for the dramatic conflict that develops later in the poem. By using syntactical inversion ("something there is.") to introduce a rambling, undisciplined series of relative clauses and compound verb phrases ("that doesn't love. that sends. and spills. and makes."), he evinces his persona's unorthodox, unrestrained imagination. Not only does this speaker believe in a strange force, a seemingly intelligent, natural or supernatural "something" that "sends the frozen-ground-swell" to ravage the wall, but his speech is also charged with a deep sensitivity to it.

The three active verbs ("sends," "spills," "makes") that impel the second, third, and fourth lines forward are completed by direct objects that suggest his close observation of the destructive process. He appreciates the subterranean dynamics of the frost, he knows how spilled boulders look in the bright winter light, and he seems so familiar with the gaps that we suspect he has walked through more than a few (evidently with a companion).

The first line of "Mending Wall" is also notable because it functions effectively as a counterpoint to the farmer's "good fences" apothegm, which appears once in the middle of the poem and then again in the final line. The farmer is summed up by his adage, fittingly his only utterance; his reiteration of it is an appropriate ending to the poem because it completes a cyclical pattern to which the speaker has no rejoinder and from which he cannot escape. Beyond expressing an attitude toward walls, it evokes the farmer's personality through its simplicity and balanced directness. The basic subject-verb-object syntax of the five-word maxim is reinforced by the repeated adjective and by the symmetrical balance and rhythmic similarity of subject ("Good fences") and object ("good neighbors") on either side of the monosyllabic verb "make." The persona's initial observation, "Something there is that doesn't love a wall," with its hesitations and indefinite circumlocutions, conveys not only a contrasting opinion, but also a different way of thinking from the tight-lipped Yankee's. Significantly, though the speaker's observation is reiterated later in the poem, it is not a self-contained statement. Unlike the farmer's encapsulated wisdom, it is a protest, a complaint leading into a series of tenuously linked explanations, digressions, and ruminations.

Throughout the first half of the poem the speaker contemplates the deterioration and repair of walls, strengthening our awareness of his two central traits; his whimsical imagination and his fine sensitivity to detail. He digresses to describe hunters who actively tear walls apart in search of rabbits. Then he returns to his own interest in a more mysterious, unseen, unheard, destructive power. With relaxed, conversational irrelevance, he launches in a discussion of the rebuilding ritual, objective physical description to a light touch of fantasy—"We have to use a spell to make them balance"—which is likely to be noticed only because of the suggestive hints made earlier to the strange force responsible for the gaps.

Frost's control of tone during this desultory ramble is responsible for the speaker's ability to hold our attention and pique our interest. Even on successive readings, we are surprised by the implications of a given line or phrase, and we find ourselves gauging how much of a smile or frown accompanies each sentence. The imagined spell of line 18 dissolves in the jocularity of line 19: "'Stay where you are until our backs are turned!'" Yet, just as quickly, the concrete, sensory images in the following line remind us of the real effort such work requires: "We wear our fingers rough with handling them."

Having touched on the seriousness of wall building, however, the speaker indulges in another irreverent speculation:

Oh, just another kind of outdoor game,
One on a side. It comes to little more.

The unceremonious sentence fragment and the deprecatory offhandedness of "just another kind" and "comes to little more" are unsuited to the earnestness of the preceding line; yet by now we are accustomed to incongruities, and we suspect that behind his capriciousness there is something on the speaker's mind. The allusion to an "outdoor game" evokes rivalry and competition, not only in wall repair, but also in wall destruction. This persona shows great appreciation of playfulness and recognizes many kinds of sport. If the wall builders participate in one "kind of outdoor game together," then they surely play another game against the wall destroyers: the hunters and those mysterious underground forces that wait strategically until the workers' backs are turned before spilling any more boulders. Hints of opposition and competitiveness soon gain strength in lines that effect a marvelous blend of natural fact and fanciful fabrication:

He is all pine and I am apple orchard.
My apple trees will never get across
And eat the cones under his pines, I tell him.

This telling passage indicates how far the persona's imagination can carry him. It is true that the acidity of pine duff would prevent apple seeds from taking root, but simple aboricultural observation leads to a fantastic—and deeply revealing—personification. Although the speaker seems merely facetious, his imagery betrays antagonism as he ridicules the farmer, implying that he is too foolish and stubborn to see the incongruity of a rapacious invasion of apples (which are edible) seeking to devour pine cones (which are not).

While attacking his neighbor's lack of open-minded amiability, the speaker is the one who exhibits antisocial tendencies. He is quick to think the worst, presuming that the farmer's concern with the wall is motivated by base selfishness, despite the latter's expressed interest in being "good neighbors." Furthermore, it is not the farmer but the speaker who initiates the mending-wall ritual. Thus these lines heighten a still undefined tension and reveal surprising complexities while preparing us for the Yankee farmer's blunt precept: "Good fences make good neighbors." Such a forceful line crystallizes the poem's dramatic conflict by standing in salient opposition to everything the persona has said and, indeed, to his mode of speech. It is a remarkable and memorable line, not because of its inherent truth or quotability, but because of Frost's effective anticipatory presentation of an extraordinarily imaginative antagonism to "good fences."

Just as the twenty-five lines preceding the farmer's aphorism contribute to its impact, so do the sixteen succeeding lines that lead up to its reiteration. But once the conflict of farmer and observer has been made overt, the last section of the poem develops a contentiousness that further elucidates the differences between the two characters and reveals how little sociability there is between them. As the poem draws to its close with a chimerical vision of the farmer as "an old stone savage" the term "neighbour" seems increasingly ironic. The farmer looms not as an associate or coworker, but as an alien being whom the speaker observes, criticizes, and reflects upon while maintaining his distance and objectivity.

The two men—farmer and observer, insider and outsider—are separated by deep differences in perception, differences that the speaker does not fully appreciate. He thinks they are building a wall, but to his neighbour it is merely fence mending. A more significant contrast is suggested by the Yankee farmer's reliance on shibboleth (a from of mental enclosure). Confident in his beliefs, he relies on traditional wisdom to suppress inquisitive or speculative tendencies. He concerns himself not with the whys and wherefores of walls but with the simple, practical fact (to him a fact) of their efficacy. His unwillingness to explain or debate his position implies that he feels there is nothing to be gained through communicating or exchanging ideas. If fences are good, then, conversely, too much closeness between neighbors must be undesirable. Indeed, there is no evidence that his "neighborly" relations with the speaker extend much beyond the laconic yearly ritual described in the poem. Satisfied to confine himself behind his personal wall of self-assumed taciturnity, he never converses with the speaker. He only repeats the aphorism he learned from his father, as if to keep from something original (or as if incapable of saying something original).

The persona, for his part, does not equate thinking with to adages; instead of accepting parental or neighborly authorities, he seems willing to "go behind" anyone's sayings, including his own. Even his tendentious investigation of whatever it is "that doesn't love a wall" is inconclusive, shifting as it does from the mysterious instability of walls to the foibles of the barrier-loving neighbour before finally dissipating in bitter complaints. But conclusiveness can hardly be the major concern of a speaker so given to equivocations (ll. 21-22, 36-38), digressions (ll. 5-9), questions (ll. 30-34), suppositions (ll. 28-29, 32-35, 41-42), and outright fantasies (ll. 18-19, 25-26, 39-40).

After ranging from careful description to seemingly frivolous speculation, from shrewdness to willful illusiveness, and from subtle irony to urgent sincerity, the persona grows diffident toward the end of the poem about his own perceptions. He is particularly uncertain about how he should respond to his neighbour. Though wanting to "put a notion" in his head, he goes no further than conjecture: "I wonder If I could." His claim that "Spring is the mischief in me" recalls the mischievous force "that doesn't love a wall," yet he does not try to make gaps in the farmer's mental fortifications. He indulges only in speculative, figmental "mischief," contemplating the crucial question he dares not ask: "Why do they make good neighbors?" He even undercuts his strongest comment with a qualifier: "He moves in darkness as it seems to me" (my emphasis).

Ironically (and there is much irony in this poem), although the speaker complains about his neighbor's unfriendliness, his own susceptibility to subjective vision and his willingness to let his imagination run away with him predispose him also to prejudicial attitudes He sees the wall and its symbolism virtually overwhelms him. By contrast, the farmer, who surely knows that "fence" is a misnomer for the country-style stone wall they are working on, sees no sinister implications in it and evidently uses the slightly imprecise adage to show his desire not "to give offense." It was a brilliant touch by Frost to use wordplay in exposing his persona's central misjudgment. For wordplay is the mark of the poet, and it is a poet's sensibility that so delightfully plays this speaker false. It is only in the imagination that the fence gives offfence, and it is only this visionary speaker who insists a wall cannot be innocent, cannot be the benign fence of the farmer's precept.

Ultimately, the persona's imahinative and indecisive dispositiņ renders him incapable of challenging the Yankee's confident maxim. But Frost has shrewdly made him both unable and unwilling to settle on an argument that might demonstarte what it is to want a wall down. The allusion to elves, though meaningful to the persona, would never appeal to the hidebound farmer; it is such a hopeless suggestion that it leads to a kind of surrender: "I'd rather He said it for himself." Yet this concession only reaffirms the personality displayed earlier. The speaker's sensitivity to what he sees may excite his desire for action, but he is neither capable nor desirous of didactic argument. Though the Yankee farmer says little in the poem, we may not notice that the persona actually has less to say to break down those walls he finds so detestable. He can only imagine saying something, for he is an observer and a commentator, not a reformer or a philosopher.

In the closing lines of "Mending Wall" the Yankee farmer may seem to get the last word and leave his antagonist circumscribed—indeed, walled in—by an alien philosophy. But truly, the speaker has mended the walls of his own personality, and instead of combating an opponent, attempting moral or philosophical sallies, and worrying about victory or defeat, he has again taken an observer's approach to his neighbour. At the end he presents a highly imaginative and appropriately climactic response to the Yankee, envisioning him as a shadowy "old-stone savage." As he completes this portrait, he brings his own drama to its denouement. His deep feelings about walls have led him to challenge what he takes neighbor's antithetical position; but after recognizing the futility of debate, he returns to his original contemplative outlook.

This study of Frost's treatment of his persona in "Mending Wall" should be sufficient to establish that the poem is not primarily an expression of moral views on neighborliness. Contrary to the burden of critical opinion, it is less about neighborliness than it is about modes of thought, about language, perhaps even about poetry itself. To the speaker, the farmer is antipathetic because he seems so antipoetic: he distrusts the flow of words, ideas, and feelings. Lacking a playful imagination and the willingness to "go behind" a saying or a concept, he seems cut off from the poetic. But we must not forget that the failure of communication in the poem is mutual.

And in truth, Frost's persona is the less communicative and the more hostile of the two. His portrait of an intractable neighbour involves feverish speculation that makes us doubt the reliability of his point of view. On the surface of it, at least, the Yankee's brief adage bespeaks more amiability than do the speaker's speculations and suspicious conjectures. Yet Frost offers no answers in "Mending Wall," no clues about who is right or wrong. He does not moralize: he demonstrates. And what he demonstrates is a conflict that commands our attention because in its origin and development it exhibits the power of imagination in flight.

George Montiero

"Mending Wall" is a meditative lyric that reports and assesses a dialogue between neighbors who have joined in the annual occupation of rebuilding the wall which separates their farms. Obviously antedating the farmers themselves, the old wall seems to serve no modern need. Has "walking the line" degenerated, the poet wonders, into bootless and vulgar ritual? Or are there fresh reasons, as yet unarticulated, for maintaining the wall? The poet's mischief—that impulse which urges him to needle his rather taciturn neighbour with this puckish question—acts to open things up.

Asked once about his intended meaning, Frost recast the question: "In my Mending Wall was my intention fulfilled with the characters portrayed and the atmosphere of the place?" Characteristically, he went on to answer obliquely.

I should be sorry if a single one of my poems stopped with either of those things—stopped anywhere in fact. My poems—I should suppose everybody's poems—are all set to trip the reader head foremost into the boundless. Ever since infancy I have had the habit of leaving my blocks carts chairs and such like ordinaries where people would be pretty sure to fall forward over them in the dark. Forward, you understand, and in the dark. I may leave my toys in the wrong place and so in vain. It is my intention we are speaking of—my innate mischievousness.

No other poem in the Frost canon better illustrates his manner—as he described it—and his overall poetic intention. "Mending Wall" is constructed around the idea of mischief. The poet's mischief ultimately erects the verbal barrier that his neighbour is bullied into trying to surmount or withstand. "Why rebuild ancient walls?" is a question offered to trip the neighbour. But one of the surprises in "Mending Wall" is that the neighbour responds with a defence. He does not fall forward. He cannot be tripped into darkness—and a new outlook. Instead, threatened, he reaches into the past for support and comes up with his father's proverb: "Good fences make good neighbors." When we fail to recognize that the neighbour replies to the poet's prodding with a proverb, we miss a good deal of Frost's point.

Current in America as early as 1850, "Good fences make good neighbors" can be traced to the Spanish, "Una pared entre dos vezinos guarda mas (haze durar) la amistad," which goes back at least to the Middle Ages. In this form, Vicesimus Knox translated it for his compendium of Elegant Extracts in 1797, and in 1832 Emerson recorded it in his journal—"A wall between both, best preserves friendship." That Frost encountered the idea in Emerson's published journals is probable, though it seems more likely that he found its precise expression elsewhere. For our purpose it is important that both Frost and Emerson were attracted to the same idea, suggesting an affinity of poetic temperament. "The sea, vocation, poverty, are seeming fences, but man is insular and cannot be touched." In senti ment this is vintage Frost, but Emerson made the remark.

Speech in proverbial form surfaces as the poem's final "wall." Since the proverb's message is sanctioned by tradition, the poet's neighbour can retreat to safety: Resorting to a proverb enables him, moreover, to have the last word in the exchange. The importance of what he chooses to say is exceeded by the import of how he has chosen to say it. Provoked into speech, the farmer hides behind a clinching proverb. Twice the proverb is offered to close the matter. Failing to understand the message the first time, the poet repeats his question. The neighbour employs his proverb to win his point, even as it is employed in some African tribes, for example, where participants are allowed to use proverbs in litigation.

What finally emerges from Frost's poem is the idea that the stock reply—unexamined wisdom from the past—seals off the possibility of further thought and communication. When thought has frozen into folk expression, language itself becomes another wall, one unresponsive to that which it encircles and given over to fulfilling a new and perhaps unintended function. Meeting once a year and insulated from anything beyond simple interaction by their well-defined duties and limits, these "good" neighbors turn out to be almost incommunicative.

It is difficult to ascertain Frost's full intent in linking "Mending Wall" with "The Tuft of Flowers." If the latter is about unexpected fellowship, then some interesting possibilities present themselves when it is paired with "Mending Wall." One way of stating the theme of "The Tuft of Flowers" is that even when a man works alone he works with others—but that is hardly the theme of "Mending Wall." On the contrary, in "Mending Wall" the poet discovers that, even when men work together, each of them works alone. "The Tuft of Flowers" also says that there can be communication without words, beyond physical presence and across time. But in "Mending Wall" we see that communication breaks down even as men converse: For Frost, "taking up a theme" did not at all entail dealing with it always in the same way. When we examine these linked poems in the light that each casts on the other, we find that their relationship really involves statement and counterstatement, or, put another way, theme and antitheme.

Yet if Frost could provide links between and among his poems to encourage the kind of cross-reading that he so much favored for poetry, he could also omit from his poems the kinds of links—in the form of pieces of information—that would show him plainly to be writing in many cases within a larger historical and mythic context. Such is the case with "Mending Wall," in which the poet deliberately withholds a piece of useful information.

"Who are bad neighbors?" asked Thoreau, for the sole purpose of answering his own question. "They who suffer their neighbors' cattle to go at large because they don't want their ill will,—are afraid to anger them. They are abettors of the ill-doers." Thoreau could as readily have asked, "Who are good neighbors?" Whereupon, following his reasoning, he could have answered, "Those who build and maintain walls which keep out their neighbors' cattle."

How, and indeed whether, the goodwill of one's neighbour is fostered by boundaries, however, was a general question that engaged Frost. Were walls and fences instrumental in the retention and renewal of human relationships? The answers presented in "Mending Wall" are somewhat less than clear-cut. The reason is at least partly that Frost has purposely and purposefully left out of his poem some important information. One key to the poet's omission lies in the final lines of the poem.

I see him there,
Bringing a stone grasped firmly by the top
In each hand, like an old-stone savage armed.
He moves in darkness as it seems to me,
Not of woods only and the shade of trees.
He will not go behind his father's saying,
And he likes having thought of it so well
He says again, 'Good fences make good neighbors.'

In these lines the poet moves back through time, no longer questioning the possible reasons for continuing annually to repair the now apparently useless boundaries, and returns to an earlier, darker age. Indeed, his neighbour seems to be moving in a "darkness" that is, suggestively, "not of woods only and the shade of trees." To the poet he is now "like an old-stone savage armed." Even on New England farms in this century the ways of the savage continue, it would seem, no matter how transformed they may be or how radically attenuated.

Indeed, Frost shrewdly and characteristically stopped his poem just short of a mythological link. That Frost and his neighbour engage in what is tantamount to a vestigial ritual and that, furthermore, prodded by the poet, the neighbour would defend his father's idea (proverbially expressed) that "Good fences make good neighbors" relates this poem to traditions and rituals antedating the Romans. The god of boundaries they named Terminus was not invented by the Romans, but he became one of their important household gods. Terminus was annually honored in a ritual that not only reaffirmed boundaries but also provided the occasion for predetermined traditional festivities among neighbors.

The festival of the Terminalia was celebrated in Rome and in the country on the 23rd of February. The neighbours on either side of any boundary gathered round the landmark [the stones which marked boundaries], with their wives, children, and servants; and crowned it, each on his own side, with garlands, and offered cakes and bloodless sacrifices. In later times, however, a lamb, or sucking pig, was sometimes slain, and the stone sprinkled with the blood. Lastly, the whole neighbourhood joined in a general feast.

If the poet's neighbour does not know that this annual ritual of walking the boundaries to repair their common wall has its obscure source in the all but totally lost mysteries of ancient man, that information could not possibly have been unknown to the serious student of the classics who wrote the poem and who had read in Walden of Thoreau's search for firewood: "An old forest fence which had seen its best days was a great haul for me. I sacrificed it to Vulcan, for it was past serving the god Terminus." What impresses itself on Frost, however, is something quite different. Whatever the reason, men continue to need marked boundaries, even when they find it difficult to justify their existence.

Katherine Kearns

It is arguable that the self-righteous speaker of "Mending Wall" is himself obsessively committed to wall building, far more intractably and instinctively committed than his cliché-bound neighbour. While the speaker of "Mending Wall" justifiably castigates his unthinking neighbour and is himself far more aware of the powers of language for good and for ill, he is nonetheless caught up, ironically perhaps, in the same actual task, wall building, which will have the same results and look no different from his neighbor's contribution despite the narrative he brings to it.

There are several possibilities for irony here, depending on the level of Frost's self-awareness. Wall imagery pervades his poetry, as a conscious poetic image and as a psychosexual marker of control and limitation. That the speaker is the one who calls the neighbour to mend the wall is vitally important, then, but it is not clear that Frost meant for the speaker to be ironically perceived as a hypocrite.

The simple explanation, that the speaker acts out of a sense of inevitability, knowing his neighbor's habits, seems hardly enough given the contextual symbolism of the wall in Frost's poetry; the psychological explanation attendant upon this version might suggest that Frost's conscious intent was subverted by his own unconscious need for walls. So while Frost might not mean the speaker to be self-parodic, the reader might judge that there is an ironic discrepancy between what is said and what is meant, both by the speaker and by the poet. On a deeper level even than this is the possibility that Frost was aware of, had taken account of and justified, his own need for barriers. One does, after all, need something against which to push. In this case, the poem might be completely unironic, for while both men are engaged in the same task, each brings a different narrative to it, the one limited to a thoughtless clichJ, the other enriched philosophically. It could be that Frost is illustrating what it means to move from delight to wisdom: the road less traveled may not look any different, but it is made different by the inner progress of the traveller. The one wall becomes, in this reading, two walls, the speaker's wall a philosophically differentiated structure, the neighbor's wall a mere landmark of past clichJ s.

Rachel Hadas

Recall that the speaker in "Mending Wall" questions his neighbor's stolid assumption that "good fences make good neighbors." What he objects to is not so much the sentiment itself as the unwillingness or inability of the other to think for himself, to "go beyond his father's saying." Just so; we must try to get beyond the apophthegm-like opening line of "Mending Wall," testing carefully for gradations of tone as we proceed. Is it the proverb-like authority of "something there is. " that makes it so natural to equate "something" with the speaker? Once this equation has been made, the reader joins the speaker in sympathizing with this mysterious "something" and hence in opposing the neighbor's unthinking defence of walls.

Frost rings subtly drastic changes on the sound of a phrase like "good fences make good neighbors." By the time the poem ends, this line has acquired some of the pat stupidity of a slogan. Similar turns of the screw affect the opening line, when to it is added the darker phrase "that wants it down" and again when the speaker refuses to name the antiwall "something." "Elves" is the closest he gets, yet "It's not elves exactly, and I'd rather He said it for himself." Elves may mean not willowy things out of Tolkien but darker forces of the wood, for the next image is one of darkness. The neighbour is viewed as subtly menacing, "an old-stone savage armed." Yet this man has been the one to defend boundaries. The apparently relaxed and leisurely pace of the poem has made us lower our own boundaries and forget who is on what side.

At any rate, although the speaker's ironic evasiveness undermines any confident interpretation, Poirier is surely right when he makes the following point:

.it is not the neighbour. a man who can only dully repeat "good fences make good neighbors"—.it is not he who initiates the fence-making. Rather it is the far more spirited, lively, and "mischievous" speaker of the poem. While admitting that they do not need the wall, it is he who each year "lets my neighbour know beyond the hill" that it is time to do the job anyway, and who will go out alone to fill the gaps made in the wall by hunters. Though the speaker may or may not think that good neighbors are made by good fences, it is abundantly clear that he likes the yearly ritual, the yearly "outdoor game" by which fences are Because if fences do not make good neighbors the making of fences can.

Part of an old-fashioned neighborliness which results from the annual wall mending is fellowship, the potential exchange of feelings and ideas. More salient still is the joint maintenance of form for its own sake, not for utility, so that wall-making also becomes "a time to talk."

At the same time, repairing the wall means renewing that structure protective of "infant industries" or "a mood apart," protective from trespass on a symbolic level, even if "My apple trees will never get across And eat the cones under his pines." As an occasion for craft, besides being a guarantee of privacy, the wall is also crucial. Frost often compared free verse to playing tennis without the net—a remark which no one has ever interpreted as an attack on nets.

Lawrence Raab

Robert Frost once said that "Mending Wall" was a poem that was spoiled by being applied. What did he mean by "applied"? Any poem is damaged by being misunderstood, but that's the risk all poems run. What Frost objects to, I think, is a reduction and distortion of the poem through practical use. When President John F. Kennedy inspected the Berlin Wall he quoted the poem's first line: "Something there is that doesn't love a wall." His audience knew what he meant and how the quotation applied. And on the other side of that particular wall, we can find another example of how the poem has been used. Returning from a visit to Russia late in his life, Frost said, "The

Russians reprinted 'Mending Wall' over there, and left that first line off." He added wryly, "I don't see how they got the poem started." What the Russians needed, and so took, was the poem's other detachable statement: "Good fences make good neighbors." They applied what they wanted. "I could've done better for them, probably," Frost said, "for the generality, by saying:

Something there is that doesn't love a wall,
Something there is that does.

"Why didn't I say that?" Frost asked rhetorically. "I didn't mean that. I meant to leave that until later in the poem. I left it there." "Mending Wall" famously contains these two apparently conflicting statements. One begins the poem, the other ends it, and both are repeated twice. Which are we supposed to believe? What does Frost mean? "The secret of what it means I keep," he said. Of course he was being cagey, but not without reason.

At a reading given at the Library of Congress in 1962 Frost told this anecdote: In England, two or three years ago, Graham Greene said to me, "The most difficult thing I find in recent literature is your having said that good fences make good neighbors." And I said, "I wish you knew more about it, without my helping you." We laughed, and I left it that way.

Why doesn't Frost want to say what he meant? When asked, he'd reply, "What do you want me to do, say it again in different and less good words?" "You get more credit for thinking," Frost wrote in a letter, "if you restate formulae or cite cases that fall in easily under formulae, but all the fun is outside: saying things that suggest formulae that won't formulate—that almost but don't quite formulate." The formula is the easy answer that turns out to be, if right or wrong in general, certainly inadequate in particular. The formula, like a paraphrase of the poem itself, is made of those "less good words" the poet has tried to resist.

"Mending Wall" seems to present us with a problem, and appears to urge us to choose up sides. I suspect most readers are eager to ally themselves with the speaker, to consider the neighbour dim-witted, block-headed, and generally dull. Such a reading is nicely represented by the following passage from a booklet on Robert Frost put out by Monarch Notes:

By the end of the poem [the wall] has become a symbol, and the two farmers have turned into allegorical figures representing opposing views of freedom and confinement, reason and rigidity of mind, tolerance and violence, civilization and savagery.... There is no mistaking the poet's meaning, or his attitude toward what the wall represents. it stands for. the barrier between human contact and understanding. It is erected by all that is primitive, fearful, irrational and hostile [in the neighbour]. It is opposed by a higher "something" that Frost recognizes as in himself. the desire not to be alone, walled in, but to be one with the rest of the world.

There is no mistaking what the authors of the Monarch Notes want to believe, and on which side of the wall they stand. And of course it's pleasant—even comforting—to believe that the poem encourages us to be "one with the rest of the world." But is that what the poem actually says?

"Mending Wall" opens with a riddle: "Something there is...." And a riddle, after all, is a series of hints calculated to make us imagine and then name its hidden subject. The poem doesn't begin, "I hate walls," or even, "Something dislikes a wall." Its first gesture is one of elaborate and playful concealment, a calculated withholding of meaning. Notice also that it is the speaker himself who repairs the wall after the hunters have broken it. And it is the speaker each year who notifies his neighbour when the time has come to meet and mend the wall. Then can we safely claim that the speaker views the wall simply as a barrier between human contact and understanding?

Speaker and neighbour work together and equally. Although the job is tedious and hard, the speaker considers it "just another kind of outdoor game One on a side." He acknowledges that his whimsical spell—"stay where you are until our backs are turned!"—is useless, and that the result is impermanent and perhaps less important than something else. For all practical purposes this particular wall is not needed. But the project of mending it has taken on significance: "Spring is the mischief in me, and I wonder If I could put a notion in his head."

The speaker's mischievous impulse is to plant an idea. He does not say that he wants to change his neighbor's mind, to make him believe what he himself believes. He wants to nudge the neighbor's imagination, just as a teacher might wish to challenge a student. So he asks questions: "'Why do they make good neighbors? Isn't it Where there are cows? But here there are no cows.'" But the neighbour is unwilling to play this game of teacher and student. He won't answer the questions or consider the riddle. The speaker could suggest "Elves" but "it's not elves exactly," and of course it's not elves at all. The speaker's frustration is beginning to get the better of him. He wants to be fanciful—he wants to talk—and his neighbour does not. More importantly, and like a good teacher, "I'd rather He said it for himself!"

"I wish you knew more about it," Frost says he told Graham Greene, "without my helping you." This is the poem's essential challenge, which the neighbour will not accept. But the challenge is ours as well—our work, our play. The relationship between speaker and neighbour is like the relationship between poem and reader, another kind of indoor game, one on a side.

But this is a relationship between poem and reader, not poet and reader. Frost, I want to believe, is not the speaker exactly. He is behind the whole poem, rather than narrowly inside it. We need to be at least little skeptical of the speaker and not associate him automatically with the side upholding freedom, reason, and tolerance. At the end, because the neighbour won't play his game, the speaker imagines him as "an old stone savage," a harsh judgment to apply even to the most recalcitrant student. Because the neighbour will only repeat what he remembers his father having said, he seems to "Move in darkness. Not of woods only and the shade of trees." But of what else? We should say it for ourselves. His ignorance? Confinement, violence, and savagery, as the Monarch authors have it? Not exactly. It's his refusal to be playful and imaginative that irks the speaker, and his unwillingness to consider work anything more than a job to be accomplished. The speaker, after all does not ask the neighbour to give up his father's notion. He wants him to "go behind" it. If, as I want to suggest, the poem is about education, this distinction is important. The poem does not merely advocate one position over another. It asks neither for advocacy nor for application, but for investigation. It is not a statement but a performance. It enacts its meanings.

Who, finally, is right about the wall? The poem does not answer that question exactly, swerving off into deeper and more interesting territory. It uses that problem to engage us and demand that we think, which is the poem's pleasure, and its strategy. Sometimes good fences do indeed make good neighbors, and we might recall that the phrase "mending fences" means to restore communication and neighborliness. Equally true is the notion that something doesn't love a wall. The riddle isn't difficult one. We know that natural forces disturb those boulders, that the frozen groundswell is frost. But not, for all the play of the pun "Robert Frost." "All the fun's in how you say a thing," says a character in another Frost poem. But fun can be serious, just as work can be turned into play. The wall in the poem is not "the barrier between human contact and understanding." Certainly a wall may be just that, but it can also serve precisely the opposite function.

I let my neighbour know beyond the hill,
And on a day we meet to walk the line
And set the wall between us once again.
We keep the wall between us as we go.

The repetition of between should give us pause and remind us of its two equally common meanings: between as separation, as in "something's come between us," and between as what might be shared and held in common, as in "a secret between two people" or "a bond between friends." The wall divides but it also connects, if you look at it that way. All the meaning is in how you look at it—how the poem encourage you to think about it.

Frost once wrote about his experience as a teacher, "I was determined to have it out with my youngers and betters as to what thinking really was. We reached an agreement that most of what they had regarded as thinking, their own and other peoples', was nothing but voting—taking sides on an issue they had nothing to do with laying down." "Mending Wall" is a poem that lures the unwary reader into believing that thinking is merely voting, choosing up sides, taking out of the poem what most fits our own preconceived ideas. It adopts this subversive tactic because its ultimate purpose is to challenge us to go behind what we might find initially appealing in the formulas that he on its surface. "We ask people to think," Frost says, "and we don't show them what thinking is." "Mending Wall" is less a poem about what to think than it is poem about what thinking is, and where it might lead.

In his essay, "Education by Poetry," Frost writes,

Poetry provides the one permissible way of saying one thing and meaning another. People say, "Why don't you say what you mean?" We never do that, we being all of us too much poets. We like to talk in parables and in hints and indirections—whether from diffidence or some other instinct.

Perhaps we are, all of us, so much poets, or might be; but Frost who certainly was, doesn't really answer his question. Surely diffidence is not the reason why writers are drawn to the indirections of figurative language. What might that "other instinct" be? One answer is the instinct of the teacher who speaks in hints, in questions, and in challenges, who refrains from saying what he means because he wants his students to discover it for themselves. Similarly, the apparent meaning of a poem remains merely a formula unless the reader has understood how the poem came to articulate and embody that meaning. The speaker of "Mending Wall" fails in his attempt to become a successful poetteacher. Each year, it seems, he fails at the same task. Frost's poem, of course, depends upon and survives this failure, recreating a similar moment each time it is encountered.

Norman Holland

This is one of Frost's most often anthologized and

analyzed poems, justifiably so. I sense from it deep and widely shared psychological issues like those of "Once by the Pacific," but first, I want to concentrate on reading toward a conscious theme.

Several phrases refer to the seasons, particularly in a repetitive, cyclic way: "spring mending-time," "frozen ground-swell," "once again," "spring is the mischief in me." One of the major themes I see, then, is the cycle of the seasons. Associated with it, critic George Monteiro points out, is an ancient ritual antedating the Romans, the Terminatia, an annual reaffirming of boundaries, surely not unknown to Robert Frost, student of the classics.

Another theme I would use to bring together a number of particular lines and images is parallelism or the lack of it. Sometimes this parallelism takes a physical form, associated with the wall, as we imagine the two men walking parallel paths: "We meet to walk the line." "We keep the wall between us as we go." "One on a side." It is a mental wall, though, as well as a physical one, and I read the gaps as making possible a meeting of minds and attitudes as well as of lands and bodies. Closing the gaps in the wall means closing off points where the two men might meet physically or mentally. As the poet says, "If I could put a notion in his head," but he can't. The two men, the two minds, will remain parallel, on opposite sides of a wall.

I find parallelism in the language as well as in the central image of the two men walking along a wall. I find it in phrasings like "To each the boulders that have fallen to each." "And some are loaves and some so nearly balls." "Walling in or walling out." I find it most centrally in "Good fences make good neighbors," whose neat parallelism contrasts in my mind with the redundancy, the tangled, circling syntax of "Something there is that doesn't love a wall."

The parallelisms in phrasing lead me to think of speech and language themselves as themes. I find many phrases like, "'I tell him," "He only says," "I'd rather he said it," "his father's saying," "He says again." The neighbour speaks "his father's saying" twice. The poet also speaks twice, and both their repetitions represent a hardening of position, a re-building of the wall. Speech can seem almost ominous, when I hear about those yelping dogs or when the poet spells out the magic he uses to balance rocks.

Richard Poirier points out that the poem is not only about the making of fences but the making of speech between men and, even more tellingly, the way the making of fences leads to the making of speech—poetry, really, against "the claustrophobias of mechanical forms." "Walls have a power of confinement which creates a counter-movement of 'mischief.'" Richard Poirier points out a significant fact: the mischievous poet "who voices his opposition to wall-building is also the man who each year informs his taciturn neighbour that it is time to build them." "Voice and nature are thus potentially allied."

The cycles of nature and the seasons; parallelism; speech and poetry; the contrast between the physical and mental—I state such themes explicitly so that I can try to make each item of the poem relevant to every other through one or more of the themes. For example, what significance can I find in, "We wear our fingers rough with handling them"? The skin, it says, is another boundary being firmed up, and I can fit this line "under" the theme of walls and parallelism. Frost's psyche has nothing to do with this way of reading. Thematizing, as today's critical jargon has it, or simply "theming" is essential to my own sense of coherence in the poem and hence to my experience of it, although the themes themselves do not describe that experience, which remains finally emotional and private.

The last step in such a theming or cohering is to phrase one central theme or meaning for my four themes or subthemes. Then I can play the details of the poem against that central theme. What idea would unite seasons, parallelism, physical and mental, speech? I can borrow from Northrop Frye's reading of this poem and speak of the centre of the poem as two human attitudes toward a wall, one wintry, one spring-like. Frank Lentricchia describes the two men in the poem this way: "One moves in a world of freedom because, aware of the resources of the mind, he nurtures the latent imaginative power within himself and makes it a factor in every-day living, while the other, unaware of the value of imagination, must live his unliberated life without it." I need not assume that Frost favors the walls-down, spring-like attitude over the walls-up, colder one, only that he is playing with the contrast between them. In fact Frost said, "Maybe I was both fellows in the poem." "I've got a man there; he's both of those people but he's man—both of them, he's a wall builder and a wall toppler. He makes boundaries and he breaks boundaries. That's man." Indeed that there are two such types and that one person can be both—those very facts make up one of the human walls that the poem, for me, is about.

Having arrived at some such centering theme, I can make parts of the poem relevant that otherwise would not make sense to me. "Some are loaves and some so nearly balls. " Why does Frost trouble to say that? I can read it as a dualism right inside the wall itself, a wan within a wall, a division within a division. (But is that enough? See the last pages of this book.) Why "elves"? I can fit them in as nature-spirits, as having to do with the "something" that takes the wall down—hence they fit under the theme of the seasons. Why cows? And what is the sense of Frost's saying his apple trees will never eat the cones under his neighbor's pines? I daresay I could rationalize these images (St. Armand, for example, notes that Frost knew pine cones could seed a nearby orchard). My task, however, is not to cohere the poem so much as to read the mind of Robert Frost.

[The basic task of our first year of life is to establish a sense of self, whether that involves separating from a mother-and-child matrix or simply developing a sense of "I." As I read it, "Mending Wall" is about just this issue: setting up and breaking down boundaries, especially boundaries between people. Shall we have separate identities or shall we get rid of the boundaries between ourselves and the world outside? Frye and Lentricchia have stated the attitudes on either side of the wall in adult terms. In terms of child development, our first "wall"—our sense of a boundary between self and not-self—

came about by means of the mouth. If so, I can imagine why Frost's poem about a wall has so many images of speaking and eating: "the yelping dogs," stones which are "loaves," the speaking of a spell, the neighbor's twice saying "his father's saying," phrases like "I tell him," "He only says," and so on.

I can also imagine why, although both Frost and his neighbour are grown men, the poet should offer his pixyish explanations through "elves." The poem itself offers something of a clue: "Spring is the mischief in me," and elves are tiny and child-like as well as imaginative and playful. Frost as a poet allies himself with that elfin playfulness but also with an impulse to lose the boundary between self and other and so return to earliest childhood, when one is an elf, living in a world where spells work.

In this way Frost projects onto nature his own playfulness: "Something there is that doesn't love a wall, That wants it down." The verb "love," by calling for an animate subject, makes the something that doesn't love more than some thing. Besides, the "frozen-ground-swell" is really frost, and that concealed pun again mixes up self and outer world as does "Spring is the mischief in me." The reference to cows, which I find somewhat puzzling, introduces other infantile themes, milk and motherhood most obviously, a note of femininity, but I also think of the cow as an eat-and-be-eaten animal. Hence I hear in Frost's "But here there are no cows" a denial of rivalry and eat-and-be-eaten anger—we don't need a wall.

It seems to me Frost is working with an infantile fantasy about breaking down the wall which marks self so as to return to a state of closeness to an Other. To lose the boundary between self and Other is to perceive one's own impulses as part of the outer world and to feel the actions of the outer world as one's own. Keats called this the essential ability for a poet: negative capability, being able to put one's own identity aside and imagine oneself into the things and persons of the world outside the self. Such a return to a child's at-oneness, however, is not without risk. One gives oneself over to "projection" and "introjection" which, Erikson remarks, "remain some of our deepest and most dangerous defence mechanisms." They may be good for poets, but they are dangerous for, say, politicians and generals or for a child frightened by the waves at the Cliff House beach. I am thinking of paranoid projections.

In the section of the poem where Frost entertains the possibility of just letting the wall fall down, I sense a faintly paranoid loss of boundary between himself and his neighbour: "I wonder If I could put a notion in his head." "I'd rather He said it for himself." There is a link, widely recognized in psychiatry, between a paranoid view of the world (It is all directed at me) and the projection of homosexual impulses (I don't love him—he loves me). In this context, the poem's fantasy of merger may not be directed at a woman ("no cows") but another man, and (in psychoanalytic terms) I can hear other levels of merger, in those hard boulders the two men carry: as weapons, as "balls," "handling them," and so on. In this vein, I am hearing wishes and fears about being close to another man, particularly a strong, primitive one, a "savage." I am hearing wishes about excrement, testicles, assault, or penetration of one man by another.

I hear, too, the primitive rage of the so-called "oral stage," in "the work of hunters," a rage that can carry over into all later hungers and desires.

they have left not one stone on a stone,
But they would have the rabbit out of hiding,
To please the yelping dogs.

Still more ominous is the picture of the neighbour holding a stone in each hand, "like an old-stone savage armed." The Palaeolithic reference images in yet another way regression to a violent, primitive state of mind. Knowing something about the sources of this rage helps me make sense out of what seem to me the oddest lines of the poem:

He is all pine and I am apple orchard.
My apple trees will never get across
And eat the cones under his pines, I tell him.

Using language to cope, Frost is telling the neighbour that he is being unrealistic. In a manifest way, Frost is simply being sarcastic: you only need a wall if you think immovable trees will cross over and eat inedible seeds. In the poem, however, as necessarily in Frost's and my minds, boundary and eating and identity and the ability to deal with reality all go together. A failure to keep one's boundaries marks the most severe mental disorders. It could indicate either a regression to the earliest stage of infancy or a failure to develop out of that oral stage. Thus, when the speaker imagines that wall down, he says, "He is all pine and I am apple orchard." If the wall comes down, individual identity will be destroyed. Unconscious anger is masked as gentle sarcasm, but the chaos comes through unchanged. I hear the neighbour (and the poem) saying, If there is no wall, craziness will break through.

That, it seems to me, is the core of fantasy that corresponds to the imagining and controlling of a sexual scene in "Once by the Pacific." When "something" takes the walls down between self and other, a chaotic, violent, irrational, primitive attack appears. As in the shorter poem, Frost uses language to imagine that aggression (the Stone Age image of the neighbour, for example). He then uses language to limit it: "He says again, 'Good fences make good neighbors.'" "Put out the light."

At the conscious level (if we adopt Northrop Frye's centering theme) the poem plays off two human attitudes, one wintry, one spring-like. The warm spring-like (but dangerous) walls-down feeling corresponds to a poet's wish for a cozy but risky return to some original one-ness. The neighbor's wintry, New England standoffishness, his walls-up sense of privacy and separateness, corresponds to the cold, hard, more grownup reality of individuation. In a theme Richard Poirier develops, the walls-down feeling corresponds to the poet's wayward imaginings, the walls-up to the control of that imagination.

Mark Richardson

The speaker of that poem allies himself with the insubordinate energies of spring, which yearly destroy the wall separating his property from his neighbor's: "Spring is the mischief in me," he says). This alliance at first has the effect of setting the speaker against the basic conservatism of his neighbour beyond the hill, who as everybody knows never "goes behind his father's saying": "Good fences make good neighbors." But the association of the speaker with insubordinate natural forces should not be permitted to obscure an important fact, which has been often enough noticed: he, not the neighbour, initiates the yearly spring repair of the wall; moreover, it is again he, not the neighbour, who goes behind hunters who destroy the wall in other seasons and makes repairs. So if the speaker is allied with the vernal mischief of spring and its insubordinations, he is nevertheless also set against them in his efforts to make the stones of the wall balance and remain in place: "Stay where you are until our backs are turned!" he wryly says to the stones. Here, in fact, the speaker is rather like those of Frost's earlier poems "Rose Pogonias" and "October," each of whom, in imagination at least, attempts to arrest the naturally entropic and destructive forces of nature in the hope of achieving a momentary stay against confusion. In "Rose Pogonias," for example, we read:

We raised a simple prayer
Before we left the spot,
That in the general mowing
That place might be forgot;
Or if not all so favored,
Obtain such grace of hours,
That none should mow the grass there
While so confused with flowers.

And in "October":

O hushed October morning mild,
Begin the hours of this day slow.
Make the day seem to us less brief.
Hearts not averse to being beguiled,
Beguile us in the way you know.
Release one leaf at break of day;
At noon release another leaf;
One from our trees, one far away.
Retard the sun with gentle mist;
Enchant the land with amethyst.
Slow, slow!

The happy irony of "Mending Wall" is this: the speaker in this case allies himself with the destructive energies of nature, not against them as in "Rose Pogonias" and "October"; but at the same time he ritually initiates the wall-building exercise that so inefficiently resists and contains those same energies. The speaker of "Mending Wall" is obviously of two minds: at once wall-builder and wall-destroyer, at once abettor and antagonist of seasonal entropies. I would point out further that his impatience with his neighbor's aphoristic turn of mind is significantly (and playfully) qualified by the admonitory aphorism he himself devises and twice repeats, clearly delighted at having thought of it himself: "Something there is that doesn't love a wall," he says in a tone that by the poem's end almost acquires an air of finger-wagging, country pedantry. The difference is that, unlike his benighted neighbour, the speaker of the poem does indeed go behind his own favored aphorism to play both sides of the fence. In short, the two opposed men in the poem fairly shape up into one, and his name is Robert Frost.

At last, then, we have alternative aphorisms about walls and fences, and the truth of the matter resides in the "gap" between them that this famously mischievous poem opens up. In this way "Mending Wall" at once acknowledges the limitations of walls (and aphorisms) and also their seductions and value. As has often been pointed out, this dual

theme is embodied even in the movement of the blank verse lines of "Mending Wall," which subtly play both within and against the metrical and structural impositions of the iambic pentameter line. When his speaker has in view the energies that disturb walls and boundaries, Frost's prosody vagrantly resists the regularities of his metrical contract:

Something there is that doesn't love a wall,
That sends the frozen-ground-swell under it
And spills the upper boulders in the sun
And makes gaps even two can pass abreast.

Enjambment and metrical variations—trochaic feet for iambic ones, spondaic and pyrrhic substitutions, and so on—contribute subtly to the theme of these lines. It is exactly as

Pope would have it. How better to, describe a disordered wall than in lines themselves disordered? At such times Frost's blank verse recalls "Tintern Abbey," in which Wordsworth describes those "hedgerows hardly hedgerows" in eloquently unruly lines. In any case, here—as at a number of moments in "Mending Wall"—metrical and rhythmical patterns work in a kind of loosely running counterpoint characterized more by "formity" than by "conformity," as Frost might say. By contrast, when Frost imagines the reconstruction of the wall as the two men labour, the rhythm and meter of his lines coincide quite exactly:

I let my neighbour know beyond the hill;
And on a day we meet to walk the line
And set the wall between us once again.
We keep the wall between us as we go.

Here, end-stopped lines are the rule: grammatical and rhetorical units more or less confine themselves to their prescribed ten-syllable boundaries. And there is little or no rhythmical variation against the basic iambic grid, which reasserts itself in these lines rather as the wall it- self is "reasserted." Other such examples of Frost's metrical dexterity in this poem might be given, but these two suffice to suggest how tightly integrated in "Mending Wall" are form and theme.

In sum, the speaker of the poem exhibits, both in his manner and in his actions, a certain flexibility. He unsettles walls that he also always repairs; he is at once Apollonian and Dionysian. Once again—as in the introduction to King Jasper and "The Future of Man"—Frost's conservative and rebellious tendencies are perfectly balanced, just as the "intransigent" and "accommodating" tendencies of the speaker of "Good Hours" are metrically and thematically balanced ....

We might also regard "Mending Wall" in light of what Frost says in his 1934 letter to his daughter Lesley about the doctrine of Inner Form. The "neighbour beyond the hill" is all on the side of conformity, the speaker of the poem (at least by his own account) all on the side of formity. Frost himself—and here we should perhaps distinguish him from his speaker—stands at the dialectical intersection of these two opposed terms, for as he says in "The Constant Symbol" about the "discipline[s]" from "within" and from "without": "He who knows not both knows neither."

On "Home Burial"

Randall Jarrell

The poem's first sentence, "He saw her from the bottom of the stairs Before she saw him," implies what the poem very soon states: that, knowing herself seen, she would have acted differently—she has two sorts of behaviour, behaviour for him to observe and spontaneous immediate behaviour: "She was starting down, Looking back over her shoulder at some fear" says that it is some fear, and not a specific feared object, that she is looking back at; and, normally, we do not look back over our shoulder at what we leave, unless we feel for it something more than fear. "She took a doubtful step" emphasizes the queer attraction or fascination that the fear has for her; her departing step is not sure it should depart. "She took a doubtful step and then undid it ": the surprising use of undid gives her withdrawal of the tentative step a surprising reality.

The poem goes on: "To raise herself and look again." It is a little vertical ballet of indecision toward and away from a fearful but mesmerically attractive object, something hard to decide to leave and easy to decide to return to. "He spoke Advancing toward her": having the old line end with "spoke," the new line begin with "advancing," makes the very structure of the lines express the way in which he looms up, gets bigger. (Five lines later Frost repeats the effect even more forcibly with: "He said to gain time: 'What is it you see,' Mounting until she cowered under him.") Now when the man asks: "What is it you see From up there always—for I want to know," the word "always" tells us that all this has gone on many times before, and that he has seen it—without speaking of it—a number of times before.

The phrase "for I want to know" is a characteristic example of the heavy, willed demands that the man makes, and an even more characteristic example of the tautological, rhetorical announcements of his actions that he so often makes, as if he felt that the announcement somehow justified or excused the action.

The poem goes on: "She turned and sank upon her skirts at that." The stairs permit her to subside into a modest, compact, feminine bundle; there is a kind of smooth deftness about the phrase, as if it were some feminine saying: "When in straits, sink upon your skirts." The next line, "And her face changed from terrified to dull," is an economically elegant way of showing how the terror of surprise (perhaps with another fear underneath it) changes into the dull lack of response that is her regular mask for him.

The poem continues: "He said to gain time"—to gain time in which to think of the next thing to say, to gain time in which to get close to her and gain the advantage of his physical nearness, his physical bulk. His next "What is it you see" is the first of his many repetitions; if one knew only this man one would say, "Man is the animal that repeats." In the poem's next phrase, "mounting until she cowered under him," the identity of the vowels in "mounting" and "cowered" physically connects the two, makes his mounting the plain immediate cause of her cowering. "I will find out now" is another of his rhetorical announcements of what he is going to do: "this time you're going to tell me, I'm ging to make you." But this heavy-willed compulsion changes into sheer appeal, into reasonable beseeching, in his next phrase: "you must tell me, dear." The "dear" is affectionate intimacy, the "must" is the "must "of rational necessity; yet the underlying form of the sentence is that of compulsion.

The poem goes on: "She, in her place, refused him any help." The separated phrase "in her place" describes and embodies, with economical brilliance, both her physical and spiritual lack of outgoingness, forthcomingness; she brims over none of her contours, remains sitting upon her skirts upon her stairstep, in feminine exclusion. "Refused him any help With the least stiffening of her neck and silence": she doesn't say Yes, doesn't say No, doesn't say; her refusal of any answer is worse than almost any answer. "The least stiffening of her neck," in its concise reserve, its slight precision, is more nearly conclusive than any larger gesture of rejection. He, in extremities, usually repeats some proverbial or rhetorical generalization; at such moments she usually responds either with a particular, specific sentence or else with something more particular than any sentence: with some motion or gesture.

The next line, "She let him look, sure that he wouldn't see," reminds one of some mother bird so certain that her nest is hidden that she doesn't even flutter off, but sits there on it, risking what is no risk, in complacent superiority. "Sure that he wouldn't see, Blind creature": the last phrase is quoted from her mind, is her contemptuous summing up. "And awhile he didn't see"; but at last when he sees, he doesn't tell her what it is, doesn't silently understand, but with heavy slow comprehension murmurs, "Oh," and then repeats, "Oh." It is another announcement of what he is doing, a kind of dramatic rendition of his understanding. (Sometimes when we are waiting for someone, and have made some sound or motion we are afraid will seem ridiculous to the observer we didn't know was there, we rather ostentatiously look at our watch, move our face and lips into a "What on earth could have happened to make him so late?" as a way of justifying our earlier action.

The principle behind our action is the principle behind many of this man's actions.) With the undignified alacrity of someone hurrying to reestablish a superiority that has been questioned, the woman cries out like a child: "What is it—what?" Her sentence is, so to speak, a rhetorical question rather than a real one, since it takes it for granted that a correct answer can't be made. His reply, "Just that I see," shows that his unaccustomed insight has given him an unaccustomed composure; she has had the advantage, for so long, of being the only one who knows, that he for a moment prolongs the advantage of being the only one who knows that he knows. The immediately following "'You don't,' she challenged. 'Tell me what it is'" is the instant, childishly assertive exclamation of someone whose human position depends entirely upon her knowing what some inferior being can never know; she cannot let another second go by without hearing the incorrect answer that will confirm her in her rightness and superiority.

The man goes on explaining, to himself, and to mankind, and to her too, in slow rumination about it and about it. In his "The wonder is I didn't see at once. I never noticed it from here before. I must be wonted to it—that's the reason," one notices how "wonder" and "once" prepare for "wonted," that provincial-, archaic-sounding word that sums up—as "used" never could—his reliance on a habit or accustomedness which at last sees nothing but itself, and hardly sees that; and when it does see something through itself, beyond itself, slowly marvels. In the next line, "The little graveyard where my people are!" we feel not only the triumph of the slow person at last comprehending, but also the tender, easy accustomedness of habit, of long use, of a kind of cozy social continuance—for him the graves are not the healed scars of old agonies, but are something as comfortable and accustomed as the photographs in the family album. "So small the window frames the whole of it," like the later "Broad-shouldered little slabs there in the sunlight On the sidehill," not only has this easy comfortable acceptance, but also has the regular feel of a certain sort of Frost nature description: this is almost the only place in the poem where for a moment we feel that it is Frost talking first and the man talking second. But the man's "Not so much larger than a bedroom, is it?"—an observation that appeals to her for agreement—carries this comfortable acceptance to a point at which it becomes intolerable: the only link between the bedroom and the graveyard is the child conceived in their bedroom and buried in that graveyard.

The sentence comfortably establishes a connection which she cannot bear to admit the existence of—she tries to keep the two things permanently separated in her mind. (What he says amounts to his saying about their bedroom: "Not so much smaller than the graveyard, is it?") "There are three stones of slate and one of marble, Broad-shouldered little slabs there in the sunlight On the sidehill " has a heavy tenderness and accustomedness about it, almost as if he were running his hand over the grain of the stone. The "little" graveyard and "little" slabs are examples of our regular way of making something acceptable or dear by means of a diminutive.

Next, to show her how well he understands, the man shows her how ill he understands. He says about his family's graves: "We haven't to mind those"; that is, we don't have to worry about, grieve over, my people: it is not your obligation to grieve for them at all, nor mine to give them more than their proper share of grief, the amount I long ago measured out and used up. But with the feeling, akin to a sad, modest, relieved, surprised pride, with which he regularly responds to his own understanding, he tells her that he does understand: what matters is not the old stones but the new mound, the displaced earth piled up above the grave which he had dug and in which their child is buried.

When he says this, it is as if he had touched, with a crude desecrating hand, the sacred, forbidden secret upon which her existence depends. With shuddering hysterical revulsion she cries: "Don't, don't, don't, don't." (If the reader will compare the effect of Frost's four don't's with the effect of three or five, he will see once more how exactly accurate, perfectly effective, almost everything in the poem is.) The poem continues: "She withdrew shrinking from beneath his arm That rested on the banister, and slid downstairs"; the word "slid" says, with vivid indecorousness, that anything goes in extremities, that you can't be bothered, then, by mere appearance or propriety; "slid" has the ludicrous force of actual fact, is the way things are instead of the way we agree they are. In the line "And turned on him with such a daunting look," the phrase "turned on him " makes her resemble a cornered animal turning on its pursuer; and "with such a daunting look" is the way he phrases it to himself, is quoted from his mind as "blind creature" was quoted from hers.

The beautifully provincial, old-fashioned, folk-sounding "daunting" reminds one of the similar, slightly earlier "wonted," and seems to make immediate, as no other word could, the look that cows him. The next line, " He said twice over before he knew himself," tells us that repetition, saying something twice over, is something he regresses to under stress; unless he can consciously prevent himself from repeating, he repeats. What he says twice over (this is the third time already that he has repeated something) is a rhetorical question, a querulous, plaintive appeal to public opinion: "Can't a man speak of his own child he's lost?" He does not say specifically, particularly, with confidence in himself: "I've the right to speak of our dead child"; instead he cites the acknowledged fact that any member of the class man has the acknowledged right to mention, just to mention, that member of the class of his belongings, his own child—and he has been unjustly deprived of this right. "His own child he's lost" is a way of saying: "You act as if he were just yours, but he's just as much just mine; that's an established fact." "Can't a man speak of his own child he's lost" has a magnificently dissonant, abject, aggrieved querulousness about it, in all its sounds and all its rhythms; "Can't a man" prepares us for the even more triumphantly ugly dissonance (or should I say consonance?) of the last two words in her "I don't know rightly whether any man can."

Any rhetorical question demands, expects, the hearer's automatic agreement; there is nothing it expects less than a particular, specific denial. The man's "Can't a man speak." means "Isn't any man allowed to speak.," but her fatally specific answer, "Not you!" makes it mean, "A man cannot—is not able to—speak, if the man is you." Her "Oh, where's my hat?" is a speech accompanied by action, means: "I'm leaving. Where's the hat which social convention demands that a respectable woman put on, to go out into the world?" The immediately following "Oh, I don't need it!" means: in extremities, in cases when we come down to what really matters, what does social convention or respectability really matter? Her "I must get out of here.

I must get air" says that you breathe understanding and suffocate without it, and that in this house, for her, there is none. Then, most extraordinarily, she gives a second specific answer to his rhetorical question, that had expected none: "I don't know rightly whether any man can." The line says: "Perhaps it is not the individual you that's to blame, but man in general; perhaps a woman is wrong to expect that any man can speak—really speak—of his dead child."

His "Amy! Don't go to someone else this time" of course tells us that another time she has gone to someone else; and it tells us the particular name of this most particular woman, something that she and the poem never tell us about the man. The man's "Listen to me. I won't come down the stairs" tells us that earlier he has come down the stairs, hasn't kept his distance. It (along with "shrinking," "cowered," and many later things in the poem) tells us that he has given her reason to be physically afraid of him; his "I won't come down the stairs" is a kind of euphemism for "I won't hurt you, won't even get near you."

The poem's next sentence, "He sat and fixed his chin between his fists"—period, end of line—with its four short i's, its "fixed " and "fists," fixes him in baffled separateness; the sentence fits into the line as he fits into the isolated perplexity of his existence. Once more he makes a rhetorical announcement of what he is about to do, before he does it: "There's something I should like to ask you, dear." The sentence tiptoes in, gentle, almost abjectly mollifying, and ends with a reminding "dear"; it is an indirect rhetorical appeal that expects for an answer at least a grudging: "Well, go ahead and ask it, then." His sentence presupposes the hearer's agreement with what it implies: "Anyone is at least allowed to ask, even if afterwards you refuse him what he asks." The woman once more gives a direct, crushing, particular answer: "You don't know how to ask it." "Anyone may be allowed to ask, but you are not because you are not able to ask"; we don't even need to refuse an animal the right to ask and be refused, since if we gave him the right he couldn't exercise it. The man's "Help me, then," has an absolute, almost abject helplessness, a controlled child-like simplicity, that we pity and sympathize with; yet we can't help remembering the other side of the coin, the heavy, brutal, equally simple and helpless anger of his later I'll come down to you.

The next line, "Her fingers moved the latch for all reply" (like the earlier "She. refused him any help With the least stiffening of her neck and silence"; like "And turned on him with such a daunting look"; like the later "She moved the latch a little"; like the last "She was opening the door wider"), reminds us that the woman has a motion language more immediate, direct, and particular than words—a language she resorts to in extremities, just as he, in extremities, resorts to a language of repeated proverbial generalizations. "Home Burial" starts on the stairs but continues in the doorway, on the threshold between the old life inside and the new life outside.

The man now begins his long appeal with the slow, heavy, hopeless admission that "My words are nearly always an offence." This can mean, "Something is nearly always wrong with me and my words," but it also can mean—does mean, underneath—that she is to be blamed for nearly always finding offensive things that certainly are not meant to offend. "I don't know how to speak of anything So as to please you" admits, sadly blames himself for, his baffled ignorance, but it also suggests that she is unreasonably, fantastically hard to please—if the phrase came a little later in his long speech he might pronounce it "so as to please you." (Whatever the speaker intends, there are no long peacemaking speeches in a quarrel; after a few sentences the speaker always has begun to blame the other again.)

The man's aggrieved, blaming "But I might be taught, I should suppose" is followed by the helpless, very endearing admission: "I can't say I see how"; for the moment this removes the blame from her, and his honesty of concession makes us unwilling to blame him. He tries to summarize his dearly bought understanding in a generalization, almost a proverb: "A man must partly give up being a man With women-folk." The sentence begins in the dignified regretful sunlight of the main floor, in "A man must partly give up being a man," and ends huddled in the basement below, in "With women-folk." He doesn't, use the parallel, coordinate "with a woman," but the entirely different "with women-folk"; the sentence tries to be fair and objective, but it is as completely weighted a sentence as "A man must partly give up being a man with the kiddies," or "A man must partly give up being a man with Bandar-log." The sentence presupposes that the real right norm is a man being a man with men, and that some of this rightness and normality always must be sacrificed with that special case, that inferior anomalous category, "women-folk."

He goes on: "We could have some arrangement [it has a hopeful, indefinite, slightly helter-skelter sound] By which I'd bind myself to keep hands off "—the phrases "bind myself" and "keep hands off" have the primitive, awkward materiality of someone taking an oath in a bad saga; we expect the sentence to end in some awkwardly impressive climax, but get the almost ludicrous anticlimax of "Anything special you're a-mind to name." And, too, the phrase makes whatever she names quite willful on her part, quite unpredictable by reasonable man. His sensitivity usually shows itself to be a willing, hopeful form of insensitivity, and he himself realizes this here, saying, "Though I don't like such things 'twixt those that love." Frost then makes him express his own feeling in a partially truthful but elephantine aphorism that lumbers through a queerly stressed line a foot too long ("Two that don't love can't live together without them") into a conclusion ("But two that do can't live together with them") that has some of the slow, heavy relish just in being proverbial that the man so often shows. (How hard it is to get through the monosyllables of the two lines!) His words don't convince her, and she replies to them without words: "She moved the latch a little." He repeats in grieved appeal: "Don't—don't go. Don't carry it to someone else this time." (He is repeating an earlier sentence, with "Don't go" changed to "Don't carry it.") The next line, "Tell me about it if it's something human," is particularly interesting when it comes from him. When is something inside a human being not human, so that it can't be told? Isn't it when it is outside man's understanding, outside all man's categories and pigeonholes—when there is no proverb to say for it? It is, then, a waste or abyss impossible to understand or manage or share with another.

His next appeal to her, "Let me into your grief," combines an underlying sexual metaphor with a child's "Let me in! let me in!" This man who is so much a member of the human community feels a helpless bewilderment at being shut out of the little group of two of which he was once an anomalous half; the woman has put in the place of this group a group of herself-and-the-dead-child, and he begs or threatens—reasons with her as best he can—in his attempt to get her to restore the first group, so that there will be a man-and-wife grieving over their dead child.

He goes on: "I'm not so much Unlike other folks as your standing there Apart would make me out." The "standing there Apart" is an imitative, expressive form that makes her apart, shows her apart. Really her apartness makes him out like other folks, all those others who make pretense of following to the grave, but who before one's back is turned have made their way back to life; but he necessarily misunderstands her, since for him being like others is necessarily good, being unlike them necessarily bad. His "Give me my chance"—he doesn't say a chance—reminds one of those masculine things fairness and sportsmanship, and makes one think of the child's demand for justice, equal shares, which follows his original demand for exclusive possession, the lion's share. "Give me my chance" means: "You, like everybody else, must admit that anybody deserves a chance—so give me mine"; he deserves his chance not by any particular qualities, personal merit, but just by virtue of being a human being. His "I do think, though, you overdo it a little" says that he is forced against his will to criticize her for so much exceeding (the phrase "a little" is understatement, politeness, and caution) the norm of grief, for mourning more than is usual or reasonable; the phrase "overdo it a little" manages to reduce her grief to the level of a petty social blunder.

His next words, "What was it brought you up to think it the thing To take your mother-loss of a first child So inconsolably—in the face of love," manage to crowd four or five kinds of condemnation into a single sentence. "What was it brought you up" says that it is not your essential being but your accidental upbringing that has made you do this-it reduces the woman to a helpless social effect. "To think it the thing" is particularly insulting because it makes her grief a mere matter of fashion; it is as though he were saying, "What was it brought you up to think it the thing to wear your skirt that far above your knees?" The phrase "To take your mother-loss of a first child " pigeonholes her loss, makes it a regular, predictable category that demands a regular, predictable amount of grief, and no more.

The phrase "So inconsolably—in the face of love" condemns her for being so unreasonable as not to be consoled by, for paying no attention to, that unarguably good, absolutely general thing, love; the generalized love makes demands upon her that are inescapable, compared to those which would be made by a more specific phrase like "in the face of my love for you." The man's "You'd think his memory might be satisfied " again condemns her for exceeding the reasonable social norm of grief; condemns her, jealously, for mourning as if the dead child's demands for grief were insatiable.

Her interruption, "There you go sneering now!" implies that he has often before done what she calls "sneering" at her and her excessive sensitivity; and, conscious of how hard he has been trying to make peace, and unconscious of how much his words have gone over into attack, he contradicts her like a child, in righteous anger: "I'm not, I'm not!" His "You make me angry" is another of his rhetorical, tautological announcements about himself, one that is intended somehow to justify the breaking of his promise not to come down to her; he immediately makes the simple childish threat, "I'll come down to you"—he is repeating his promise, "I won't come down to you," with the "not" removed. "God, what a woman!" righteously and despairingly calls on God and public opinion that voice of the people which is the voice of God) to witness and marvel at what he is being forced to put up with: the fantastic, the almost unbelievable wrongness and unreasonableness of this woman. "And it's come to this," that regular piece of rhetorical recrimination in quarrels, introduces his third use of the sentence "Can't a man speak of his own child he's lost"; but this time the rhetorical question is changed into the factual condemnation of "A man can't speak of his own child that's dead." This time he doesn't end the sentence with the more sentimental, decorous, sympathy—demanding "that's lost," but ends with the categorical "that's dead."

Earlier the woman has given two entirely different, entirely specific and unexpected answers to this rhetorical question of his; this time she has a third specific answer, which she makes with monosyllabic precision and finality: "You can't because you don't know how to speak." He has said that it is an awful thing not to be permitted to speak of his own dead child; she replies that it is not a question of permission but of ability, that he is too ignorant and insensitive to be able to speak of his child.

Her sentence is one line long, and it is only the second sentence of hers that has been that long. He has talked at length during the first two-thirds of the poem, she in three- or four-word phrases or in motions without words; for the rest of the poem she talks at length, as everything that has been shut up inside her begins to pour out. She opens herself up, now—is far closer to him, striking at him with her words, than she has been sitting apart, in her place. His open attack has finally elicited from her, by contagion, her open anger, so that now he is something real and unbearable to attack, instead of being something less than human to be disregarded.

This first sentence has indicted him; now she brings in the specific evidence for the indictment. She says: "If you had any feelings, you that dug With your own hand "—but after the three stabbing, indicting stresses of your own hand she breaks off the sentence, as if she found the end unbearable to go on to; interjects, her throat tightening, the incredulous rhetorical question, "how could you?"—and finishes with the fact that she tries to make more nearly endurable, more euphemistic, with the tender word "little": "his little grave." The syntax of the sentence doesn't continue, but the fact of things continues; she says, "I saw you from that very window there."

That very window there has the same stabbing stresses, the same emphasis on a specific, damning actuality, that your own hand had—and that, soon my own eyes and your own baby's grave and other such phrases Will have. She goes on: "Making the gravel leap and leap in air, Leap up, like that, like that, and land so lightly And roll back down the mound beside the hole." As the sentence imitates with such terrible life and accuracy the motion of the gravel, her throat tightens and aches in her hysterical repetition of "like that, like that": the sounds of "leap and leap in air, Leap up, like that, like that, and land so lightly" are "le! le! le! li! li! la! li!" and re-create the sustained hysteria she felt as she first watched; inanimate things, the very stones, leap and leap in air, or when their motion subsides land "so lightly," while the animate being, her dead child, does not move, will never move. (The foxes have holes, and the birds of the air have nests; but the Son of man hath not where to lay his head.)

Her words "leap and leap in air, Leap up, like that, like that" keep the stones alive! alive! alive!—in the words "and land" they start to die away, but the following words "So lightly" make them, alive again, for a last moment of unbearable contradiction, before they "roll back down the mound beside the hole. " The repeated o's (the line says "oh! ow! ow! oh!") make almost crudely actual the abyss of death into which the pieces of gravel and her child fall, not to rise again. The word "hole" (insisted on even more by the rhyme with "roll") gives to the grave the obscene actuality that watching the digging forced it to have for her.

She says: "I thought, Who is that man? I didn't know you." She sees the strange new meaning in his face (what, underneath, the face has meant all along) so powerfully that the face itself seems a stranger's. If her own husband can do something so impossibly alien to all her expectations, he has never really been anything but alien; all her repressed antagonistic knowledge about his insensitivity comes to the surface and masks what before had masked it. In the next sentence, "And I crept down the stairs and up the stairs To look again," the word "crept" makes her a little mouselike thing crushed under the weight of her new knowledge. But the truly extraordinary word is the "and" that joins "down the stairs" to "up the stairs." What is so extraordinary is that she sees nothing extraordinary about it: the "and" joining the two coordinates hides from her, shows that she has repressed, the thoroughly illogical, contradictory nature of her action; it is like saying: "And I ran out of the fire and back into the fire," and seeing nothing strange about the sentence.

Her next words, "and still your spade kept lifting," give the man's tool a dead, mechanical life of its own; it keeps on and on, crudely, remorselessly, neither guided nor halted by spirit. She continues: "Then you came in. I heard your rumbling voice Out in the kitchen"; the word "rumbling" gives this great blind creature an insensate weight and strength that are, somehow, hollow. Then she says that she did something as extraordinary as going back up the stairs, but she masks it, this time, with the phrase "and I don't know why." She doesn't know why, it's unaccountable, "But I went near to see, with my own eyes." Her "I don't know why" shows her regular refusal to admit things like these; she manages by a confession of ignorance not to have to make the connections, consciously, that she has already made unconsciously.

She now says a sentence that is an extraordinarily conclusive condemnation of him: "You could sit there with the stains on your shoes Of the fresh earth from your own baby's grave And talk about your everyday concerns." The five hissing or spitting s's in the strongly accented "sit," "stains," "shoes"; the whole turning upside down of the first line, with four trochaic feet followed by one poor iamb; the concentration of intense, damning stresses in fresh earth from your own baby's grave all these things give an awful finality to the judge's summing up, so that in the last line, "And talk about your everyday concerns," the criminal's matter-of-fact obliviousness has the perversity of absolute insensitivity: Judas sits under the cross matching pennies with the soldiers. The poem has brought to life an unthought-of literal meaning of its title: this is home burial with a vengeance, burial in the home; the fresh dirt of the grave stains her husband's shoes and her kitchen floor, and the dirty spade with which he dug the grave stands there in the entry. As a final unnecessary piece of evidence, a last straw that comes long after the camel's back is broken, she states: "You had stood the spade up against the wall Outside there in the entry, for I saw it." All her pieces of evidence have written underneath them, like Goya's drawing, that triumphant, traumatic, unarguable I SAW IT.

The man's next sentence is a kind of summing-up-in-little of his regular behaviour, the ways in which (we have come to see) he has to respond. He has begged her to let him into her grief, to tell him about it if it's something human; now she lets him into not her grief but her revolted, hating condemnation of him; she does tell him about it and it isn't human, but a nightmare into which he is about to fall. He says: "I shall laugh the worst laugh I ever laughed. I'm cursed. God, if I don't believe I'm cursed." The sounds have the gasping hollowness of somebody hit in the stomach and trying over and over to get his breath—of someone nauseated and beginning to vomit: the first stressed vowel sounds are "agh! uh! agh! uh! agh1 uh!" He doesn't reply to her, argue with her, address her at all, but makes a kind of dramatic speech that will exhibit him in a role public opinion will surely sympathize with, just as he sympathizes with himself. As always, he repeats: "laugh," "laugh," and "laughed," "I'm cursed" and "I'm cursed" (the rhyme with "worst" gives almost the effect of another repetition): as always, he announces beforehand what he is going to do, rhetorically appealing to mankind for justification and sympathy. His "

I shall laugh the worst laugh I ever laughed " has the queer effect of seeming almost to be quoting some folk proverb. His "I'm cursed" manages to find a category of understanding in which to pigeonhole this nightmare, makes him a reasonable human being helpless against the inhuman powers of evil—the cursed one is not to blame. His "God, if I don't believe I'm cursed" is akin to his earner "God, what a woman!"—both have something of the male's outraged, incredulous, despairing response to the unreasonableness and immorality of the female. He responds hardly at all to the exact situation; instead he demands sympathy for, sympathizes with himself for, the impossibly unlucky pigeonhole into which Fate has dropped him.

His wife then repeats the sentence that, for her, sums up everything: "I can repeat the very words you were saying. 'Three foggy mornings and one rainy day Will rot the best birch fence a man can build.'" We feel with a rueful smile that he has lived by proverbs and—now, for her—dies by them. He has handled his fresh grief by making it a part of man's regular routine, man's regular work; and by quoting man's regular wisdom, that explains, explains away, pigeonholes, anything. Nature tramples down man's work, the new fence rots, but man still is victorious, in the secure summing up of the proverb.

The best birch fence is, so far as its stresses are concerned, a firm, comfortable parody of all those stabbing stress systems of hers. In his statement, as usual, it is not I but a man. There is a resigned but complacent, almost relishing wit about this summing up of the transitoriness of human effort: to understand your defeat so firmly, so proverbially, is in a sense to triumph. He has seen his ordinary human ambition about that ordinary human thing, a child, frustrated by death; so there is a certain resignation and pathos about his saying what he says.

The word "rot " makes the connection between the fence and the child, and it is the word "rot" that is unendurable to the woman, since it implies with obscene directness: how many foggy mornings and rainy days will it take to rot the best flesh-and-blood child a man can have? Just as, long ago at the beginning of the poem, the man brought the bedroom and the grave together, he brings the rotting child and the rotting fence together now. She says in incredulous, breathless outrage: "Think of it, talk like that at such a time!" (The repeated sounds) th, t, t, th, t, t, are thoroughly expressive.) But once more she has repressed the connection between the two things: she objects to the sentence not as what she knows it is, as rawly and tactlessly relevant, but as something absolutely irrelevant, saying: "What had how long it takes a birch to rot To do with"—and then she puts in a euphemistic circumlocution, lowers her eyes and lowers the shades so as not to see—"what was in the darkened parlor."

But it is time to go back and think of just what it was the woman saw, just how she saw it, to make her keep on repeating that first occasion of its sight. She saw it on a holy and awful day. The child's death and burial were a great and almost unendurable occasion, something that needed to be accompanied with prayer and abstention, with real grief and the ritual expression of grief. It was a holy or holi-day that could only be desecrated by "everyday concerns"; the husband's digging seemed to the wife a kind of brutally unfeeling, secular profanation of that holy day, her holy grief. Her description makes it plain that her husband dug strongly and well.

And why should he not do so? Grief and grave digging, for him, are in separate compartments; the right amount of grief will never flow over into the next compartment. To him it is the workaday, matter-of-fact thing that necessarily comes first; grieving for the corpse is no excuse for not having plenty of food at the wake.

If someone had said to him: "You dig mighty well for a man that's just lost his child," wouldn't he have replied: "Grief's no reason for doing a bad job"? (And yet, the muscles tell the truth; a sad enough man shovels badly.) When, the grave dug and the spade stood up in the entry, he went into the kitchen, he may very well have felt: "A good job," just as Yakov, in Rothschild's Fiddle, taps the coffin he has made for his wife and thinks: "A good job."

But unconsciously, his wife has far more compelling reasons to be appalled at this job her husband is doing. Let me make this plain. If we are told how a woman dreams of climbing the stairs, and of looking out through a window at a man digging a hole with a spade—digging powerfully, so that the gravel leaps and leaps into the air, only to roll back down into the hole; and still the man's spade keeps lifting and plunging down, lifting and plunging down, as she watches in fascinated horror, creeps down the stairs, creeps back up against her will, to keep on watching; and then, she doesn't know why, she has to go to see with her own eyes the fresh earth staining the man's shoes, has to see with her own eyes the man's tool stood up against the wall, in the entrance to the house—if we are told such a dream, is there any doubt what sort of dream it will seem to us? Such things have a sexual force, a sexual meaning,.

That day of the funeral the grieving woman felt only misery and anguish, passive suffering; there was nobody to blame for it all except herself. the woman's feeling of guilt about other things is displaced onto the child's death. Now when this woman sees her husband digging the grave (doing what seems to her, consciously, an intolerably insensitive thing; unconsciously, an indecent thing) she does have someone to blame, someone upon whom to shift her own guilt: she is able to substitute for passive suffering and guilt an active loathing and condemnation—as she blames the man's greater guilt and wrongness her own lesser guilt can seem in comparison innocence and rightness. (The whole matrix of attitudes available to her, about woman as Madonna-and-child and man as brute beast, about sexuality as a defiling thing forced upon woman, helps her to make this shift.)

The poem has made it easy for us to suspect a partial antagonism or uncongeniality, sexually, between the weak oversensitive woman and the strong insensitive man, with his sexual force so easily transformed into menace. (The poem always treats it in that form.) The woman's negative attitudes have been overwhelmingly strengthened, now; it is plain that since the child's death there has been no sort of sexual or emotional union between them.

She has put grief, the dead child, apart on an altar, to be kept separate and essential as long as possible—forever, if possible. He has immediately filed away the child, grief, in the pigeonhole of man's wont, man's proverbial understanding: the weight is off his own separate shoulders, and the shoulders of all mankind bear the burden. In this disaster of her child's death, her husband's crime, her one consolation is that she is inconsolable, has (good sensitive woman) grieved for months as her husband (bad insensitive man) was not able to grieve even for hours. Ceasing to grieve would destroy this consolation, would destroy the only way of life she has managed to find. And yet she has begun to destroy them. When she says at the end of the poem: "How can I make you—" understand, see, she shows in her baffled, longing despair that she has tried to make him understand; has tried to help him as he asked her to help him.

Her "You couldn't care," all her lines about what friends and the world necessarily are, excuse him in a way, by making him a necessarily insensitive part of a necessarily insensitive world that she alone is sensitive in: she is the one person desperately and forlornly trying to be different from everyone else, as she tries to keep death and grief alive in the middle of a world intent on its own forgetful life.

At these last moments she does not, as he thinks, "set him apart" as "so much Unlike other folks"; if he could hear and respond to what she actually has said, there would be some hope for them. But he doesn't; instead of understanding her special situation, he dumps her into the pigeonhole of the crying woman—any crying woman—and then tries to manage her as one manages a child. She does try to let him into her grief, but he won't go; instead he tells her that now she's had her cry, that now he feels better, that the heart's gone out of it, that there's really no grief left for him to be let into.

The helpless tears into which her hard self-righteous separateness has dissolved show, underneath, a willingness to accept understanding; she has denounced him, made a clean breast of things, and now is accessible to the understanding or empathy that he is unable to give her. Women are oversensitive, exaggerate everything, tell all, weep, and then are all right: this is the pigeonhole into which he drops her. So rapid an understanding can almost be called a form of stupidity, of not even trying really to understand. The bewitched, un canny, almost nauseated helplessness of what he has said a few lines before: "I shall laugh the worst laugh I ever laughed.

I'm cursed. God, if I don't believe I'm cursed," has already changed into a feeling of mastery, of the strong man understanding and managing the weak hysterical woman. He is the powerful one now. His "There, you have said it all and you feel better. You won't go now" has all the grown-up's condescension toward the child, the grown-up's ability to make the child do something simply by stating that the child is about to do it. The man's "You're crying. Close the door. The heart's gone out of it: why keep it up" shows this quite as strikingly; he feels that he can manipulate her back into the house and into his life, back out of the grief that—he thinks or hopes—no longer has any heart in it, so that she must pettily and exhaustingly "keep it up."

But at this moment when the depths have been opened for him; at this moment when the proper management might get her back into the house, the proper understanding get her back into his life; at this moment that it is fair to call the most important moment of his life, someone happens to come down the road. Someone who will see her crying and hatless in the doorway; someone who will go back to the village and tell everything; someone who will shame them in the eyes of the world. Public opinion, what people will say, is more important to him than anything she will do; he forgets everything else, and expostulates: "Amy! There' s someone coming down the road! " His exclamation is full of the tense, hurried fear of social impropriety, of public disgrace; nothing could show more forcibly what he is able to understand, what he does think of primary importance. Her earlier "Oh, where's my hat? Oh, I don't need it!" prepares for, is the exact opposite of, his "Amy! There's someone coming down the road!"

She says with incredulous, absolute intensity and particularity, "You—"

That italicized you is the worst, the most nearly final thing that she can say about him, since it merely points to what he is. She doesn't go on; goes back and replies to his earlier sentences: "oh, you think the talk is all." Her words have a despairing limpness and sadness: there is no possibility of his being made to think anything different, to see the truth under the talk. She says: "I must go—" and her words merely recognize a reality—"Somewhere out of this house." Her final words are full of a longing, despairing, regretful realization of a kind of final impossibility: "How can I make you—" The word that isn't said, that she stops short of saying, is as much there as anything in the poem. All her insistent anxious pride in her own separateness and sensitiveness and superiority is gone; she knows, now, that she is separate from him no matter what she wants. Her "How can I make you—" amounts almost to "If only I could make you—if only there were some way to make you—but there is no way."

He responds not to what she says but to what she does, to "She was opening the door wider." He threatens, as a child would threaten: "If—you—do!" He sounds like a giant child, or a child being a giant or an ogre. The "If—you—do!" uses as its principle of being the exaggerated slowness and heaviness, the willedness of his nature. (Much about him reminds me of Yeats's famous definition: "Rhetoric is the will trying to do the work of the imagination"; "Home Burial" might be called the story of a marriage between the will and the imagination.) The dashes Frost inserts between the words slow down the words to the point where the slowedness or heaviness itself, as pure force and menace, is what is communicated. Then the man says, trying desperately—feebly—to keep her within reach of that force or menace: "Where do you mean to go? First tell me that. I'll follow and bring you back by force. I will!— " The last sentences of each of her previous speeches (her despairing emotional "Oh, I won't, I won't!" and her despairing spiritual "How can I make you—") are almost the exact opposite of the "I will!" with which he ends the poem.

It is appropriate that "force," "I," and "will" are his last three words: his proverbial, town-meeting understanding has failed, just as his blankly imploring humility has failed; so that he has to resort to the only thing he has left, the will or force that seems almost like the mass or inertia of a physical body. We say that someone "throws his weight around," and in the end there is nothing left for him to do but throw his weight around. Appropriately, his last line is one more rhetorical announcement of what he is going to do: he will follow and bring her back by force; and, appropriately, he ends the poem with one more repetition—he repeats: " I will!"

Richard Poirier

In "Home Burial," the couple are trapped inside the house, which is described as a kind of prison, or perhaps more aptly, a mental hospital. Even the wife's glance out the window can suggest to the husband the desperation she feels within the confines of what has always been his family's "home"; it looks directly on the family graveyard which now holds the body of their recently dead child:

He saw her from the bottom of the stairs
Before she saw him. She was starting down,
Looking back over her shoulder at some fear.
She took a doubtful step and then undid it
To raise herself and look again. He spoke
Advancing toward her: "What is it you see
From up there always — for I want to know." [always?]
She turned and sank upon her skirts at that,
And her face changed from terrified to dull.
He said to gain time: "What is it you see," [see?]
Mounting until she cowered under him.
"I will find out now — you must tell me, dear."

The remarkable achievement here is that the husband and wife have become so nearly inarticulate in their animosities that the feelings have been transferred to a vision of household arrangements and to their own bodily movements. They and the house conspire together to create an aura of suffocation. For a comparable sense of divorcement communicated mostly by silent uses of space in a "home," a supposedly shared area, perhaps the best analogy is not to be found in literature but in film, such as the opening of Antonioni's La Notte. But of course Frost's special genius is in the placement of words. The first line poses the husband as a kind of spy; the opening of the second line suggests a habituated wariness on her part, but from that point to line 5 we are shifted back to his glimpse of her as she moves obsessively again, as yet unaware of being watched, to the window. Suggestions of alienation, secretiveness, male intimidation ("advancing toward her") within a situation of mutual distrust, a miasmic fear inside as well as outside the house - we are made to sense this before anyone speaks. Initially the fault seems to lie mostly with the husband. But as soon as she catches him watching her, and as soon as he begins to talk, it is the grim mutuality of their dilemma and the shared responsibilities for it that sustain the dramatic intelligence and power of the poem.

I have indicated in the margin a number of the emendations made by Lathem in his edition - which is assumed to be "authoritative" - because his version substantially loses the poignant delicacy with which Frost treats the estrangement between husband and wife.

Lathem chose to make two emendations wholly on his own: he added a question mark after "always" in line 7, and he put a comma after "help" in line 13. He also arbitrarily chose to follow early editions by allowing a question mark at the end of line 10, though Frost had deleted it in all the editions he supervised after 1936, including the 1949 Complete Poems. These textual matters are worth considering, because while Lathem's choices hurt the poem, they make us aware of punctuation in ways that considerably increase our appreciation of nuances which might otherwise go unremarked.

We can note, for example, the scrupulous justice with which Frost tries to locate, even through the use of a comma, the sources of conflict in this "home." There is a marvelously managed shifting in the apportionment of blame. Thus the man's initial speech, while impatient, is meant to be more gentle than it is in the assertively interrogative form that Lathem's question mark gives it. Without the question mark, there is the implication that the husband has learned, after many trying experiences, not to expect an answer to his questions. And the strength of her obstinacy with regard to him is then confirmed by the fact that instead, of showing fear at his "advancing on her," her face, on his near approach, changes from "terrified to dull."

Nonetheless, the choice of "until" and "under" in the phrase "mounting until she cowered under him" suggests that there indeed is a calculated masculine imposition of will in the way he acts, though this possibility is as quickly muffled by his then speaking more gently still ("'I will find out now - you must tell me, dear"') with its allowable lack of stress on the word "now" and the especially strong beat, after a comma, on the word "dear." Frost did not choose to put a comma after the word "help" ("She, in her place, refused him any help With the least stiffening of her neck and silence"), and its absence is crucial to our recognition of how perverse and stubbornly uncompliant she can be.

With the comma added, the line suggests that her stiffness and silence merely accompanied her refusal to tell him what she had seen out the window; without the comma, we are allowed to infer that she would choose not to stiffen her neck lest she thereby give him any clue at all about what she has been staring at: "Sure that he wouldn't see Blind creature." These surges of surreptitious feeling between the two of them obviously result not from their immediate juxtaposition on the stairs but from a customary incapacity to share any feelings with one another.

Of course he does see what is out there, the child's grave. And her challenge then to "'Tell me what it is"' is merely the first of many instances in which differences are defined, as they so often are in Frost, as differences in the use of words, in the way one speaks or hears things, in the uses to which a metaphor is put, be it sane or crazy, brutal or insensitive: "'You don't know how to ask it"' (line 43), she complains, and he - "'My words are nearly always an offense. I don't know how to speak of anything' " (lines 45-46); or, again (line 70), "'A man can't speak of his own child that's dead,'" to which in the next line she replies, "'You can't because you don't know how to speak."' Her lengthy indictment of him near the end of the poem begins with her claim, "'I can repeat the very words that you were saying. think of it, talk like that at such a time!'" (lines 91, 94).

One of the husband's initial mentions of the graveyard does betray a certain tactless predominance and possessiveness ("'The little graveyard where my people are!"'), but this is immediately followed by a metaphor of diminishment that somewhat restores a balance ("'So small the window frames the whole of it"'). However, this in turn gives way to yet another metaphor of dangerously thoughtless implication: "'Not so much larger than a bedroom, is it?"' In its very casualness, really a kind of stupidity, the husband's comparison of the graveyard to a bedroom is a sign that, having been made so nervous about the inadequacy of his language, he has to double or triple his illustration of anything he wants to communicate.

He seems unaware of his tastelessness, which is of course all the more reason to think that his bedroom metaphor reveals some of his deepest feelings about what has happened to their marriage. But if the bedroom is like a graveyard, the reason has as much to do with her excessive (possibly neurotic) sensibility as with the obvious deficiencies of his. And if he is insensitive, he is at least not without gentleness. When he asks her " 'Don't - Don't go. Don't carry it to someone else this time"' (lines 56-57), he is less peremptory than is she: "'Don't, don't, don't, don't' she cried" (line 29), a line that is as remarkably powerful in its effect as a similar one in Hemingway's "Hills Like White Elephants": "Will you Please please please please please please please stop talking?" She is asking him not to speak; he is asking her not to leave him.

Out of some terrible fastidiousness she seems to want to abridge even what is left of their relationship, while he, because of love, and some incipient pride of place in the community, is doing his best to maintain some sort of contact. Sexuality in Frost has been noted, when at all, with a kind of surprise. And yet in a very great number of his poems it figures, as it does here, as a submerged metaphor for his all-consuming interest in the relational and transitional nature of poetry, of thinking, of talking itself.

The husband and wife here cannot "ask" anything of one another or "tell" anything without giving offense partly because they both are flawed in their sense of time and of timing. With her desire to stop everything in the interest of mourning the death of an infant, she cannot understand his apparent incapacity to mourn at all and his choosing to talk, instead, of everyday concerns. She does not see that this is his only way of managing grief, of not letting it consume his or her life. And the words she accuses him of using as he sat there talking on the day he buried his child - "'Three foggy mornings and one rainy day Will rot the best birch fence a man can build"' - form hemselves without his knowing it, but with complete appropriateness, into a metaphor for the way nature, if only by some accident of weather, will erode whatever human beings might make to protect themselves from the reality of change and death. The wife sees and then describes her husband's actions on that day with an angry exactitude, a kind of novelistic passion for detail, characteristic of country women in the poems we have been looking at:

"If you had any feelings, you that dug
With your own hand — how could you?
— his little grave;
I saw you from that very window there,
Making the gravel leap and leap in air,
Leap up, like that, like that, and land so lightly
And roll back down the mound beside the hole.
I thought, Who is that man? I didn't know you.
And I crept down the stairs and up the stairs
To look again, and still your spade kept lifting.
Then you came in. I heard your rumbling voice
Out in the kitchen, and I don't know why,
But I went near to see with my own eyes.
You could sit there with the stains on your shoes
Of the fresh earth from your own baby's grave
And talk about your everyday concerns.
You had stood the spade up against the wall
Outside there in the entry, for I saw it."

There is a genius here of a sort found in the brilliantly right sentence in Joyce's "The Dead" when Gretta remembers how her dead lover of long ago stood under her window in a cold that was to chill him to his death: "'I can see his eyes as well as well!"' she says to Gabriel. "'He was standing at the end of the wall where there was a tree."' Allen Tate remarks on how a vision of the past is framed with startling immediacy by the mention of that "tree," how it lets us share a reality vividly present to the person speaking. The same peculiar convergence of past and present occurs here, thanks to Frost's keen sense of the power of variation and repetition: "'Making the gravel leap and leap in air, Leap up, like that, like that, and land so lightly.'" Her charge continues, and with the same haunted exactness of recollection:

"I can repeat the very words you were saying:
'Three foggy mornings and one rainy day
Will rot the best birch fence a man can build.'
Think of it, talk like that at such a time!
What had how long it takes a birch to rot
To do with what was in the darkened parlor?"

It is important here to notice the comparative bareness of the attendant language when she quotes the metaphor of the "birch fence." His inability to respond effectively to her charges is understandable: an indictment cannot be answered when it is only more or less a description, as if certain words and acts are inherently contemptible. "'I'm cursed. God, if I don't believe I'm cursed,'" he says, and indeed he is being "cursed": there is no word more apt for what she says to him. It is worth recollecting here something that Frost wrote in a letter to Wilbert Snow, a poet and professor of English at Wesleyan University, in 1933:

My mind goes back to how true Turgeneff holds the balance between protagonists and antagonists in the death of Bayarov in Fathers and Sons. He is perfect in his non-partizanship. I never quite like to hear a wife turned on against her husband or vice versa. They know too much about each other and they are not disinterested. They lack, what they should lack, detachment. Maybe it bothers me as a breach of manners (Thompson, Letters, p. 393).

On the chance that the wife's accusations might prove more persuasive than they should, Frost corrects the flow of our sympathies by allowing for a curious imbalance in that part of the poem (lines 97-107) given to her complaints about the brevity of all human sorrow. It is as if even the proportions of the poem - its form and decorum - much less those of mourning, must be swelled out of proper shape by the wife's obsession with her grievances.

The catalogue of her complaints is a symptom of how for her they have become a way of deadening a deeper grief too painful to be borne. Her list of grievances is no adequate metaphor, that is, for the grief she feels. All she can do is insist that " 'I won't have grief so,' " won't have it, that is, dissipated by the passage of time. In response, one might think of a poem called "Good Relief" never collected by Frost in any volume, in which he says that "No state has found a perfect cure for grief In law, in gospel, or in root or herb." "Grief without grievance" - this, we have seen, was a dictum for Frost; the limits of sympathy were no less prescribed by the nature of things than were the limits of metaphor. A bit like the wife here was his sister Jeanie, as described in a letter of April 12, 1920, to Louis Untermeyer:

She has always been antiphysical and a sensibilitist. I must say she was pretty well broken by the coarseness and brutality of the world before the war [World War I] was thought of. She was willing to go almost too far to show her feeling about it, the more so that she couldn't find anyone who would go far enough. One half the world seemed unendurably bad and the other half unendurably indifferent. She included me in the unendurably indifferent. A mistake. I belong to the unendurably bad.

And I suppose I am a brute in that my nature refuses to carry sympathy to the point of going crazy just because someone else goes crazy, or of dying just because someone else dies. As I get older, I find it easier to lie awake nights over other peoples' troubles. But that's as far as I go to date. In good time I will join them in death to show our common humanity.

The experience in the reading of the poem is that the wife's talk in this long peroration has a driven and dissociated quality with respect not only to the form of the poem but to the conversation going on in it. That is why the husband feels that she has somehow purged herself and that the "talk" will of itself have relieved her and the situation of a kind of swelling:

"There, you have said it all and you feel better.
You won't go now. You're crying. Close the door.
The heart's gone out of it: why keep it up?

Amy! There's someone coming down the road!"
"You — oh, you think the talk is all. I must go —
Somewhere out of this house. How can I make you —
"If-you-do!" She was opening the door wider.
"Where do you mean to go? First tell me that.
I'll follow and bring you back by force. I will! —"

Clearly, she cannot say "it all" because her grievances are not and cannot be the equivalent of her grief, and so she necessarily rejects what to her cannot help but sound like condescension. Her movement out of the house, out of discord, and into a literal "extravagancy" on the road leads again to his assertion of masculine threat and will, though this is now so tempered by an evident love and toleration and concern that the threat sounds more like a plea and an admission of helplessness.

Besides being a moving and powerful human drama, "Home Burial" is about the limits, as revealed through the consciousness of these two unique people, of "home" as a place, a form, a mode of discourse in which often unmanageably extreme states of feeling occur. But if the limits are sad and terrifying, Frost seems nonetheless sure of their necessity. His decorums, he would have it, are consistent with reality and, if respected, can make life at least manageable. Violations of decorum in a poem or in any other formed relationship are a cause as well as a symptom of induced terror. "Poetry is measured in more senses than one," Frost wrote to Sidney Cox in September 1929. "It is measured feet, but more important still it is a measured amount of all we could say an we would.

We shall be judged finally by the delicacy of our feeling of where to stop short" (Thompson, Letters, p. 361). It could be said that the central subject of this poem is poetic form seen in the metaphor of domestic form - a debate between a husband and wife about how each "shall be judged finally by the delicacy of our feeling of where to stop short." She claims that he has violated any possible decorums of grief by his lack of expressiveness. Hence, she "must get out of here" (line 37), "somewhere out of this house" (line 113) - this poem, too. He insists that she restrict her expression of grief to the house and to the boundaries of their marital contract, but he is in all this too peculiarly willful for her or for his own good. The poem ends on his exclamation " 'I will!' " Our only sure indication that she has by then gone through the door she has been gradually opening while they talk.

Mordecai Marcus

"Home Burial" may not be as popular as "Mending Wall" and "The Death of the Hired Man," but it is Frost's most critically acclaimed and intensively analyzed narrative. Again, Frost deals with barriers between people—in this case a husband and wife who have recently lost their first child and who handle their grief in strikingly different ways—according to their characters and expressive capacities.

The locale is a New England farm with a family burial plot in the yard, illustrating familiarity with death, which partly accounts for the husband's taciturn handling of his grief. The poem opens with intense looking and severe gestures between the man and woman, as she gazes from a stairway window at the backyard grave of her recently dead child, defensively and accusatorially, both calling attention to herself and refusing her husband's concern for her grief. He seems not to have noticed the view from the window, but his tender description of the gravestones and the child's mound—not yet marked with a stone—show that he is not unfeeling but that such family deaths have become an everyday part of his life.

In the initial action the wife moves away from the husband and he pursues her with hesitating dominance, but her continued withdrawal is partly a provocation, which helps account for his protest that he's not allowed to grieve in his own way. Her desire for air and her explanation that perhaps his reaction is just masculine show that her criticism may not be strictly personal.

Struggling to restrain himself, the husband sits down, speaking and reflecting on the fact that his wife goes to other people with her troubles instead of discussing them with him. He is attempting reconciliation, but she continues to taunt him with words and actions, insisting that he can't say the right thing. He musingly half-apologizes for his ways and tries to account for their communication barrier by the difference between male and female.

Tentatively offering to consider certain subjects off limits for them, he cleverly notes that such a tactic is necessary for strangers living together but not good for lovers. Again she makes a taunting gesture, and again he asks her not to take her grief to someone else but rather to share it with him. Still, he shows that he is reconciled to the child's death in a way she can't be, and she regards his view that their love casts a blessing on the lost child, and expresses a promise for the future, as a sneer at the reality of their loss. His repeated protest that he's not allowed to grieve in his own way leads her to a full-scale attack on what she takes to have been his grossly unfeeling burial of the child.

Here she projects her own insistence on his unfeelingness onto images of his burial activities, not seeing that he buried the child himself to maintain his intimacy with it, to make it a part of his past, and to work out his own grieves. The spade and the stains on his shoes, which she took for signs of indifference, show his bond to the processes of life and death, just as his everyday talk after digging the grave was a way of holding back pain.

But he is either incapable of an analytic answer or too stubbornly proud to offer one, so instead of protesting that she misunderstands, he can only toss out grimly oblique anger. She revels in the fact that everyone must die alone, and sets herself up as a philosopher, condemning humanity's supposed insensitivity to everyone else's grief and proposing the impossible task of changing the world.

His assumption that she has talked out her grief and his concern with the possibility of being spied by a neighbour suggest either a stronger sense of privacy than his wife's or a superficial concern about the judgments of others. The wife's obsession suggests an inflated pride in something that distinguishes her from others. Her repeated assertion that she must get away shows that she doesn't really want a break with her husband, that she can see her way to internal change. His apparently irrational insistence that she tell where she's going so he can bring her back by force suggests that he knows she wants to be subdued or at least to have her irrationality brought back to earth.

Each character evinces more sympathy than the other from some readers; Amy is sometimes seen as being over the edge of madness, and her husband is sometimes seen as self-righteously callous. The poem has some relationship to Elinor and Robert Frost's loss of their first child, and although the characters do not seem much like the poet and his wife, Frost may have put into them some of her tendency toward exaggeration and his own almost willful and defensive pretense that he does not understand things that he thinks are improper. A balanced view might be that the poem shows compassion for two different human types in view of not only their loss but also their covert insistence on and exaggeration of their differences.

Katherine Kearns

It one may use a metrical yardstick to evaluate a given speaker's control, then it becomes profitable to compare the dramatic speeches within, for example, "Home Burial, " where one crucial theme is the perceived failure of language to communicate adequately the bereaved couple's shared dilemma. Does one speaker show more control, and thus by extension for Frost, more good sense than the other? Neither of them, in fact, is said by the other to be able to use language authoritatively, and this, if it is true, condemns them both to ineffectuality.

The husband "can't. speak of his own child he's lost" because his "words are nearly always an offense" (another pun, perhaps, as his words are barriers), and he can't ask the right question because, the wife says, he doesn't "know how to ask it." The wife is herself inarticulate with despair, and while she asserts that her husband has no right to talk because he doesn't "know how to speak," she herself knows that nothing she says will be sufficient.

When her husband says to her, "There, you have said it all and you feel better, " she reacts with contempt: "You - oh, you think the talk is all. I must go -" Both of them use eleven- to twelve-syllable lines, which come in the context of the iambic pentameter base to represent a kind of spillage, a profligacy of language that, for them, is without its desired effect - to communicate their separate griefs. The wife uses about 10 percent more of these extrasyllabic lines, a difference that does not seem conclusive in establishing the husband's authority even as it suggests the direction of Frost's sympathies (of the husband's forty-nine lines, fifteen are extrasyllabic; of the wife's forty-one lines, seventeen are extrasyllabic). Thus the metrical virtuosity of the poet-narrator in lines like the appropriately eleven-syllable "She took a doubtful step and then undid it" is used by Frost within the dialogue to reveal the uncontrol and frustration of both husband and wife. Such uncontrived speech argues for their complete sincerity; neither has an agenda beyond personal need, neither defends an unreasonable position, and neither is capable of the rhetorical control demanded by irony.

"Home Burial epitomizes Frost's intimate relationships between sex, death, and madness: that "a bedroom" - not, significantly, the bedroom by the husband's terms - and the graveyard are of the same size and shape suggests the geometrical precision by which desire becomes correlated with burial itself. The wife is in the process of leaving the house, crossing the threshold from marital asylum into freedom. The house is suffocating her. Her window view of the graveyard is not enough and is, in fact, a maddening reminder that she could not enter the earth with her son.

With its transparent barrier, the window is a mockery of a widened vision throughout Frost's poetry and seems to incite escape rather than quelling it; in "Home Burial" the woman can "see" through the window and into the grave in a way her husband cannot, and the fear is driving her down the steps toward the door - "She was starting down - Looking back over her shoulder at some fear" - even before she sees her husband.

He threatens to follow his wife and bring her back by

force, as if he is the cause of her leaving, but his gesture will be futile because it is based on the mistaken assumption that she is escaping him. Pathetically, he is merely an obstacle toward which she reacts at first dully and then with angry impatience; he has lost all authority and all power, a truth manifested most potently in his linguistic failures whereby he is reduced to the stuttering refrain, "A man can't speak." Without language he is unmanned. He "think[s] the talk is all" and yet he cannot speak. He has become merely an animate part of the embattled household, but her real impetus for movement comes from the grave.

The house itself, reduced to a narrow passageway between the bedroom and the threshold and triangulated to the graveyard, is a correlative for the sexual tension generated by the man's preoccupation with his marital rights and the woman's rejection of them. He offers to "give up being a man" by binding himself "to keep hands off," but quite clearly their marriage is already sexually damaged and empty.

That he makes this concession suggests that his wife has repulsed his sexual advances in the past: in this refusal she empowers herself, symbolically and literally rejecting the role as servant-wife by refusing to acknowledge the conjugal "rights" of the husband and by refusing to provide him with an heir. Her egress from the house will be symbolic verification of her husband's impotence, and if she leaves it and does not come back, the house will rot like the best birch fence will rot. Unfilled, without a woman with child, it will fall into itself, an image that recurs throughout Frost's poetry and suggests analogously Frost's sense that the poetic structure must be pushed taut by the erotic energy of its language.

Thus the child's grave predicts the dissolution of household, a movement toward the open cellar of "The Generations of Men," almost a literal "home burial." Randall Jarrell explicates the grave-digging scene in "Home Burial" as perceived by the grieving mother: as if in a dream, she climbs the stairs and looks out to see her husband plunging his spade again and again into the earth.

Then she walks down to see her husband's shoes stained

with fresh earth, his spade standing against the wall in the entryway. Jarrell says, "Such things have a sexual force, a sexual meaning, as much in our waking hours as in our dreams. When the plowman digs his plow into the earth, Mother Earth, to make her bear, this does not have a sexual appropriateness only in the dreams of neurotic patients - it is something we all understand, whether or not we admit we understand." "Home Burial," in its committing to earth the proof of a couple's sexual love, predicts a pattern of imagery, rich and ambivalent, that throughout Frost's poetry relates earth both to sexuality and to death. The grave, with its natural and domestic correlatives, becomes a remarkably potent conflation of the point at which desire and death merge into inextricable ecstasy and despair.

Karen L. Kilcup

Interestingly for our purposes, a central source of friction between the couple is the divergence between their self-conceptions, expressed in their different attitudes toward grief; while he mourns inwardly, she affirms the necessity of its outward expression. In her pain and anger she threatens him with her physical absence (her emotional absence is only too evident), yet, when she makes this threat, his real fears of sexual inadequacy surface: "'Amy! Don't go to someone else this time.'" What stands out for me at this moment—and elsewhere—is the duplicity of the language in which the husband couches his desire, for this line represents both plea and command. Furthermore, his words exhibit a wide veering from his behaviour: "'Listen to me.

I won't come down the stairs.' He sat and fixed his chin between his fists. 'There's something I should like to ask you, dear"' (emphasis added). Throughout the poem a language of endearment masks and conventionalizes the subverbal menace emblematized in his physical gestures. Echoing an issue that emerges differently in poems like "The Housekeeper" and "The Fear," Frost understands—only too well, perhaps— the psychic weight carried by the threat physical violence embodied here by the husband, and his is deeply sensitive to the wife's vulnerability. If masculinity requires bodily supremacy, it also collides, however unwittingly, with psychological dominance. Yet the consequence of this dominance seems to be only greater alienation, sexual as well is emotional. [T]he portrait of the husband on the verge of a violent brutishness both reflects and interrogates early-twentieth-century notions of muscular masculinity.

In "Home Burial" we are left a capacious space in which to imagine the transformation of a prior intimacy into an utter fracture of relationship. As the husband reflects on his wife's kind of grief, he pleads, "You'd think his memory might be satisfied—," and she responds,

"There You go sneering now!"
"I'm not, I'm not!"

Frost breaks this line in the middle to suggest how profoundly at odds they are, how much psychic as well as literal space separates them. Once again, the relationship between the husband and wife's creativity emerges most clearly in language: his language wounds powerfully, and, however unwittingly, he, not she, is the metaphor-maker, the poet who speaks of fences when his heart aches. When the wife accuses, "'You can't because you don't know how to speak,"' she is unable to hear the pain and beauty in his lament: "'Three foggy mornings and one rainy day Will rot the best birch fence a man can build!"' We see a moment in which the poet urges and encodes the efficacy of language but only to an audience that can understand it—the reader willing to respond emotionally as much as intellectually. Frost acknowledges that Amy—like Elinor, perhaps—is confined by the literal creativity that her role as wife demands and by the emotions that such limitation imposes. Being only a place of "confinement" for her, home is too much where the heart is.

Working against the stereotype of the nostalgic regionalist idyll, Frost is especially critical of representations of home as merely a source of renewal and refuge. Amy is home-less, and the religion that sometimes filled the Frost household is echoed in her circumscription, in her repeated affirmations that she has to escape, get out, go, "'Somewhere out of this house.'" She wonders, "'How can I make you—'" understand, we assume, but she is inadequate even to complete her sentence. The husband's "sentence" that concludes the poem—"I'll follow and bring you back by force. I will!"—represents both desperate plea and the final, overt expression of the menace that has underscored his speech throughout the poem. Structurally as well as semantically, the poem enacts the enclosure of the feminine self and feminine speech; to read this last line as merely desperate is seriously to underread the danger that the husband poses. Echoing the voice of cultural authority, he becomes both judge and author of his wife's fate: house arrest.

Robert Faggen

. In "Home Burial" a wife's angry reticence becomes a moral rebuke to what she perceives as her husband's brutal and selfish way of mourning the death of their first child; the gender hierarchy of civilized and uncivilized, ordered and chaotic, male and female, becomes remarkably fluid. The death of their child, one of the most disturbing possible events in a marriage and an undermining of a fundamental biological order, threatens the purpose of their relationship and reveals, instead of love, a void. The drama of their argument reveals the intensity of her personal interests beneath her mask of piety and the force of her husband's will beneath his postures of care and reasonableness. Their debate about the limits of grief becomes defined by gender and whether there is any common human ground on which to continue their relationship and a family.

Amy's declaration of the loneliness of death and others' inability to grieve appears to conform to the Aristotelian view that excessive grief is "unmanly," associated with women who are closer to chaotic nature than men. In "Home Burial" this ancient distinction becomes complicated. Amy remains impervious to fellow mourners and provides a powerful though flawed rebuke to her husband's grief and temporary control, which may be little more than the virtue of maintaining his own power within the home. Amy becomes the relentless idealist in a world of survival demands.

Though "Home Burial" focuses on Amy's need to escape the confines of the house and marriage, we learn that her husband found some of his own escape outside the house digging his son's grave, no doubt a form of relief from his wife 's moral control. When the narrative begins, we find Amy in a position of metaphoric superiority, at the top of the stairs, silent and refusing her husband's gaze from the bottom. Her silence becomes a barrier she has created to torment her husband and force him into a confrontation with her fears, one of which is the physical force he exhibits as he "mounts" above her seeking to penetrate her reticence. The absence of question marks at the end of the husband's "questions" reveal the extent to which they are more accurately demands, if not threats:

She was first the object of his gaze, and one senses that her extra looks back were intended to offset his controlling stare. The narrator tells us that she was "looking back at some fear."

Here, as in "The Witch of Coos" or "The Fear," the woman's ability to reanimate fear, while seemingly irrational, serves an important moral role, to unsettle the complacency of civil and domestic control. Amy has succeeded in rousing fear in her husband, sufficient fear for him to break his own barrier of silence and demand to know what it is she sees. She denies his ability to see, and she demeans him as imperceptive and crude, becoming a "blind creature." The husband, not Amy, has been reduced to brutishness and lower mental capacity.

The husband's response to the challenge reveals part of what Amy fears: she is being used as a childbearing instrument in her husband's house. The husband "frames" the family graveyard with the window—diminishing its size and, figuratively its import—turning it into a portrait in his family gallery. And he makes the terrifying analogy between the bedroom and the graveyard, revealing his own ability to lacerate Amy with but a few words. Love leads not only to death but to the memorial of his people:

He refers to his own relatives in an extraordinarily cold way, nuking an analogy between their persons, "broad-shouldered," and the "slabs." The "child's mound" remains the one as yet indeterminate part of the "family plot," to which Amy has become destined to contribute. Her pain and anger bear resemblance to the feelings and actions of Laban's third wife in "Place for a Third," as she refuses to be buried with the previous two and become another of his "children in a burial row." In the death of Amy's child she sees her own death and burial as part of his family story.

Having penetrated the mystery of her fear and revealed his own capacities for cruelty and his own less than elevated motives, she erects new barriers, pleading that he desist: "Don't, don't, don't, don't," as though her words portended violence. Retreating to a posture of male reason—"Can't a man speak of his own child he's lost?"—the husband irritates Amy even more by referring to it as "his child." The underlying issue here on both sides is possession, self-interest, and control. She seizes control again by attacking his innate lack of ability to speak, a crudeness inherent in men: "I don't know rightly whether any man can" (rightly could refer both to her "knowledge" and to the ways of men).

But I doubt that Amy believes that her husband does not know how to speak. His words and her silences speak powerfully of their individual and conflicting interests. Amy makes him dance, forcing him back on himself and demanding behaviour that suits her interests. We wonder who the "someone else" was that Amy fled to after an earlier argument—a lover or comforter. No doubt Amy fears her husband's violence, revealed not only by her desire to leave the house but also by his promise not to come down the stairs:

The narrator's observation of the husband sitting with his "chin between his fists" calls attention ominously to physical force that might have been used in the past. Any wants her husband to bend to her demands, but she may also want to be independent of him altogether. The husband feels the strain of meeting his wife's demands of beauty, and, while he wants to please her, he also wants to remain true to his sense of self and purpose, which is inextricably bound up with his "being a man." As soon as he asks to be "given a chance," he then veers to reducing her concerns to her sex, to her "mother-loss." Frustrated that he must "partly give up being a man With women-folk," he suggests an "arrangement" by which he'd "keep hands off" anything she might name. Language on her part has become not a source of miscommunication but, instead, a barrier that she can erect. But words alone may not be the only failure or offense. He may well be "hands on" in other ways that are terrifying. In a couplet riddled with negatives, what seems to be a plea for no barriers, he seems on the verge of recognizing that there is no love in their marriage, only fear and competing interests:

His maxim that "Two that don't love can't live together without them. But two that do can't live together with them" indicates how little actual love exists without completing the dialectic with a child, both a bond and a barrier.

The husband feels the pressure of her moral judgment, pleading for her to talk about her grief "if it's something human," a phrase that barely conceals his anger at being reduced to a brute. Her sentimental unworldliness becomes to him just as inhuman. Both their excesses threaten to undermine the possibility of any domestic order and leave the question of what it means to be human balanced across gender lines: He emphasizes Amy's grief as particular to her sex, a "mother-loss," even while wondering whether this way of grieving may not be innate but taught, something she was "brought up" to think. Referring to her upbringing reduces her to the status of a selfish child, one who does not recognize that sacrifice (or waste) is the essence of the larger scheme. Amy retaliates by reducing her husband to a brute, his logic nothing more than a "sneer."

In recounting his digging of their child's grave, Amy demonstrates her ability to speak and characterize in a way that reinforces her husband's lack of verbal ability and, thereby, his lack of humanity. Her portrait of him depicts a coarse unfeeling laborer, associated with dirt and "everyday concerns":

Richard Poirier notes the novelistic detail with which Amy recounts her husband's activity right down to "the stains on your shoes Of fresh earth from your own baby's grave." More than detail, the hurling of the phrase "stains on your shoes" becomes a metaphor for her heaping sin on his soul. Her husband's response of laughing and accepting his curse echoes the urging of Job 's wife to "Curse God and die" (Job 2:9), only in this situation the wife has replaced God as the moral authority. The husband feels cursed both by the loss of a child as well as his inability to make his wife understand him, something she attributes to the innate qualities of his sex.

Amy's interpretation of her husband's words in the kitchen reveals, ironically, that her husband may be far more subtle and sophisticated in expressing himself than she understands. Her question is really an accusation, and she believes not only that he would not care but that he is fundamentally incapable of caring:

She takes his saying "Three foggy mornings and one rainy day Will rot the best birch fence a man can build" quite literally as some musing about the weather and fence building and fails to recognize the power of his own metaphor. The time it takes for a birch to rot represents the husband's naturalistic way of talking about what his loss means and has everything to do with what is in "the darkened parlor." Amy thinks in terms of civilization and parlor culture, her husband in terms of survival against the natural decay of elements. The birch fence is, like the child, a barrier between the threatening environment and his future as well as a barrier between himself and Amy.

Amy charges that her husband and the world are "evil" because they cannot grieve sufficiently, cannot follow the dead into the beyond. The inescapable self-interest of all human beings, or at least her husband, leads her far into the position of an ascetic Christian's denial of the world, one that would make life impossible:

Her eloquent expression of despair—"from the time when one is sick to death, One is alone, and he dies more alone"—reverses Jesus' words in John 11 after the resurrection of Lazarus: "This sickness is not unto death, but for the glory of

God, that the son of God might be glorified thereby." Her despair denies a facile Christianity and affirms the necessity of a heroic existential suffering similar to what Kierkegaard described in The Sickness unto Death as evidence of man's ascendancy over beast:. Amy comes close, then, to sounding like a representative not of nature but of Christian philosophy and its assertion of the distinction of man from other creatures. She sees her own being "sick to death," a sickness that is unending because "To be saved from this sickness by death is an impossibility, for the sickness and its torment—and death—are precisely to be unable to die." Though powerful, Amy's stance renders family survival impossible, a form of immoral purity as it attempts to transcend the demands of survival. She may not sound like Antigone or Cordelia, but her piety may be at least as damaging as theirs.

Her attitude describes a crisis in civilization that Freud commented on in "Our Attitude toward Death" (1915), published the year after North of Boston; "Consideration for the dead, who no longer need it, is dearer to us than the truth, and certainly, for most of us, is dearer also than concern for the living." Freud and Frost challenge Christian culture to conform to a conception of truth provided by science, one in which the demands of survival reign. Amy refuses to conform to manly and scientific conceptions of the limits of grief, and her war with her husband is an attempt to make the world conform to her standards and accept her authority: "I won't have grief so If I can change it. Oh, I won't, I won't!" Her husband must realise that failure to meet her demands will result in the dissolution of the home and his concern for furthering his people.

In treating her complaint as a form of therapy, her husband condescends to her and makes her pain seem just talk. For her to give in would be to give up being who she is, and she pushes her threat beyond "talk." Her husband's lack of tender love and rationality is unmasked in the final exchange, as her refusals push him to threaten force to keep her. Her "I won't" is met with a decidedly passionate "I will":

The proliferation of dashes in the last two parts indicates

a world of emotional reality beyond words, a world that is actively, physically threatening. The dash after "will!" indicates that she has escaped the house and brought him to taking action. The drama lacks closure or "settling down," but this ambiguity is precisely what reveals the power struggle lurking beneath moral and ethical positions.

The line between grief and madness is a fine one, and Amy's desire to escape can be seen as a response to the suffocation of servitude.

Joseph Brodsky

In "Home Burial" we have an arena reduced to a staircase, with its Hitchcockian banister. The opening line tells you as much about the actors' positions as about their roles: those of the hunter and his prey. Or, as you'll see later, of Pygmalion and Galatea, except that in this case the sculptor turns his living model into stone. In the final analysis, "Home Burial" is a love poem, and if only on these grounds it qualifies as a pastoral. But let's examine this line and a half

He saw her from the bottom of the stairs
Before she saw him

Frost could have stopped right here. It is already a poem, it is already a drama. Imagine this line and a half sitting on the page all by itself, in minimalist fashion. It's an extremely loaded scene—or, better yet, a frame. You've got an enclosure, the house, with two individuals at cross—no, diverse—purposes. He's at the bottom of the stairs, she's at the top. He's looking up at her, she, for all we know thus far, doesn't register his presence at all. Also, you've got to remember that it's in black and white. The staircase dividing them suggests a hierarchy of significances. It is a pedestal with her atop (at least, in his eyes) and him at the bottom (in our eyes and, eventually, in hers). The angle is sharp. Place yourself here in either position—better in his—and you'll see what I mean. Imagine yourself observing, watching somebody, or imagine yourself being watched. Imagine yourself interpreting someone's movements—or immobility—unbeknownst to that person. That's what turns you into a hunter, or into Pygmalion.

So let's watch the deportment of the model
She was starting down,
Looking back over her shoulder at some fear.
She took a doubtful step and then undid it
To raise herself and look again.

On the literal level, on the level of straight narrative, we have the heroine beginning to descend the steps with her head turned to us in profile, her glance lingering on some frightful sight. She hesitates and interrupts her descent, her eyes still trained, presumably, on the same sight neither on the steps nor on the man at the bottom. But you are aware of yet another level present here, aren't you?

Let's leave that level as yet unnamed. Each piece of information in this narrative comes to you in an isolated manner, within a pentameter line. The isolation job is done by white margins framing, as it were, the whole scene, like the silence of the house, and the lines themselves are the staircase. Basically, what you get here is a succession of frames. "She was starting down" is one frame. "Looking back over her shoulder at some fear" is another, in fact, it is a close-up, a profile—you see her facial expression. "She took a doubtful step and then undid it" is a third again a close-up—the feet. "To raise herself and look again" is a fourth—full figure.

But this is a ballet, too. There is a minimum of two pas de deux here, conveyed to you with a wonderful euphonic, almost alliterative precision. I mean the ds in this line, in "doubtful" and in "undid it," although the ts matter also. "Undid it" is particularly good, because you sense the spring in that step. And that profile in its opposition to the movement of the body—the very formula of a dramatic heroine—is straight out of a ballet as well.

But the real faux pas de deux starts with "He spoke Advancing toward her." For the next twenty-five lines, a conversation occurs on the stairs. The man climbs them as he speaks, negotiating mechanically and verbally what separates them. "Advancing" bespeaks self-consciousness and apprehensiveness. The tension grows with the growing proximity. However, the mechanical and, by implication, physical proximity is more easily attained than the verbal—i e, the mental—and that's what the poem is all about. "'What is it you see From up there always?—for I want to know'" is very much a Pygmalion question, addressed to the model on the pedestal atop the staircase. His fascination is not with what he sees but with what he imagines it conceals—what he has placed there. He invests her with mystery and then rushes to uncloak it: this rapacity is always Pygmalion's double bind. It is as though the sculptor found himself puzzled by the facial expression of his model: she "sees" what he does not "see." So he has to climb to the pedestal himself, to put himself in her position. In the position of "up there always"—of topographical (vis-à-vis the house) and psychological advantage, where he put her himself. It is the latter, the psychological advantage of the creation, that disturbs the creator, as the emphatic "'for I want to know'" shows.

The model refuses to cooperate. In the next frame ("She turned and sank upon her skirts at that"), followed by the close-up of "And her face changed from terrified to dull," you get that lack of cooperation plain. Yet the lack of cooperation here is cooperation. The less you cooperate, the more you are a Galatea. For we have to bear in mind that the woman's psychological advantage is in the man's self-projection. He ascribes it to her. So by turning him down she only enhances his fantasy. In this sense, by refusing to cooperate she plays along. That's basically her whole game here. The more he climbs, the greater is that advantage, he pushes her into it, as it were, with every step.

Still, he is climbing: in "he said to gain time" he does, and also in

"What is it you see?"
Mounting until she cowered under him.
"I will find out now—you must tell me, dear

The most important word here is the verb "see," which we encounter for the second time. In the next nine lines, it will be used four more times. We'll get to that in a minute. But first let's deal with this "mounting" line and the next. It's a masterly job here. With "mounting," the poet kills two birds at once, for "mounting" describes both the climb and the climber. And the climber looms even larger, because the woman "cowers"—i.e, shrinks under him. Remember that she looks "at some fear." "Mounting" versus "cowered" gives you the contrast, then, between their respective frames, with the implicit danger contained in his largeness. In any case, her alternative to fear is not comfort. And the resoluteness of "'I will find out now'" echoes the superior physical mass, not alleviated by the cajoling "dear" that follows a remark—"'you must tell me'"—that is both imperative and conscious of this contrast.

And now we come to this verb "see." Within fifteen lines it's been used six times. Every experienced poet knows how risky it is to use the same word several times within a short space. The risk is that of tautology. So what is it that Frost is after here? I think he is after precisely that tautology. More accurately, non-semantic utterance. Which you get, for instance, in "'Oh,' and again, 'Oh.'" Frost had a theory about what he called "sentence-sounds." It had to do with his observation that the sound, the tonality, of human locution is as semantic as actual words.

For instance, you overhear two people conversing behind a closed door, in a room. You don't hear the words, yet you know the general drift of their dialogue; in fact, you may pretty accurately figure out its substance. In other words, the tune matters more than the lyrics, which are, so to speak, replaceable or redundant. Anyway, the repetition of this or that word liberates the tune, makes it more audible. By the same token, such repetition liberates the mind—rids you of the notion presented by the word. (This is the old Zen technique, of course, but, come to think of it, finding it in an American poem makes you wonder whether philosophical principles don't spring from texts rather than the other way around.)

The six "see"s here do precisely that. They exclaim rather than explain. It could be "see," it could be "Oh," it could be "yes," it could be any monosyllabic word. The idea is to explode the verb from within, for the content of the actual observation defeats the process of observation, its means, and the very observer. The effect that Frost tries to create is the inadequacy of response when you automatically repeat the first word that comes to your tongue. "Seeing" here is simply reeling from the unnameable. The least seeing our hero does is in "'Just that I see,'" for by this time the verb, having already been used four times, is robbed of its "observing" and "understanding" meaning (not to mention the fact— draining the word even further of content—that we readers are ourselves still in the dark, still don't know what there is to see out that window). By now, it is just sound, denoting an animal response rather than a rational one.

This sort of explosion of bona-fide words into pure, non-semantic sounds will occur several times in the course of this poem. Another happens very soon, ten lines later. Characteristically, these explosions occur whenever the players find themselves in close physical proximity. They are the verbal—or, better yet, the audial—equivalents of a hiatus. Frost directs them with tremendous consistency, suggesting his characters' profound (at least, prior to this scene) incompatibility. "Home Burial" is, in fact, the study of that, and on the literal level the tragedy it describes is the characters' comeuppance for violating each other's territorial and mental imperatives by having a child. Now that the child is lost, the imperatives play themselves out with vehemence they claim their own.

By standing next to the woman, the man acquires her vantage point. Because he is larger than she, and also because this is his house (as line 23 shows), where he has lived, presumably, most of his life, he must, one imagines, bend somewhat to put his eyes on her line of vision. Now they are next to each other, in an almost intimate proximity, on the threshold of their bedroom, atop the stairs. The bedroom has a window, a window has a view. And here Frost produces the most stunning simile of this poem, and perhaps of his entire career:

"'The little graveyard where my people are'" generates an air of endearment, and it's with this air that "'So small the window frames the whole of it'" starts, only to tumble itself into "'Not so much larger than a bedroom, is it?'" The key word here is "frames," because it doubles as the window's actual frame and as a picture on a bedroom wall. The window hangs, as it were, on the bedroom wall like a picture, and that picture depicts a graveyard. "Depicting," though, means reducing to the size of a picture. Imagine having that in your bedroom. In the next line, though, the graveyard is restored to its actual size and, for that reason, equated with the bedroom. This equation is as much psychological as it is spatial. Inadvertently, the man blurts out the summary of the marriage (foreshadowed in the grim pun of the title). And, equally inadvertently, the "is it?" invites the woman to agree with this summary, almost implying her complicity.

As if that were not enough, the next two lines, with their stones of slate and marble, proceed to reinforce the simile, equating the graveyard with the made-up bed, with its pentametrically arranged pillows and cushions—populated by a family of small, inanimate children. "Broad-shouldered little slabs." This is Pygmalion unbound, on a rampage. What we have here is the man's intrusion into the woman's mind, a violation of her mental imperative—if you will, an ossification of it. And then this ossifying hand—petrifying, actually—stretches toward what's still raw, palpably as well as in her mind:

"But I understand it is not the stones,
But the child's mound—"

It's not that the contrast between the stones and the mound is too stark, though it is, it is his ability—or, rather, his attempt—to articulate it that she finds unbearable. For, should he succeed, should he find the words to articulate her mental anguish, the mound will join the stones in the "picture," will become a slab itself, will become a pillow of their bed. Moreover, this will amount to the total penetration of her inner sanctum that of her mind. And he is getting there:

The poem is gathering its dark force. Four "don't"s are that non-semantic explosion, resulting in hiatus. We are so much in the story line now—up to the eyebrows—that we may forget that this is still a ballet, still a succession of frames, still an artifice, stage-managed by the poet. In fact, we are about to take sides with our characters, aren't we? Well, I suggest we pull ourselves out of this by our eyebrows and think for a moment about what it all tells us about our poet. Imagine, for instance, that the story line has been drawn from experience—from, say, the loss of a firstborn. What does all that you've read thus far tell you about the author, about his sensibility? How much he is absorbed by the story and—what's more crucial—to what degree he is free from it?

Were this a seminar, I'd wait for your answers. Since it is not, I've got to answer this question myself And the answer is: He is very free. Dangerously so. The very ability to utilize—to play with—this sort of material suggests an extremely wide margin of detachment. The ability to turn this material into a blank-verse, pentameter monotone adds another degree to that detachment. To observe a relation between a family graveyard and a bedroom's fourposter—still another. Added up, they amount to a considerable degree of detachment. A degree that dooms human interplay, that makes communication impossible, for communication requires an equal.

Remember the hiatus, and what causes it, and remember that this is an artifice. Actually, the author himself reminds you of it with

She withdrew, shrinking from beneath his arm
That rested on the banister, and slid downstairs.

It is still a ballet, you see, and the stage direction is incorporated into the text. The most telling detail here is the banister. Why does the author put it here? First, to reintroduce the staircase, which we might by now have forgotten about, stunned by the business of ruining the bedroom. But, secondly, the banister prefigures her sliding downstairs, since every child uses banisters for sliding down. "And turned on him with such a daunting look" is another stage direction:

He said twice over before he knew himself:
"Can't a man speak of his own child he's lost?"

Now, this is a remarkably good line. It has a distinctly vernacular, almost proverbial air. And the author is definitely aware of how good it is. So, trying both to underscore its effectiveness and to obscure his awareness of it, he emphasizes the unwittingness of this utterance: "He said twice over before he knew himself."

This whole section of the poem, from "'Don't, don't, don't, don't'" on, obviously has some sexual connotations, of her turning the man down. That's what the story of Pygmalion and his model is all about. On the literal level, "Home Burial" evolves along similar "hard to get" lines. However, I don't think that Frost, for all his autonomy, was conscious of that. (After all, North of Boston shows no acquaintance with Freudian terminology.) And, if he was not, this sort of approach on our part is invalid. Nevertheless, we should bear some of it in mind as we are embarking on the bulk of this poem:

What we've got here is the desire to escape: not so much the man as the enclosure of the place, not to mention the subject of their exchange. Yet the resolution is incomplete, as the fidgeting with the hat shows, since the execution of this desire will be counterproductive for the model as far as being the subject of explication goes. May I go so far as to suggest that that would mean a loss of advantage, not to mention that it would be the end of the poem? In fact, it does end with precisely that, with her exit. The literal level will get into conflict, or fusion, with the metaphorical. Hence "'I don't know rightly whether any man can,'" which fuses both these levels, forcing the poem to proceed, you don't know any longer who is the horse here, who is the cart. I doubt whether the poet himself knew that at this point. The fusion's result is the release of a certain force, which subordinates his pen, and the best it can do is keep both strands— literal and metaphorical—in check.

We learn the heroine's name, and that this sort of discourse had its precedents, with nearly identical results. Given the fact that we know the way the poem ends, we may judge—well, we may imagine—the character of those occasions. The scene in "Home Burial" is but a repetition. By this token, the poem doesn't so much inform us about their life as replace it. We also learn, from "'Don't go to someone else this time,'" about a mixture of jealousy and sense of shame felt by at least one of them. And we learn, from "'I won't come down the stairs'" and from "He sat and fixed his chin between his fists," about the fear of violence present in their physical proximity. The latter line is a wonderful embodiment of stasis, very much in the fashion of Rodin's Penseur, albeit with two fists, which is a very telling self-referential detail, since the forceful application of fist to chin is what results in a knockout.

The main thing here, though, is the reintroduction of the stairs. Not only the literal stairs but the steps in "he sat," too. From now on, the entire dialogue occurs on the stairs, though they have become the scene of an impasse rather than a passage. No physical steps are taken. Instead, we have their verbal, or oral, substitute. The ballet ends, yielding to the verbal advance and retreat, which is heralded by "'There's something I should like to ask you, dear.'" Note again the air of cajoling, colored this time with the recognition of its futility in "dear." Note also the last semblance of actual interplay in "'You don't know how to ask it.' 'Help me, then'"—this last knocking on the door, or, better yet, on the wall. Note "Her fingers moved the latch for all reply," because this feint of trying for the door is the last physical movement, the last theatrical or cinematic gesture in the poem, save one more latch-trying.

The speaker's hectic mental pacing is fully counterbalanced by his immobility. If this is a ballet, it is a mental one. In fact, it's very much like fencing not with an opponent or a shadow but with one's self. The lines are constantly taking a step forward and then undoing it ("She took a doubtful step and then undid it.") The main technical device here is enjambment, which physically resembles descending the stairs. In fact, this back-and-forth, this give-and-take almost gives you a sense of being short of breath. Until, that is, the release that is coming with the formulaic, folksy "'A man must partly give up being a man With womenfolk.'"

After this release, you get three lines of more evenly paced verse, almost a tribute to iambic pentameter's proclivity for coherence, ending with the pentametrically triumphant "'Though I don't like such things 'twixt those that love.'" And here our poet makes another not so subdued dash toward the proverbial: "'Two that don't love can't live together without them But two that do can't live together with them'"—though this comes off as a bit cumbersome, and not entirely convincing.

Frost partly senses that: hence "She moved the latch a little." But that's only one explanation. The whole point of this qualifier-burdened monologue is the explication of its addressee. The man is groping for understanding. He realizes that in order to understand he's got to surrender—if not suspend entirely—his rationality. In other words, he descends. But this is really running down stairs that lead upward. And, partly from rapidly approaching the end of his wits, partly out of purely rhetorical inertia, he summons here the notion of love. In other words, this quasi-proverbial two-liner about love is a rational argument, and that, of course, is not enough for its addressee.

For the more she is explicated, the more remote she gets the higher her pedestal grows (which is perhaps of specific importance to her now that she is downstairs). It's not grief that drives her out of the house but the dread of being explicated, as well as of the explicator himself. She wants to stay impenetrable and won't accept anything short of his complete surrender. And he is well on the way to it:

"Don't—don't go
Don't carry it to someone else this time.
Tell me about it if it's something human."

The last is the most stunning, most tragic line, in my view, in the entire poem. It amounts practically to the heroine's ultimate victory—i.e, to the aforementioned rational surrender on the part of the explicator. For all its colloquial air, it promotes her mental operations to supernatural status, thus acknowledging infinity—ushered into her mind by the child's death—as his rival. Against this he is powerless, since her access to that infinity, her absorption by and commerce with it, is backed in his eyes by the whole mythology of the opposite sex—by the whole notion of the alternative being impressed upon him by her at this point rather thoroughly. That's what he is losing her to by staying rational. It is a shrill, almost hysterical line, admitting the man's limitations and momentarily bringing the whole discourse to a plane of regard that the heroine could be at home on—the one she perhaps seeks. But only momentarily. He can't proceed at this level, and succumbs to pleading:

He tumbles down, as it were, from the hysterical height of "'Tell me about it if it's something human.'"

But this tumble, this mental knocking about the metrically lapsing stairs, restores him to rationality, with all its attendant qualifiers. That brings him rather close to the heart of the matter—to her taking her "'mother-loss of a first child So inconsolably'"—and he evokes the catchall notion of love again, this time somewhat more convincingly, though still tinged with a rhetorical flourish: "'in the face of love.'" The very word—"love"— undermines its emotional reality, reducing the sentiment to its utilitarian application as a means of overcoming tragedy. However, overcoming tragedy deprives its victim of the status of hero or heroine. This, combined with the resentment over the explicator's lowering of his explication's plane of regard, results in the heroine's interruption of "'You'd think his memory might be satisfied—'" with "'There you go sneering now!'" It's Galatea's self-defence, the defence against the further application of the chiseling instrument to her already attained features.

Because of its absorbing story line, there is a strong temptation to bill "Home Burial" as a tragedy of incommunicability, a poem about the failure of language, and many have succumbed to this temptation. In fact, it is just the reverse: it is a tragedy of communication, for communication's logical end is the violation of your interlocutor's mental imperative. This is a poem about language's terrifying success, for language, in the final analysis, is alien to the sentiments it articulates. No one is more aware of that than a poet, and if "Home Burial" is autobiographical, it is so in the first place by revealing Frost's grasp of the collision between his métier and his emotions. To drive this point home, may I suggest that you compare the actual sentiment you may feel toward an individual in your company and the word "love." A poet is doomed to resort to words. So is the speaker in "Home Burial." Hence, their overlapping in this poem; hence, too, its autobiographical reputation.

But let us take it a step further. The poet here should be identified not with one character but with both. He is the man here, all right, but he is the woman also. Thus you've got a clash: not just of two sensibilities but of two languages. Sensibilities may merge—say, in the act of love; languages can't. Sensibilities may result in a child, languages won't. And, now that the child is dead, what's left is two totally autonomous languages, two non-overlapping systems of verbalization. In short, words. His versus hers, and hers are fewer. This makes her enigmatic. Enigmas are subject to explication, which they resist— in her case, with all she's got. His job, or, more exactly, the job of his language, is, therefore, the explication of her language, or, more exactly, her reticence. Which, when it comes to human interplay, is a recipe for disaster. When it comes to a poem, an enormous challenge.

Small wonder, then, that this "dark pastoral" grows darker with every line; it proceeds by aggravation, reflecting not so much the complexity of the author's mind as words' own appetite for disaster. For the more you push reticence, the greater it gets, having nothing to fall back upon but itself. The enigma thus grows bigger.

This is the voice of a very foreign territory indeed: a foreign language. It is a view of the man from a distance he can't possibly fathom, since it is proportionate to the frequency with which the heroine creeps up and down the stairs. Which, in its own right, is proportionate to the leaps of his gravel in the course of his digging the grave. Whatever the ratio, it is not in favour of his actual or mental steps toward her on that staircase. Nor in his favour is the rationale behind her creeping up and down the stairs while he is digging. Presumably, there is nobody else around to do the job. (That they lost their firstborn suggests that they are fairly young and thus not very well off.) Presumably also, by performing this menial task, and by doing it in a particularly mechanical way—as a remarkably skillful mimetic job in the pentameter here indicates (or as is charged by the heroine)—the man is quelling, or controlling, his grief, that is, his movements, unlike the heroine's, are functional.

In short, this is futility's view of utility. For obvious reasons, this view is usually precise and rich in judgment: "'If you had any feelings,'" and "'Leap up, like that, like that, and land so lightly And roll back down the mound beside the hole.'" Depending on the length of observation—and the description of digging runs here for nine lines—this view may result, as it does here, in a sensation of utter disparity between the observer and the observed: "'I thought, Who is that man? I didn't know you.'" For observation, you see, results in nothing, while digging produces at least a mound, or a hole. Whose mental equivalent in the observer is also, as it were, a grave. Or, rather, a fusion of the man and his purpose, not to mention his instrument. What futility and Frost's pentameter register here above all is rhythm. The heroine observes an inanimate machine. The man in her eye is a gravedigger, and thus her alternative.

Now, the sight of our alternative is always unwelcome, not to say threatening. The closer your view of it, the sharper your general sense of guilt and of a deserved comeuppance. In the mind of a woman who has lost her child, that sense may be fairly sharp. Add to that her inability to translate her grief into any useful action, save a highly agitated creeping up and down, as well as the recognition—and subsequent glorification—of that inability. And add a cross-purpose correspondence between her movements and his: between her steps and his spade What do you think it would result in? And remember that she is in his house, that this is the graveyard where his people are. And that he is a gravedigger.

"Then you came in I heard your rumbling voice
Out in the kitchen, and I don't know why,
But I went near to see with my own eyes."

Note this "and I don't know why," for here she unwittingly drifts toward her own projection. All that she needs now is to check that projection with her own eyes. That is, she wants to make her mental picture physical.

"You could sit there with the stains on your shoes
Of the fresh earth from your own baby's grave
And talk about your everyday concerns.
You had stood the spade up against the wall
Outside there in the entry, for I saw it."

So what do you think she sees with her own eyes, and what does that sight prove? What does the frame contain this time? What does she have a close-up of? I am afraid she sees a murder weapon: she sees a blade. The fresh earth stains either on the shoes or on his spade make the spade's edge shine: make it into a blade. And does earth "stain," however fresh? Her very choice of noun, denoting liquid, suggests—accuses—blood. What should our man have done? Should he have taken his shoes off before entering the house? Perhaps. Perhaps he should have left his spade outside, too. But he is a farmer, and acts like one—presumably out of fatigue. So he brings in his instrument—in her eyes, the instrument of death. And the same goes for his shoes, and it goes for the rest of the man. A gravedigger is equated here, if you will, with the reaper. And there are only the two of them in this house.

The most awful bit is "for I saw," because it emphasizes the perceived symbolism of that spade left standing against the wall outside there in the entry: for future use. Or as a guard. Or as an unwitting memento mori. At the same time, "for I saw it" conveys the capriciousness of her perception and the triumph of somebody who cannot be fooled, the triumph of catching the enemy. It is futility in full bloom, engulfing and absorbing utility into its shadow.

"I shall laugh the worst laugh I ever laughed.
I'm cursed God, if I don't believe I'm cursed."

This is practically a nonverbal recognition of defeat, coming in the form of a typical Frostian understatement, studded with tautological monosyllables quickly abandoning their semantic functions. Our Napoleon or Pygmalion is completely routed by his creation, who still keeps pressing on.

"I can repeat the very words you were saying:
'Three foggy mornings and one rainy day
Will rot the best birch fence a man can build.'
Think of it, talk like that at such a time!
What had how long it takes a birch to rot
To do with what was in the darkened parlor?"

Now, this is where our poem effectively ends. The rest is simply denouement, in which our heroine goes rambling on in an increasingly incoherent fashion about death, the world being evil, uncaring friends, and feeling alone. It is a rather hysterical monologue, whose only function, in terms of the story line, is to struggle toward a release for what has been pent up in her mind. It does not, and in the end she resorts to the door, as though only landscape were proportionate to her mental state and thus could be of solace.

So what was it that he was after in this, his very own poem? He was, I think, after grief and reason, which, while poison to each other, are language's most efficient fuel—or, if you will, poetry's indelible ink. Frost's reliance on them here and elsewhere almost gives you the sense that his dipping into this ink pot had to do with the hope of reducing the level of its contents, you detect a sort of vested interest on his part. Yet the more one dips into it, the more it brims with this black essence of existence, and the more one's mind, like one's fingers, gets soiled by this liquid.

For the more there is of grief, the more there is of reason. As much as one may be tempted to take sides in "Home Burial," the presence of the narrator here rules this out, for while the characters stand, respectively, for reason and for grief, the narrator stands for their fusion. To put it differently, while the characters' actual union disintegrates, the story, as it were, marries grief to reason, since the bond of the narrative here supersedes the individual dynamics—well, at least for the reader. Perhaps for the author as well. The poem, in other words, plays fate.

If this poem is dark, darker still is the mind of its maker, who plays all three roles the man, the woman, and the narrator.

Their equal reality, taken separately or together, is still inferior to that of the poem's author, since "Home Burial" is but one poem among many. The price of his autonomy is, of course, in its coloration, and perhaps what you ultimately get out of this poem is not its story but the vision of its ultimately autonomous maker. The characters and the narrator are, as it were, pushing the author out of any humanly palatable context: he stands outside, denied re-entry, perhaps not coveting it at all.

This is the dialogue's—alias the Life Force's— doing And this particular posture, this utter autonomy, strikes me as utterly American. Hence this poet's monotone, his pentametric drawl a signal from a far-distant station. One may liken him to a spacecraft that, as the downward pull of gravity weakens, finds itself nonetheless in the grip of a different gravitational force: outward. The fuel, though, is still the same' grief and reason. The only thing that conspires against this metaphor of mine is that American spacecraft usually return.

On "The Wood-Pile"

J. Donald Crowley

"The Wood-Pile" is thoroughly typical of many of Frost's mature nature poems. At once narrative and dramatic, the poem seems astonishingly clear even on first encounter. There at its centre are the solitary speaker, a familiar figure, and his story, this one—like Frost's others—told in the inevitably simple, straightforward and calm, almost laconic language that characterizes dozens of Frost's other narrative lines.

There is the typical stripped minimum of physical action—walking. Here, as elsewhere, the walking is seemingly aimless, has no manifest destination: it is an epitome of Frost's conviction that "Calculation is usually no part in the first step of any walk" (402). But, again as elsewhere, however much the walking appears to lack direction, it is clearly mysterious in that it radiates a high sense of personal destiny. "Every poem," Frost once remarked, "is an epitome of the great predicament; a:figure of the will braving alien entanglements"

(401). The speaker simply appears in our field of vision and—to use Yvor Winters' negative criticism in a positive way—seems to be "spiritually drifting." There is the familiar winter landscape, bleak, desolate, initially amorphous and forbidding.

There is the appearance of the small bird and the speaker's curious pretense of talking with such creatures. There is the woodpile itself, like the tuft of flowers, the mending wall, the road not taken, the west-running brook, so enigmatically and hypnotically there. And there is the almost dreamlike state of meditation it induces, in some ways calling to mind the sleepy vision of "After Apple-Picking." Finally, there is what Frost called "the vocal imagination," the speaker's voice, his style: that particular quality of sound "which indicates how the writer takes himself and what he is saying., the way he carries himself toward his ideas and deeds" (403).

Frost once joked: "Let the sound of [Robert Louis] Stevenson go through your mind empty and you will realise that he never took himself other than as an amusement. Do the same with Swinburne and you will see that he took himself as a wonder" (298). In "The Wood-Pile" Frost clearly takes himself neither simply as an amusement nor as a wonder but as both.

On another level of its structure, beneath the relaxed surface of the language, the poem progresses by way of a series, almost a system, of oppositions, ambiguities, and contrarieties that might be called Hawthornian. "In order to know where we are," Frost has noted, "we must know opposites." The "frozen swamp" is the first obvious instance of this characteristic structural phenomenon and suggests immediately multiple ambiguities in the external landscape: hardness-softness, cold-heat, solidity-fluidity, stability-instability, a surface level and a dimension—as yet untouched but present—beneath the surface. All this is registered against the blankness, the flatness of the minimally specified "one gray day." In the first line, then, we have concentrated an action, a place, a time. There is also a typically Frostian subtlety in the simple prepositions surrounding the action and thus wrapping it in still another operative ambiguity: "Out walking in"—the phrase is so solidly idiomatic, so much a mode of common speech, that all its powers of suggestion (namely, the juxtaposition of externality and internality) are playfully hidden, buried beneath the plainness of the words themselves.

This particular tension is elaborated in the relationships between lines 1 and 2. Whereas the first line addresses itself to a continuous physical action and the external landscape, the second is concerned with a pause and a turning inward to the mind of the persona and his fearful response to that landscape. The speaker's decision to "turn back" emphasizes the sharp disjunction existing between this particular mind and this particular reality.

The fear and confusion are isolated only momentarily, however, since they are immediately answered to by the courage of the counter-resolution of line 3. There, as the grammatical shift from "I" to "we" signifies, it is not Frost's purpose to annihilate the fear but to use it: the fear and the courage, the will to proceed and the hesitancy to do it, now almost formally define two dimensions of the persona.

He has become at once his own reassuring guide and cautious initiate. And since it is the "we" who shall see, what is to be discovered will be informed by both. Still another ironic opposition is in Frost's use of the negative qualifier "No" to decisively introduce the positive affirmation of "going on" and thus to undermine the negative preference to "turn back." It is as if there is in the persona's emotions a mathematical logic in which two negatives interpenetrate to form a positive. The playful blending of "amusement" and "wonder" here illustrates what Reuben Brower calls Frost's "delight of saying the ordinary thing and discovering that it is art."

We might at this juncture turn back to ask what gives rise to the fear in the first place. The question leads back to that "frozen swamp" and to the realization that the place is forbidding and inscrutable because it suggests nature in its least regenerate aspects. It is essentially primordial, totally unformed. Hinting as it does at a sweeping geological sense of time and age, it provides another, prehistoric tension with the fragile minuteness and ephemerality of the mere "one gray day." In line 4 the speaker, going on, now, as it were, gives himself to the place. He is no longer "out" altogether but in some sense "in."

The distance between mind and reality is now diminished even to the point of tactile intimacy implied in the word "held." He who would see submits willingly to being acted upon by the still undefined force within that which he would see. But the explicit oppositions and tensions persist: in the "now" an the "then," the one foot and the implied other, the "here" and the "Somewhere else." Even the syntax displays similarly precarious balances: "The hard snow held me" announces a categorical, absolute condition, and points to a sureness of footing and, concomitantly, an intellectual and emotional security.

But the line moves on by way of a concessive clause that turns back on the earlier statement and attaches exceptional circumstances contrary to it. The sentence contains elaborated images of impenetrability and penetrability that are quietly paradoxical because of the conditions they are associated with. The impenetrability suggests sureness and constancy, the penetrability doubt and instability, even danger. What normally seem to be positive and negative connotations are equally mixed in each of these syntactical units, then, and they are joined in fact by a conjunction—"save"—whose playful punning transforms the usual logic of "except" and suggests that the categories of positive and negative have again interpenetrated.

To see is, of course, to penetrate into the truth or meaning of a phenomenon or thing. In a Frost poem, however, to see is always to know that there is a point at which the thing to be seen resists and defies penetrability, a point of its being beyond which it is alas unknowable. "The Wood-Pile," like "Neither Out Far nor In Deep," is from this angle a metaphor about the process of penetration and the ultimate limits of that process: a metaphor about the process of the interpenetration of him who sees and that which is seen. It is at once, like so much of Hawthorne's work, an exploration into the wilderness and into the self, a journey at once out and in.

What the persona sees in lines 5 to 9 is merely a "view,"

since he has as yet penetrated very little—only enough, in fact, to be confronted with an overwhelmingly confusing verticality. He sees merely one-dimensional lines without shape, and the measure of his plight is that he cannot find a language to give a name to the place. But, although he is thus suspended between his desire for certainty and the fact of his fearful uncertainty, his uneasiness and doubt are now informed by his awareness of them. Trying to solve the riddle of the landscape, he comes to know something not so much about that landscape as about himself. He is, he says, "just far from home." If "just" points up the severe, even terrifying, limits of his knowledge at this point of the process, it also simultaneously emphasizes his diminished anxiety regarding those limits. The word at once generates a sense of terror and dispels it. The effect is almost that the terrors of "homelessness," of being lost in undifferentiated space, comprise a condition the speaker has known before and finds so persistent and multifarious as to demand his constant re-engagement.

The small bird now appears, and in a way that seems equally fortuitous and gratuitous. The speaker responds immediately by recognizing it as a dramatic projection of his own fearfulness. In the following lines, the bird's activity adds a horizontal dimension to the speaker's growing spatial consciousness; and, giving the scene intersecting lines, if not shape, it permits the speaker to have for the first time a perspective. Again, the process moves by way of the artful opposition between bird and tree and the little joke by which physical laws seem overturned: the bird "puts" a tree—that is, assigns it a specific material place—between itself and the speaker. The bird is clearly what the speaker has come so far to know best, and he comes to know it by way of what he has previously come to know about himself. As Frost's deliberately confusing pronoun references in lines 12 and 13 imply, the speaker intimately identifies with the bird at the same time he tries to assert his superiority to it. The condition that allows him this intimacy, however, is his physical separation from the bird, marked by the one tree standing between subject and object.

The tree, like the mending wall, signifies one of those barriers without which the world would, for Frost, not make sense. The speaker's teasing identification with the bird leads to his awareness of himself as the source of the bird's fearfulness; and this, in turn, clarifies his own relationship with the larger, unredeemed scene, the source of his own fear, which is thus brought further under the control of consciousness. The speaker's awareness is now many- layered, and he now has words for what is at stake. The bird's white tail feather is, of course, that by which he is what he is: it is the unmistakable mark of his irreducible identity and, paradoxically, the sign of his surrender. His fear of its loss turns back on and elucidates the speaker's recognition of his homelessness. "Home" is now understood to mean that point in space where one is at ease, where the self "belongs," where identity is safe.

Counterbalancing the gradual emergence of clarity and shape in the landscape is the gradually emerging personality of the speaker: at every stage of the poem, we know the speaker only to that extent which the speaker himself has come to know and understand the landscape. Frost once remarked that if the style of a poem "is with outer seriousness, it must be with inner humor. If it is with outer humor, it must be with inner seriousness. Neither one alone without the other under it will do" (351).

The cautious sobriety and reserve within the vocal imagination as it initially addressed the outer terror are now cut across by a tone of humorous self-parody as the speaker engages in reflection. Now he can indulge in the quietly extravagant joke of a pathetic fallacy—"like one who takes Everything said as personal to himself." Now too, however, the speaker's enlarged awareness and confidence are juxtaposed to, and measured by, his own self-deception. The speaker is himself deceived in thinking that the way for the bird to become "undeceived" is simply to flee the scene—to go "the way I might have gone." The bird, given free play, does not flee but, willing to get lost in order, apparently, to find itself, goes behind the woodpile.

He seeks it out as a refuge, a home, in a final effort to

discover and preserve identity in this place. Bird and man now embrace the woodpile, bind it by both courage and fear; and what the speaker sees there is conditioned, then, by his awareness of the bird on the opposite side. The logic of this perceptual symmetry, of course, is that the pile of wood has consolations to offer the man—consolations against the threat of formlessness, mindlessness, absence of order. And consolations there are indeed, in the lovely wholeness, the solid three-dimensionality of the woodpile.

Here is, at last, the physical universe filled out in shapely and substantial form, caught in a moment of exacting perception that sees into it with a clarity and completeness incorporating at once modes of analysis and synthesis, modes of physical labour and intellectual love: "It was a cord of maple, cut and split And piled—and measured, four by four by eight." The moment of perception constitutes a symbolic reenactment of the original building of the woodpile.

The cutting and splitting and piling refer us simultaneously to the fact of the pile of wood and to that process by which it came to be. The speaker imaginatively duplicates all of the separate, divisible stages of the process of physical activity and then, in an evaluative act of measuring, finds a language—"four by four by eight"—that expresses perfectly the fact of its fully unitary and integrated wholeness of being. Process and fact, energy and form, coalesce and become one in a single continuous act of perception, and in that act the courage and fear have themselves been transformed into love and meditative forgetfulness.

The moment is a perfect illustration of Frost's distinction between what it means to believe in things and what it means, on the other hand, to believe things in (339). The latter is the special task of him who would be poet and person. In this symbolic reenactment, the speaker believes into existence an entity which was potentially there in the emerging but partial lines of the earlier stages of his journey inward. The woodpile, according to Frost's poetic theory, had its beginnings "in something more felt than known" (339). While in one sense, then, the speaker only "reveals" and "discovers" the woodpile, in another he can be said to have "made" it. We have here what William James, in "Humanism and Truth," called a quasi-paradox: "A fact virtually pre-exists when every condition of its realization save one is already there. In this case the condition lacking is the act of the counting and comparing mind. Undeniably something comes by the counting that was not there before. And yet that something was always true. In one sense you create it, and in another sense you find it."

Like the white tail feather, the woodpile is totally singular. It is a far larger, more elaborate and complex symbol of individual form and identity. In its four-by-four-by-eightness there is a marvelous solidity as well as form, a substantiality that makes it not only palpable but, at least initially, permanent. In its apparent permanence it has a homeostatic capacity that heroically confronts the ephemeral and formless flux of the entropic environment.

But just as soon as the speaker has become aware of its shape and form—its thereness—he is compelled, notice, to describe it in terms of what is not there: "And not another like it could I see." Thus, in the very process of celebrating the magnificence of its being, he uses language, has a perception, that points ironically to a sad sense of the diminishedness of things. Frost was himself fascinated by what he called "carrying numbers into the realm of space and at the same time into the realm of time" (333). In the same essay, he later quotes Einstein that "In the neighborhood of matter space is something like curved" (334).

What Frost has done in "making his count" of the woodpile's dimensions is to carry those numbers into time, and in doing so he has transformed the straightness and angularity of the landscape into curves, into roundness and sphericity. This transformation is initially hinted at, I think, in the multiple suggestiveness of "cord," which is not only the specific name given to 128 cubic feet of fuel wood but, here, a pun on the mathematical term denoting a straight line which joins two points on an arc or curve. The change wrought in the speaker's perception of the scene is a brilliant poetic realization of Frost's conviction that "We are what we are by elimination and by deflection from the straight line." Once he exists in a definitively three-dimensional physical universe, the speaker muses on the fourth dimension in trying to penetrate further into the meaning of the physical fact. Immediately, he meditates on—has a creative vision about—what is not there, what is quintessentially impalpable and increasingly indefinite, what is further and further back in time and of completely mysterious origin. Whereas the physical journey moves forward in space, its ultimate outcome is an inward journey, a meditation, which is a heightened mode of "turning back from here," an action no longer informed by fear alone.

The implied and emergent curves of the woodpile the speaker's vision now makes explicit in the imagined loops of the runner tracks he cannot see; and these imagined curves in turn lead the speaker back into an awareness of the actual curved lines explicit in the woodpile itself: the warping bark, the sunkenness, the strings of clematis circling round and round. But the Hawthornian tensions and polarities, of which those curves are the ultimate expression, persist: between the imagined facts and the observable realities, in the references to different points in time, between the one side and the other, between what the clematis had done, what the tree is still doing, what the stake and prop are about to do.

All these details catch, in a single, powerful image, a moment of process in which exquisite physical and spiritual form and imminent formlessness, growth and decay, stasis and flux fully interpenetrate, the implications of each participating in and giving value to the other. Now, although the speaker is completely at home in this place, his meditation does not lead to any reassuring consolation or benevolent resolution that would cancel these tensions and contrarieties; instead, it reaffirms and heightens them. For if the speaker's turning inward to the mind is a turning outward to the imagined identity of the woodcutter, and thus implies a consoling movement from solitude to human relationship, it also leads simultaneously to the speaker's recognition of his still distant separation from that imagined home with the "useful fireplace." The very process by which the speaker, along with the frozen swamp, has been warmed by the woodcutter's selfless and forgetful act of love issues in no comfortable, Emersonian notion of transcendent compensation.

The condition of distance, of being "far from home," still attaches, as does the implied need to continually "turn to fresh tasks." Space and time have indeed been redeemed within the process of the speaker's vision to the extent that the woodpile as fact and process—as seemingly senseless material waste—is now endowed with a poignant significance and spiritual usefulness. But the implications of that redemption presuppose the necessity of continual other ones at different times, in different places. Seeing the woodpile in all its magnificence, the speaker sees also that its heat warms "only as best it could." And while there are duration, clarity, and beauty in the "slow, smokeless burning," they are apprehended in a vision that focuses on the inexorable fact of decay. The woodpile and the loving vision it induces only momentarily stay the confusion of a universe moving toward nothingness.

The condition of lostness, of homelessness, is not finally overcome; we are, at the end, still more aware of tensions than of unities. Whatever triumph there is lies in the fact that homelessness has now been defined and formalized by intelligence and love, by the process of growing awareness by which the woodpile and the poem have simultaneously come to be. In one sense, Frost himself provides the best gloss on the way the poem works when he says that "it makes us remember what we didn't know we knew" (394). He would agree with William James, I think, that "All homes are in finite experience" and that "finite experience as such is homeless." The process of the poem does not take us from an attitude of fearful doubt to one of certainty in the immutable. Instead, it begins with a felt doubt that arises out of the formless inscrutability of a new place and takes us to an affirmation of that doubt, which, now formalized, persists even after the loveliest but inevitably mutable forms of that place are fully understood.

Frost's persona cannot stay there at the woodpile: his existence, it is clear, presupposes the necessity of perpetually walking on to an endless series of other new places equally unformed. What he walks on to, conscious all the while of the roads he does not take, is most often, as Frost says in "Directive," "a house that is no more a house Upon a farm that is no more a farm. in a town that is no more a town."

Richard Poirier

"The Wood-Pile" is like a sequel to "Home Burial," with the man in this instance wandering from a "home" that seems little more than an abstraction to him and to us. More a meditation than a dramatic narrative, it offers the soliloquy of a lone figure walking in a winter landscape. It is a desolate scene possessed of the loneliness of "Desert Places." Attention is focused on the activity of consciousness in this isolated wanderer, and nothing characterizes him as a social being or as having any relationships to another person. While the poem has resemblances, again, to Wordsworth's "Tintern Abbey," or Coleridge's "Dejection: An Ode," it is more random in its structuring and has none of the demarcations of the descriptive-reflective mode. A better way to describe the poem is suggested in a talk by A. R. Ammons, "A Poem as a Walk." "A walk involves the whole person; it is not reproducible; its shape occurs, unfolds; it has a motion characteristic of the walker" (Epoch, Fall, 1968, p. 118).

The man in the poem is not, like Stevens' Crispin, "a man come out of luminous traversing," but more like the "listener" in Stevens' "The Snow Man." In each poem is a recognition of a wintry barrenness made more so in Frost by a reductive process by which possibilities of metaphor - of finding some reassuring resemblances - are gradually disposed of. At the end, the speaker in Frost's poem is as "cool" as is the listener in Stevens, and also as peculiarly unanguished by the situation in which he finds himself. It is as if the wintry prospect, the arrival at something like Stevens' First Idea, a cold clarity without redeeming deceptions, has in itself been an achievement of the imagination. It is something won against all such conventional blandishments as the "misery" of what Harold Bloom calls the "Shelleyan wind" in "The Snow Man" or the flirtatious bird in "The Wood-Pile." The persistent difference between Frost and Stevens applies here, too, however. It resides in the kind of context the reader is asked to supply for each of the poems.

Thus, despite the absence of characterizing detail, the speaker in "The Wood-Pile" shapes, from his very opening words, a human presence for us in his sentence sounds, his voice; he makes us imagine him as someone in a human plight "far from home." By comparison, the "voice" in "The Snow Man" belongs not to a person but to a quality of rumination, and Bloom is succinctly generalizing about the poem - he calls it Stevens' "most crucial poem" - when he remarks of its author that "the text he produces is condemned to offer itself for interpretation as being already an interpretation of other interpretations, rather than as what it asserts itself to be, an interpretation of life" (Poetry and Repression, p. 270).

"The Wood-Pile" is about being impoverished, being on the dump - to recall two related states of consciousness in Stevens - with no clues by which to locate yourself in space. All you can assuredly know about "here" is that you are far from "home":

Out walking in the frozen swamp one gray day,
I paused and said, "I will turn back from here.
No, I will go on farther — and we shall see."
The hard snow held me, save where now and then
One foot went through. The view was all in lines
Straight up and down of tall slim trees
Too much alike to mark or name a place by
So as to say for certain I was here
Or somewhere else: I was just far from home.

If this is a situation that resembles winter visions of Stevens, the sound resists any effort to bring visionary possibilities into being. The voice of this man ("So as to say for certain I was here Or somewhere else") cannot be expected to test the poetic potentialities of what is seen and heard and can even less be expected to cheer itself up by indulging in the hyperbolic or the sublime vocabularies.

There is an informality even in the initial placements - "out walking. one gray day" - of the spondaic effect of "gray day," as if it were a scheduled occurrence (like "pay day") and of the possible metaphoric weight in what he says, as in the allusion (but not really) to the lack of adequate support he can expect in this landscape ("The hard snow held me, save where now and then One foot went through"). Such anxious and innocuous precision about the relative hardness of the snow or the size and contour of the trees is humanly and characterologically right. It expresses the kind of paranoia that goes with any feeling of being lost and of losing thereby a confident sense of self. Paranoia, displaced onto a small bird chancing by, becomes the motive for metaphor: the bird is endowed with the characteristics being displayed by the man observing him:

A small bird flew before me. He was careful
To put a tree between us when he lighted,
And say no word to tell me who he was
Who was so foolish as to think what he thought,
He thought that I was after him for a feather —
The white one in his tail; like one who takes
Everything said as personal to himself.
One flight out sideways would have undeceived him.
And then there was a pile of wood for which
I forgot him and let his little fear
Carry him off the way I might have gone,
Without so much as wishing him good-night.

There is a combination here of yearning, competitiveness, and resentment that threatens to become ludicrous, a parody of the romantic search for associations and resemblances. And the parodistic possibility is increased by the syntax of the lines about the bird's tail-feathers.

They could mean that the bird was foolish to think that the man had this particular design upon him. But the lines could also be the speaker's rendition or imitation of what he thought the bird was thinking, i.e., "Who does that man think he is to think that he can get hold of my tail-feathers?" In any event, there is more "thinking" proposed than could possibly or profitably be going on.

That the paranoia and self-regard confusingly attributed to the bird are really a characterization of the man who is observing the bird is further suggested by the accusation that the bird is "like one who takes Everything said as personal to himself" - a jocular simile, given the fact that there is only "one" person around to whom the comparison might apply. If all this is to some degree comic, it is feverishly so, the product of intense loneliness and displacement. From its opening moment the poem becomes a human drama of dispossession, of failed possessiveness, and of the need to structure realities which are not "here," to replace, in the words of Stevens, "nothing that is not there" with "the nothing that is."

The only probable evidence of structure that he does find, already put together, is the "wood-pile," a forgotten remnant of earlier efforts to make a "home" by people who, when they did it, were also away from home. The pile of wood, which lets the speaker promptly forget the bird, once more excites his anxious precisions.

He still needs to find some human resemblances, evidences in zones and demarcations for the human capacity to make a claim on an alien landscape. What he discovers is sparse indeed, his reassurance equally so, as we can note in his rather pathetic exactitudes:

It was a cord of maple, cut and split
And piled — and measured, four by four by eight.
And not another like it could I see.
No runner tracks in this year's snow looped near it.
And it was older sure than this year's cutting,
Or even last year's or the year's before.
The wood was gray and the bark warping off it
And the pile somewhat sunken. Clematis
Had wound strings round and round it like a bundle.
What held it, though, on one side was a tree
Still growing, and on one a stake and prop,
These latter about to fall. I thought that only
Someone who lived in turning to fresh tasks
Could so forget his handiwork on which
He spent himself, the labour of his ax,

And leave it there far from a useful fireplace
To warm the frozen swamp as best it could
With the slow smokeless burning of decay.

The poem here could be read as a commentary on the earlier "The Tuft of Flowers" where, instead of a bird, a butterfly acts as a kind of pointer who "led my eye to look At a tall tuft of flowers beside a brook" and where these flowers, in turn, direct his attention to signs of work having been done by another man with "A spirit kindred to my own; So that henceforth I worked no more alone." "The Wood-Pile" is obviously a much starker poem. The "tuft of flowers" was left as a kind of signature, a greeting and communication; the pile of wood was simply forgotten by the man who cut and carefully stacked it, as he went on to the distractions of other things.

The wood-pile cannot therefore prompt the gregarious aphorisms which bring "The Tuft of Flowers" to a close: "'Men work together,' I told him from the heart,'Whether they work together or apart.'" Remnants of a human presence in the swamp only remind the walker that he is completely alone in a place that has been deserted. And his aloneness is the more complete because there are no alternatives outside the present circumstances which give him any comfort.

Even when he thinks of a fireplace it is not with images of conviviality but only with the observation that it would be "useful." The wood burns of itself, with a warmth that cannot be felt and without giving any evidence whatever that it belongs in the world of men and women. "With the slow smokeless burning of decay" is a line whose sound carries an extraordinary authority and dignity because it has emerged out of the more sauntering vernacular movements at the beginning of the poem. It induces a kind of awe because it is the acknowledgment of nature as a realm wholly independent of human need or even human perception, and it belongs not only in what it says but in its very cadence with Wordsworth's evocation at the end of his sonnet "Mutability" of "the unimaginable touch of Time."

If the speaker "resembles" anything at the end of the

poem, it is the wood-pile itself, something without even a semblance of consciousness; it is wholly self-consuming. As in "Desert Places," another poem about a lonely man walking in a landscape of snow, the man in "The Wood-Pile" could say that "The loneliness includes me unawares." This line is a little poem in itself.

It has a syntactical ambiguity more common in Stevens than in Frost. It can mean both that the loneliness includes him but is unaware of doing so, and that the loneliness includes him and he is not aware of its doing so by virtue of his near obliteration. In either case he is not so much included as wiped out; he is included as if he were inseparable from, indistinguishable from, the thing that includes him. He is on the point of being obliterated by the landscape, rather than allowed to exist even as an observer of it, much less a mediating or transcending presence.

William H. Pritchard

The "persona" narratives from the book - "Mending Wall," "After Apple-Picking," and "The Wood-Pile" - also strive for inclusiveness although they are spoken throughout by a voice we are tempted to call "Frost." This voice has no particular back-country identity, nor is it obsessed or limited in its point of view; it seems rather to be exploring nature, other people, ideas, ways of saying things, for the sheer entertainment they can provide. Unlike poems such as "Home Burial" and "A Servant to Servants," which are inclined toward the tragic or the pathetic, nothing "terrible" happens in the personal narratives, nor does some ominous secret lie behind them. In "The Wood-Pile," for example, almost nothing happens at all; its story, its achieved idea or wisdom, the whole air with which it carries itself, is quite unmemorable. A man out walking in a frozen swamp decides to turn back, then decides instead to go farther and see what will happen. He notes a bird in front of him and spends some time musing on what the bird must be thinking, then sees it settle behind a pile of wood.

The pile is described so as to bring out the fact that it has been around for some time. With a reflection about whoever it was who left it there, "far from a useful fireplace," the poem concludes. And the reader looks up from the text, wonders if he has missed something, perhaps goes back and reads it again to see if he can catch some meaning which has eluded him. But "The Wood-Pile" remains stubbornly unyielding to any attempt at ransacking it for a meaning not evidently on the surface. This surface is a busy one, as when the speaker meets the bird:

A small bird flew before me. He was careful
To put a tree between us when he lighted,
And say no word to tell me who he was
Who was so foolish as to think what he thought.
He thought that I was after him for a feather —
The white one in his tail; like one who takes
Everything said as personal to himself.

One flight out sideways would have undeceived him.

The bird is teased for its egoism in thinking that the world revolves around his subjective hopes and fears, and his nervousness is amusing because never was there a less predatory or even purposeful figure than the walker in this poem, who early along - in deciding to continue rather than turn back - put it this way:

"No, I will go on farther - and we shall see." See what? See things like a bird lighting in a tree, and be free to make up a story about why it doesn't speak, or how jealously protective it is of the white feather in its tail? Being free to "see" means indulging in such harmless playful fantasies the freedom of whose play is a measure of its solitary creation, far from any human or social situation. Perhaps the point of maximum play occurs in the lines about the bird's caution as he lights in the tree and determines to look only: "And say no word to tell me who he was Who was so foolish as to think what he thought." The monosyllabic tongue-twisting aspect of these lines is effective in mixing up the reader: who is more "foolish," man or bird, and how on earth can one tell?

Then there is the wood-pile itself,
a cord of maple, split, piled and measuredz

four by four by eight.
And not another like it could I see.
No runner tracks in this year's snow looped near it.
And it was older sure than this year's cutting,
Or even last year's or the year's before.
The wood was grey and the bark warping off it
And the pile somewhat sunken. Clematis
Had wound strings round and round it like a bundle.
What held it, though, on one side was a tree
Still growing, and on one a stake and prop,
These latter about to fall.

This is a thoroughly unexciting presentation of what might lay claim to be the world's most unexceptional phenomenon, yet it engages the man enough to occupy him for the remainder of the poem. More interesting than anything it "says" is the way the presentation resists, as solidly as does the sunken woodpile, our readerly efforts to find a message in it, to take it as a symbol for something or other important. In so resisting us, the woodpile confirms the teasing character of the whole poem, always leading us on, promising that around the next corner, past the next tree, we shall see something, if we but have faith to follow the walker: and then, sure enough, there it is - an old woodpile with clematis wound round it, its very situation (its "stake and prop" about to collapse) precarious.

This is all we see, except that Frost moves to reflection, concluding the poem with these lines in which the pile of wood is extended into something more:

I thought that only
Someone who lives in turning to fresh tasks
Could so forget his handiwork on which
He spent himself, the labour of his ax,
And leave it there far from a useful fireplace
To warm the frozen swamp as best it could
With the slow smokeless burning of decay.

The final line has been rightly admired, but its brilliance almost blinds us to the fact that the reflection which it concludes is in no sense a stunning or profound one. The thought that "someone" who abandoned this pile of wood must be one who "lived in turning to fresh tasks," is certainly uncontroversial and hardly provocative of further speculation. Again the interest lies not in "content" but in the way a sentence develops over seven lines, winding from the "I" to the "someone" and finally to the "handiwork" whose thermal activity is celebrated in the ingenuity of the final three lines. As with other moments in the poem, no great claims are made, no meanings are held out for everyone to use, no praise or blame is assigned to motive or action.

Early in "The Wood-Pile" the walker is surrounded by "tall slim trees Too much alike to mark or name a place by So as to say for certain I was here Or somewhere else." By the poem's end a marking has been taken, a place named, though in a way so fanciful as to establish that it is poetry we are responding to when we try to think of that decaying pile, warming the frozen swamp as best it can.

To alter the walker's final thought: only someone, like a poet, who lives in turning to fresh tropes could write a poem like the one Frost has written here, and it is an appropriate conclusion to what remains the most original, even revolutionary, book he would ever write.

We need to recall once more the language Edward Thomas used in defining and in praising it, about how Frost trusted his convictions about the validity of speech in poetry, of sentence sounds employed with "no purpose to serve beyond expressing it, when he has no audience to be bullied or flattered, when he is free, and speech takes one form and no other."

Despite the presence of back-country characters and scenes in this "book of people," it is as a book of sentence sounds that it most truly exists, as a triumphant vindication of the poetic theory Frost had designed, and as a monument to how much could be accomplished by trusting to the rendering of speech.

At the end of "Home Burial," the wife lashes out at her husband in exasperation: "You - oh, you think the talk is all." But for the composer of these poems, the talk is all, whether that of his imagined characters or of himself speaking aloud.

On "The Road Not Taken"

William H. Pritchard

On December 16, 1916, he received a warm letter from Meiklejohn, looking forward to his presence at Amherst and saying that that morning in chapel he had read aloud "The Road Not Taken," "and then told the boys about your coming. They applauded vigorously and were evidently much delighted by the prospect."

Alexander Meiklejohn was an exceptionally high-minded educator whose principles and whose moral tone toward things may be illustrated most briefly and clearly by some statements from his essay "What the College Is." This, his inaugural address as president of Amherst, was printed for a time as an introduction to the college catalogue. What the college was, or should be -what Meiklejohn hoped to make Amherst into - was a place to be thought of as "liberal," that is, "essentially intellectual": "The college is primarily not a place of the body, nor of the feelings, nor even of the will; it is, first of all, a place of the mind." Introducing "the boys" to the intellectual life led for its own sake, would save them from pettiness and dullness, would save them from being one of what Meiklejohn referred to as "the others":

There are those among us who will find so much satisfaction in the countless trivial and vulgar amusements of a crude people that they have no time for the joys of the mind. There are those who are so closely shut up within a little round of petty pleasures they that have never dreamed of the fun of reading and conversing and investigating and reflecting.

A liberal education would rescue boys from stupidity, its purpose being to draw from that "reality-loving American boy" something like "an intellectual enthusiasm." But this result could not be achieved, Meiklejohn added, without a thorough reversal of the curriculum: "I should like to see every freshman at once plunged into the problems of philosophy," he said with enthusiasm.

Now, five years after his address, he was bringing to Amherst someone outside the usual academic orbit, a poet who lacked even a college degree. But despite - or perhaps because of - this lack, the poet had escaped triviality, was an original mind who knew about living by ideas. For he had written among other poems "The Road Not Taken," given pride of place in the just-published Mountain Interval as not only its first poem but also printed in italics, as though to make it also a preface to and motto for the poems which followed.

It was perfect for Meiklejohn's purposes because it was no idle reverie, no escape through lovely language into a soothing dream world, but a poem rather which announced itself to be "about" important issues in life: about the nature of choice, of decision, of how to go in one direction rather than another and how to feel about the direction you took and didn't take. For President Meiklejohn and for the assembled students at compulsory chapel, it might have been heard as a stirring instance of what the "liberal college" was all about, since it showed how, instead of acceding to the petty pleasures, the "countless trivial and vulgar amusements" offered by the world or the money-god or the values of the marketplace, an individual could go his own way, live his own life, read his own books, take the less traveled road:

I shall be telling this with a sigh
Somewhere ages and ages hence;
Two roads diverged in a wood, and I —
I took the one less traveled by,
And that has made all the difference.

The poem ended, the boys "applauded vigorously," and surely Meiklejohn congratulated himself just a bit on making the right choice, taking the less traveled road and inviting a poet to join the Amherst College faculty.

What the president could hardly have imagined, committed as he was in high seriousness to making the life of the college truly an intellectual one, was the unruliness of Frost's spirit and its unwillingness to be confined within the formulas - for Meiklejohn, they were the truths - of the "liberal college." On the first day of the new year, 1917, just preparatory to moving his family down from the Franconia farm into a house in Amherst, Frost wrote Untermeyer about where the fun lay in what he, Frost, thought of as "intellectual activity": You get more credit for thinking if you restate formulae or cite cases that fall in easily under formulae, but all the fun is outside saying things that suggest formulae that won't formulate - that almost but don't quite formulate. I should like to be so subtle at this game as to seem to the casual person altogether obvious. The casual person would assume I meant nothing or else I came near enough meaning something he was familiar with to mean it for all practical purposes. Well, well, well.

The "fun" is "outside," and lies in doing something like teasing, suggesting formulae that don't formulate, or not quite. The fun is not in being "essentially intellectual" or in manifesting "intellectual enthusiasm" in Meiklejohn's sense of the phrase, but in being "subtle," and not just subtle but so much so as to fool "the casual person" into thinking that what you said was obvious.

If we juxtapose these remarks with his earlier determination to reach out as a poet to all sorts and kinds of people, and if we think of "The Road Not Taken" as a prime example of a poem which succeeded in reaching out and taking hold, then something interesting emerges about the kind of relation to other people, to readers - or to students and college presidents - Frost was willing to live with, indeed to cultivate.

For the large moral meaning which "The Road Not Taken" seems to endorse - go, as I did, your own way, take the road less traveled by, and it will make "all the difference"-does not maintain itself when the poem is looked at more carefully. Then one notices how insistent is the speaker on admitting, at the time of his choice, that the two roads were in appearance "really about the same," that they "equally lay In leaves no step had trodden black," and that choosing one rather than the other was a matter of impulse, impossible to speak about any more clearly than to say that the road taken had "perhaps the better claim." But in the final stanza, as the tense changes to future, we hear a different story, one that will be told "with a sigh" and "ages and ages hence." At that imagined time and unspecified place, the voice will have nobly simplified and exalted the whole impulsive matter into a deliberate one of taking the "less traveled" road:

Two roads diverged in a wood, and I —
I took the one less traveled by,
And that has made all the difference.

Is it not the high tone of poignant annunciation that really makes all the difference? An earlier version of the poem had no dash after "I"; presumably Frost added it to make the whole thing more expressive and heartfelt. And it was this heartfelt quality which touched Meiklejohn and the students.

Yet Frost had written Untermeyer two years previously that "I'll bet not half a dozen people can tell you who was hit and where he was hit in my Road Not Taken," and he characterized himself in that poem particularly as "fooling my way along." He also said that it was really about his friend Edward Thomas, who when they walked together always castigated himself for not having taken another path than the one they took.

When Frost sent "The Road Not Taken" to Thomas he was disappointed that Thomas failed to understand it as a poem about himself, but Thomas in return insisted to Frost that "I doubt if you can get anybody to see the fun of the thing without showing them and advising them which kind of laugh they are to turn on." And though this sort of advice went exactly contrary to Frost's notion of how poetry should work, he did on occasion warn his audiences and other readers that it was a tricky poem. Yet it became a popular poem for very different reasons than what Thomas referred to as "the fun of the thing." It was taken to be an inspiring poem rather, a courageous credo stated by the farmer-poet of New Hampshire. In fact, it is an especially notable instance in Frost's work of a poem which sounds noble and is really mischievous. One of his notebooks contains the following four-line thought:

Nothing ever so sincere
That unless it's out of sheer
Mischief and a little queer
It wont prove a bore to hear.

The mischievous aspect of "The Road Not Taken" is what

makes it something un-boring, for there is little in its language or form which signals an interesting poem. But that mischief also makes it something other than a "sincere" poem, in the way so many readers have taken Frost to be sincere. Its fun is outside the formulae it seems almost but not quite to formulate.

Jay Parini

A close look at the poem reveals that Frost's walker encounters two nearlv identical paths: so he insists, repeatedly. The walker looks down one, first, then the other, "as just as fair." Indeed, "the passing there Had worn them reallv about the same." As if the reader hasn't gotten the message, Frost says for a third time. "And both that morning equally lay In leaves no step had trodden black." What, then, can we make of the final stanza? My guess is that Frost, the wily ironist, is saying something like this: "When I am old, like all old men, I shall make a myth of my life.

I shall pretend, as we all do, that I took the less traveled road. But I shall be lying." Frost signals the mockingly self-inflated tone of the last stanza by repeating the word "I," which rhymes - several times - with the inflated word "sigh." Frost wants the reader to know that what he will be saying, that he took the road less traveled, is a fraudulent position, hence the sigh.

George Montiero

"THE ROAD NOT TAKEN" can be read against a literary and pictorial tradition that might be called "The Choice of the Two Paths, " reaching not only back to the Gospels and beyond them to the Greeks but to ancient English verse as well. In Reson and Sensuallyte, for example, John Lydgate explains how he dreamt that Dame Nature had offered him the choice between the Road of Reason and the Road of Sensuality.

In art the same choice was often represented by the letter "Y" with the trunk of the letter representing the careless years of childhood and the two paths branching off at the age when the child is expected to exercise discretion. In one design the "Two Paths" are shown in great detail. "On one side a thin line of pious folk ascend a hill past several churches and chapels, and so skyward to the Heavenly City where an angel stands proffering a crown.

On the other side a crowd of men and women are engaged in feasting, music, love-making, and other carnal pleasures while close behind them yawns the flaming mouth of hell in which sinners are writhing. But hope is held out for the worldly for some avoid hell and having passed through a dark forest come to the rude huts of Humility and Repentance." Embedded in this quotation is a direct reference to the opening of Dante's Inferno:

Midway upon the journey of our life
I found myself within a forest dark,
For the straightforward pathway had been lost.
Ah me! how hard a thing it is to say
What was the forest savage, rough, and stern,
Which in the very thought renews the fear.
So bitter is it, death is little more.

From the beginning, when it appeared as the first poem in Mountain Interval (1916), many readers have overstated the importance of "The Road Not Taken" to Frost's work. Alexander Meiklejohn, president of Amherst College, did so when, announcing the appointment of the poet to the school's faculty he recited it to a college assembly.

"The Choice of Two Paths" is suggested in Frost's decision to make his two roads not very much different from one another, for passing over one of them had the effect of wearing them "really about the same." This is a far cry from, say, the description of the "two waies " offered in the seventeenth century by Henry Crosse:

Two waies are proposed and laide open to all, the one inviting to vertue, the other alluring to vice; the first is combersome, intricate, untraded, overgrowne, and many obstacles to dismay the passenger; the other plaine, even beaten, overshadowed with boughes, tapistried with flowers, and many objects to feed the eye; now a man that lookes but only to the outward shewe, will easily tread the broadest pathe, but if hee perceive that this smooth and even way leads to a neast of Scorpions: or a litter of Beares, he will rather take the other though it be rugged and unpleasant, than hazard himselfe in so great a daunger.

Frost seems to have deliberately chosen the word "roads" rather than "waies" or "paths" or even "pathways." In fact, on one occasion when he was asked to recite his famous poem, "Two paths diverged in a yellow wood," Frost reacted with such feeling—"Two roads!"—that the transcription of his reply made it necessary both to italicize the word "roads" and to follow it with an exclamation point. Frost recited the poem all right, but, as his friend remembered, "he didn't let me get away with 'two paths!'"

Convinced that the poem was deeply personal and directly self-revelatory Frost's readers have insisted on tracing the poem to one or the other of two facts of Frost's life when he was in his late thirties. (At the beginning of the Inferno Dante is thirty-five, "midway on the road of life," notes Charles Eliot Norton.) The first of these, an event, took place in the winter of 1911-1912 in the woods of Plymouth, New Hampshire, while the second, a general observation and a concomitant attitude, grew out of his long walks in England with Edward Thomas, his newfound Welsh-English poet-friend, in 1914.

In Robert Frost: The Trial by Existence, Elizabeth Shepley Sergeant locates in one of Frost's letters the source for "The Road Not Taken." To Susan Hayes Ward the poet wrote on February 10, 1912:

Two lonely cross-roads that themselves cross each other I have walked several times this winter without meeting or overtaking so much as a single person on foot or on runners. The practically unbroken condition of both for several days after a snow or a blow proves that neither is much travelled. Judge then how surprised I was the other evening as I came down one to see a man, who to my own unfamiliar eyes and in the dusk looked for all the world like myself, coming down the other, his approach to the point where our paths must intersect being so timed that unless one of us pulled up we must inevitably collide.

I felt as if I was going to meet my own image in a slanting mirror. Or say I felt as we slowly converged on the same point with the same noiseless yet laborious stride as if we were two images about to float together with the uncrossing of someone's eyes. I verily expected to take up or absorb this other self and feel the stronger by the addition for the three-mile journey home. But I didn't go forward to the touch. I stood still in wonderment and let him pass by; and that, too, with the fatal omission of not trying to find out by a comparison of lives and immediate and remote interests what could have brought us by crossing paths to the same point in a wilderness at the same moment of nightfall. Some purpose I doubt not, if we could but have made out. I like a coincidence almost as well as an incongruity.

This portentous account of meeting "another" self (but not encountering that self directly and therefore not coming to terms with it) would eventually result in a poem quite different from "The Road Not Taken" and one that Frost would not publish for decades. Elizabeth Sergeant ties the moment with Frost's decision to go off at this time to some place where he could devote more time to poetry. He had also, she implies, filed away his dream for future poetic use.

That poetic use would occur three years later. In 1914 Frost arrived in England for what he then thought would be an extended sabbatical leave from farming in New Hampshire. By all the signs he was ready to settle down for a long stay. Settling in Gloucestershire, he soon became a close friend of Edward Thomas. Later, when readers persisted in misreading "The Road Not Taken," Frost insisted that his poem had been intended as a sly jest at the expense of his friend and fellow poet. For Thomas had invariably fussed over irrevocable choices of the most minor sort made on daily walks with Frost in 1914, shortly before the writing of the poem.

Later Frost insisted that in his case the line "And that has made all the difference"—taken straight—was all wrong. "Of course, it hasn't," he persisted, "it's just a poem, you know." In 1915, moreover, his sole intention was to twit Thomas. Living in Gloucestershire, writes Lawrance Thompson, Frost had frequently taken long countryside walks with Thomas.

Repeatedly Thomas would choose a route which might enable him to show his American friend a rare plant or a special vista; but it often happened that before the end of such a walk Thomas would regret the choice he had made and would sigh over what he might have shown Frost if they had taken a "better" direction. More than once, on such occasions, the New Englander had teased his Welsh-English friend for those wasted regrets. Frost found something quaintly romantic in sighing over what might have been. Such a course of action was a road never taken by Frost, a road he had been taught to avoid.

If we are to believe Frost and his biographer, "The Road Not Taken" was intended to serve as Frost's gentle jest at Thomas's expense. But the poem might have had other targets. One such target was a text by another poet who in a different sense might also be considered a "friend": Henry Wadsworth Longfellow, whose poem, "My Lost Youth," had provided Frost with A Boy's Will, the title he chose for his first book.

"The Road Not Taken " can be placed against a passage in Longfellow's notebooks: "Round about what is, lies a whole mysterious world of might be,—a psychological romance of possibilities and things that do not happen. By going out a few minutes sooner or later, by stopping to speak with a friend at a corner, by meeting this man or that, or by turning down this street instead of the other, we may let slip some great occasion of good, or avoid some impending evil, by which the whole current of our lives would have been changed. There is no possible solution to the dark enigma but the one word, 'Providence.'"

Longfellow's tone in this passage is sobre, even somber, and anticipates the same qualities in Edward Thomas, as Frost so clearly perceived. Elizabeth Shepley Sergeant had insisted that Frost's dream encounter with his other self at a crossroads in the woods had a " subterranean connection " with the whole of "The Road Not Taken," especially with the poem's last lines:

I shall be telling this with a sigh
Somewhere ages and ages hence:

Two roads diverged in a wood, and I—
I took the one less traveled by,
And that has made all the difference.

Undoubtedly. But whereas Longfellow had invoked Providence to account for acts performed and actions not taken, Frost calls attention only to the role of human choice. A second target was the notion that "whatever choice we make, we make at our peril." The words just quoted are Fitz-James Stephen's, but it is more important that Frost encountered them in William James's essay "The Will to Believe." In fact, James concludes his final paragraph on the topic: "We stand on a mountain pass in the midst of whirling snow and blinding mist, through which we get glimpses now and then of paths which may be deceptive.

If we take the wrong road we shall be dashed to pieces. We do not certainly know whether there is any right one. What must we do? 'Be strong and of a good courage.' Act for the best, hope for the best, and take what comes. If death ends all, we cannot meet death better." The danger inherent in decision, in this brave passage quoted with clear-cut approval by the teacher Frost "never had," does not playa part in "The Road Not Taken." Frost the "leaf-treader" will have none of it, though he will not refuse to make a choice. Nothing will happen to him through default. Nor, argues the poet, is it likely that anyone will melodramatically be dashed to pieces.

It is useful to see Frost's projected sigh as a nudging criticism of Thomas's characteristic regrets, to note that Frost's poem takes a sly poke at Longfellow's more generalized awe before the notion of what might have happened had it not been for the inexorable workings of Providence, and to see "The Road Not Taken" as a bravura tossing off of Fitz-James Stephen's mountainous and meteorological scenario. We can also project the poem against a poem by Emily Dickinson that Frost had encountered twenty years earlier in Poems, Second Series (1891).

Our journey had advanced;
Our feet were almost come
To that odd fork in Being's road,

Eternity by term.
Our pace took sudden awe,
Our feet reluctant led.
Before were cities, but between,
The forest of the dead.
Retreat was out of hope,—
Behind, a sealed route,
Eternity's white flag before,
And God at every gate.

Dickinson's poem is straightforwardly and orthodoxically religious. But it can be seen that beyond the "journey" metaphor Dickinson's poem employs diction—"road" and "forest"—that recalls "The Choice of the Two Paths" trope, the opening lines of the Inferno, and Frost's secular poem "The Road Not Taken."

Katherine Kearns

"The Road Not Taken," perhaps the most famous example of Frost's own claims to conscious irony and "the best example in all of American poetry of a wolf in sheep's clothing." Thompson documents the ironic impulse that produced the poem as Frost's "gently teasing" response to his good friend, Edward Thomas, who would in their walks together take Frost down one path and then regret not having taken a better direction. According to Thompson, Frost assumes the mask of his friend, taking his voice and his posture, including the un-Frostian sounding line, "I shall be telling this with a sigh," to poke fun at Thomas's vacillations; Frost ever after, according to Thompson, tried to bring audiences to the ironic point, warning one group, "You have to be careful of that one; it's a tricky poem - very tricky).

Thompson's critical evaluation is simply that Frost had, in that particular poem, "carried himself and his ironies too subtly," so that the poem is, in effect, a failure. Yet is it simply that - a too exact parody of a mediocre poetic voice, which becomes among the sentimental masses, ironically, one of the most popularly beloved of Frost's "wise" poems? This is the easiest way to come to terms critically with the popularity of

"The Road Not Taken" but it is not, perhaps, the only or best way: in this critical case, the road less traveled may indeed be more productive.

For Frost by all accounts was genuinely fond of Thomas. He wrote his only elegy to Thomas and he gives him, in that poem, the highest praise of all from one who would, himself, hope to be a "good Greek": he elegizes Thomas as "First soldier, and then poet, and then both, Who died a soldier-poet of your race." He recalls Thomas to Amy Lowell, saying "the closest I ever came in friendship to anyone in England or anywhere else in the world I think was with Edward Thomas" (. Frost's protean ability to assume dramatic masks never elsewhere included such a friend as Thomas, whom he loved and admired, tellingly, more than "anyone in England or anywhere else in the world" (Letters 220). It might be argued that in becoming Thomas in "The Road Not Taken," Frost momentarily loses his defensive preoccupation with disguising lyric involvement to the extent that ironic weapons fail him. A rare instance in Frost's poetry in which there is a loved and reciprocal figure, the poem is divested of the need to keep the intended reader at bay.

Here Frost is not writing about that contentiously erotic love which is predicated on the sexual battles between a man and a woman, but about a higher love, by the terms of the good Greek, between two men. As Plato says in the Symposium (181, b-c), "But the heavenly love springs from a goddess [Aphrodite] whose attributes have nothing of the female, but are altogether male, and who is also the elder of the two, and innocent of any hint of lewdness.

And so those who are inspired by this other Love turn rather to the male, preferring the more vigorous and intellectual bent." If the poem is indeed informed by such love, it becomes the most consummate irony of all, as it shows, despite one level of Frost's intentions, how fraternal love can transmute swords to plowshares, how, indeed, two roads can look about the same, be traveled about the same, and be utterly transformed by the traveller. Frost sent this poem as a letter, as a communication in the most basic sense, to a man to whom he says, in "To E. T.," "I meant, you meant, that nothing should remain Unsaid between us, brother. " When nothing is meant to remain unsaid, and when the poet's best hope is to see his friend "pleased once more with words of mine," all simple ironies are made complex. "The Road Not Taken," far from being merely a failure of ironic intent, may be seen as a touchstone for the complexities of analyzing Frost's ironic voices.

Frank Lentricchia

Self-reliance in "The Road Not Taken" is alluringly embodied as the outcome of a story presumably representative of all stories of self-hood, and whose central episode is that moment of the turning-point decision, the crisis from which a self springs: a critical decision consolingly, for Frost's American readers, grounded in a rational act when a self, and therefore an entire course of life, are autonomously and irreversibly chosen. The particular Fireside poetic structure in which Frost incarnates this myth of selfhood is the analogical landscape poem, perhaps most famously executed by William Cullen Bryant in "To a Waterfowl," a poem that Matthew Arnold praised as the finest lyric of the nineteenth century and that Frost had by heart as a child thanks to his mother's enthusiasm.

The analogical landscape poem draws its force from the culturally ancient and pervasive idea of nature as allegorical book, in its American poetic setting a book out of which to draw explicit lessons for the conduct of life (nature as self-help text). In its classic Fireside expression, the details of landscape and all natural events are cagily set up for moral summary as they are marched up to the poem's conclusion, like little imagistic lambs to slaughter, for their payoff in uplifting message. Frost appears to recapitulate the tradition in his sketching of the yellow wood and the two roads and in his channeling of the poem's course of events right up to the portentous colon ("Somewhere ages and ages hence:") beyond which lies the wisdom that we jot down and take home:

Two roads diverged in a wood, and I —
I took the one less traveled by,

And that has made all the difference.

If we couple such tradition-bound thematic structure with Frost's more or less conventional handling of metric, stanzaic form and rhyme scheme, then we have reason enough for Ellery Sedgwick's acceptance of this poem for the Atlantic: no "caviar to the crowd" here.

And yet Frost has played a subtle game in an effort to have it both ways. In order to satisfy the Atlantic and its readers, he hews closely to the requirements of popular genre writing and its mode of poetic production, the mass circulation magazine. But at the same time he has more than a little undermined what that mode facilitates in the realm of American poetic and political ideals.

There must be two roads and they must, of course, be different if the choice of one over the other is to make a rational difference ("And that has made all the difference"). But the key fact, that on the particular morning when the choice was made the two roads looked "about the same," makes it difficult to understand how the choice could be rationally grounded on (the poem's key word) perceptible, objective "difference." The allegorical "way" has been chosen, a self has been forever made, but not because a text has been "read" and the "way" of nonconformity courageously, ruggedly chosen. The fact is, there is no text to be read, because reading requires a differentiation of signs, and on that morning clear signifying differences were obliterated. Frost's delivery of this unpleasant news has long been difficult for his readers to hear because he cunningly throws it away in a syntax of subordination that drifts out of thematic focus.

The unpleasant news is hard to hear, in addition, because Fireside form demands, and therefore creates the expectation of, readable textual differences in the book of nature. Frost's heavy investment in traditional structure virtually assures that Fireside literary form will override and cover its mischievous handling in this poem.

For a self to be reliant, decisive, nonconformist, there must already be an autonomous self out of which to propel decision. But what propelled choice on that fateful morning? Frost's speaker does not choose out of some rational capacity; he prefers, in fact, not to choose at all. That is why he can admit to what no self-respecting self-reliant self can admit to: that he is "sorry" he "could not travel bothAnd be one traveller." The good American ending, the last three lines of the poem, is prefaced by two lines of storytelling self-consciousness in which the speaker, speaking in the present to a listener (reader) to whom he has just conveyed "this," his story of the past - everything preceding the last stanza - in effect tells his auditor that in some unspecified future he will tell it otherwise, to some gullible audience, tell it the way they want to hear it, as a fiction of autonomous intention.

The strongly sententious yet ironic last stanza in effect predicts the happy American construction which "The Road Not Taken" has been traditionally understood to endorse — predicts, in other words, what the poem will be sentimentally made into, but from a place in the poem that its Atlantic Monthly reading, as it were, will never touch. The power of the last stanza within the Fireside teleology of analogical landscape assures Frost his popular audience, while for those who get his game — some member, say, of a different audience, versed in the avant-garde little magazines and in the treacheries of irony and the impulse of the individual talent trying, as Pound urged, to "make it new" against the literary and social American grain - for that reader, this poem tells a different tale: that our life-shaping choices are irrational, that we are fundamentally out of control. This is the fabled "wisdom" of Frost, which he hides in a moralizing statement that asserts the consoling contrary of what he knows.

Mark Richardson

The ironies of this poem have been often enough remarked. Not least among them is the contrast of the title with the better-remembered phrase of the poem's penultimate line: "thc [road] less travelled by" Which road, after all, is the road "not taken"? Is it the one the speaker takes, which, according to his last description of it, is "less travelled"-that is to say, not taken by others? Or does the title refer to the supposedly better-traveled road that the speaker himself fails to take?

Precisely who is not doing the taking? This initial ambiguity sets in play equivocations that extend throughout the poem. Of course, the broadest irony in the poem derives from the fact that the speaker merely asserts that the road he takes is "less travelled": the second and third stanzas make clear that "the passing there" had worn these two paths "really about the same" and that "both that morning equally lay In leaves no step had trodden black."

Strong medial caesurae in the poem's first ten lines comically emphasize the "either-or" deliberations in which the speaker is engaged, and which have, apparently, no real consequence: nothing issues from them. Only in the last stanza is any noticeable difference between the two roads established, and that difference is established by fiat: the speaker simply declares that the road he took was less travelled. There is nothing to decide between them. There is no meaningful "choice" to make, or rather no more choice than is meaningfully apparent to the "step-careless" politician of Frost's parable of decision in "The Constant Symbol."

Comical as "The Road Not Taken" may be, there is serious matter in it, as my reading of "The Constant Symbol" is meant to suggest. "Step-carelessness" has its consequences; choices—even when they are undertaken so lightly as to seem unworthy of the name "choice"—are always more momentous, and very often more providential, than we suppose. There may be, one morning in a yellow wood, no difference between two roads—say, the Democratic and the Republican parties. But "way leads on to way," as Frost's speaker says, and pretty soon you find yourself in the White House.

As I argue throughout this chapter, this is the indifference that Frost wants us to see: "youthful step-carelessness" really is a form of "step-carefulness." But it is only by setting out, by working our way well into the wood, that we begin to understand the meaning of the choices we make and the character of the self that is making them; in fact, only then can we properly understand our actions as choices. The speaker vacillates in the first three stanzas of "The Road Not Taken," but his vacillations, viewed in deeper perspective, seem, and in fact really are, "decisive." We are too much in the middle of things, Frost seems to be saying, ever to understand when we are truly "acting" and "deciding" and when we are merely reacting and temporizing. Our paths unfold themselves to us as we go. We realise our destination only when we arrive at it, though all along we were driven toward it by purposes we may rightly claim, in retrospect, as our own. Frost works from Emerson's recognition in "Experience":

> Where do we find ourselves? In a series of which we do not know the extremes, and believe that it has none. We wake and find ourselves on a stair; there are stairs below us, which we seem to have ascended; there are stairs above us, many a one, which go upward and out of sight. But the Genius which, according to the old belief, stands at the door by which we enter, and gives us the lethe to drink, that we may tell no tales, mixed the cup too strongly, and we cannot shake off the lethargy now at noonday.If any of us knew what we were doing, or where we are going, then when we think we best know! We do not know today whether we are busy or idle. In times when we thought ourselves indolent, we have afterwards discovered, that much was accomplished, and much was begun in us.

Frost's is an Emersonian philosophy in which indecisiveness and decision feel very much alike—a philosophy in which acting and being acted upon form indistinguishable aspects of a single experience. There is obviously a contradiction in "The Road Not Taken" between the speaker's assertion of difference in the last stanza and his indifferent account of the roads in the first three stanzas. But it is a contradiction more profitably described—in light of Frost's other investigations of questions about choice, decision, and action—as a paradox.

He lets us see, as I point out above, that every action is in some degree intemperate, incalculable, "step-careless." The speaker of "The Road Not Taken," like the politician described in "The Constant Symbol," is therefore a figure for us all. This complicates the irony of the poem, saving it from platitude on the one hand (the M. Scott Peck reading) and from sarcasm on the other (the biographical reading of the poem merely as a joke about Edward Thomas). I disagree with Frank Lentricchia's suggestion in Modernist Quartet that "The Road Not Taken" shows how "our life- shaping choices are irrational, that we are fundamentally out of control" (75). The author of "The Trial by Existence" would never contend that we are fundamentally out of control—or at least not do so in earnest.

Robert Faggen

"The Road Not Taken" is an ironic commentary on the autonomy of choice in a world governed by instincts, unpredictable contingencies, and limited possibilities. It parodies and demurs from the biblical idea that God is the "way" that can and should be followed and the American idea that nature provides the path to spiritual enlightenment. The title refers doubly to bravado for choosing a road less traveled but also to regret for a road of lost possibility and the eliminations and changes produced by choice. "The Road Not Taken " reminds us of the consequences of the principle of selection in al1 aspects of life, namely that al1 choices in knowledge or in action exclude many others and lead to an ironic recognitions of our achievements. At the heart of the poem is the romantic mythology of flight from a fixed world of limited possibility into a wilderness of many possibilities combined with trials and choices through which the pilgrim progresses to divine perfection. I agree with Frank Lentricchia's view that the poem draws on "the culturally ancient and pervasive idea of nature as allegorical book, out of which to draw explicit lessons for the conduct of life (nature as self-help text)." I would argue that what it is subverting is something more profound than the sentimental expectations of genteel readers of fireside poetry.

The drama of the poem is of the persona making a choice between two roads. As evolved creatures, we should be able to make choices, but the poem suggests that our choices are irrational and aesthetic. The sense of meaning and morality derived from choice is not reconciled but, rather obliterated and canceled by a nonmoral monism. Frost is trying to reconcile impulse with a con- science that needs goals and harbors deep regrets.

The verb Frost uses is taken, which means something less conscious than chosen. The importance of this opposition to Frost is evident in the way he changed the tide of "Take Something Like a Star" to "Choose Something Like a Star," and he continued to alter tides in readings and publications. Take suggests more of an unconscious grasp than a deliberate choice. (Of course, it also suggests action as opposed to deliberation.) In "The Road Not Taken" the persona's reasons wear thin, and choice is confined by circumstances and the irrational: Both roads had been worn "about the same," though his "taking" the second is based on its being less worn. The basis of selection is individuation, variation, and "difference": taking the one "less traveled by." That he "could not travel both And be one traveller" means not only that he will never be able to return but also that experience alters the traveller; he would not be the same by the time he came back. Frost is presenting an antimyth in which origin, destination, and return are undermined by a nonprogressive development. And the hero has only illusory choice.

This psychological representation of the developmental principle of divergence strikes to the core of Darwinian theory. Species are made and survive when individuals diverge from others in a branching scheme, as the roads diverge for the speaker. The process of selection implies an unretracing process of change through which individual kinds are permanently altered by experience. Though the problem of making a choice at a crossroads is almost a commonplace, the drama of the poem conveys a larger mythology by including evolutionary metaphors and suggesting the passage of eons.

The change of tense in the penultimate line—to took—is part of the speaker's projection of what he "shall be telling," but only retrospectively and after "ages and ages." Though he cannot help feeling free in selection, the speaker's wisdom is proved only through survival of an unretraceable course of experience:

The poem leaves one wondering how much "difference" is implied by all, given that the "roads" already exist, that possibilities are limited. Exhausted possibilities of human experience diminish great regret over "the road not taken" or bravado for "the road not taken" by everyone else. The poem does raise questions about whether there is any justice in the outcome of one's choices or anything other than aesthetics, being "fair," in our moral decisions. The speaker's impulse to individuation is mitigated by a moral dilemma of being unfair or cruel, in not stepping on leaves, "treading" enough to make them "black. " It might also imply the speaker's recognition that individuation will mean treading on others.

On "Birches"

Frank Lentricchia

In "Birches" (Mountain Interval, 1916) Frost begins to probe the power of his redemptive imagination as it moves from its playful phase toward the brink of dangerous transcendence. The movement into transcendence is a movement into a realm of radical imaginative freedom where (because redemption has succeeded too well) all possibilities of engagement with the common realities of experience are dissolved. In its moderation, a redemptive consciousness motivates union between selves as we have seen in "The Generations of Men," or in any number of Frost's love poems. But in its extreme forms, redemptive consciousness can become self-defeating as it presses the imaginative man into deepest isolation. "Birches" begins by evoking its core image against the background of a darkly wooded landscape:

When I see birches bend to left and right
Across the lines of straighter darker trees,
I like to think some boy's been swinging them.
But swinging doesn't bend them down to stay
As ice storms do.

The pliable, malleable quality of the birch tree captures the poet's attention and kicks off his meditation. Perhaps young boys don't bend birches down to stay, but swing them they do and thus bend them momentarily. Those "straighter, darker trees," like the trees of "Into My Own" that "scarcely show the breeze," stand ominously free from human manipulation, menacing in their irresponsiveness to acts of the will. The malleability of the birches is not total, however, and the poet is forced to admit this fact into the presence of his desire, like it or not. The ultimate shape of mature birch trees is the work of objective natural force, not human activity. Yet after conceding the boundaries of imagination's subjective world, the poet seems not to have constricted himself but to have been released.

> *Often you must have seen them*
> *Loaded with ice a sunny winter morning*
> *After a rain. They click upon themselves*
> *As the breeze rises, and turn many-colored*
> *As the stir cracks and crazes their enamel.*
> *Soon the sun's warmth makes them shed crystal shells*
> *Shattering and avalanching on the snow crust—*
> *Such heaps of broken glass to sweep away*
> *You'd think the inner dome of heaven had fallen.*

Fascinated as he is by the show of loveliness before him, and admiring as be is of nature as it performs the potter's art, cracking and crazing the enamel of ice coating on the birch trees, it is not finally the thing itself (the ice-coated trees) that interests the poet but the strange association be is tempted to make: "You'd think the inner dome of heaven had fallen." Certainly there is no question of belief involved here.

The linkage of the scientifically discredited medieval sphere with the heaps of cracked ice suggests rather the poet's need to break beyond the rigid standard of empirical truth, that he himself has already allowed into the poem, and faintly suggests as well the kind of apocalyptic destruction that the imagination seeks when unleashed (the idea that the inner dome has been smashed clearly pleases the speaker). Eventually Frost in "Birches" comes round to exploring in much more sophisticated ways the complex problem broached by this statement from a later poem, "On Looking Up By Chance At the Constellations":

The sun and moon get crossed, but they never touch,
Nor strike out fire from each other, nor crash out loud.
The planets seem to interfere in their curves,
But nothing ever happens, no harm is done.
We may as well go patiently on with our life,
And look elsewhere than to stars and moon and sun
For the shocks and changes we need to keep us sane.

In "Birches" Frost looks not to natural catastrophe for those "shocks and changes" that "keep us sane" but to his resources as a poet:

You may see their trunks arching in the woods
Years afterwards, trailing their leaves on the ground
Like girls on hands and knees that throw their hair
Before them over their heads to dry in the sun.

Manipulating the simile, the overt figure of comparison, is a dangerous ploy for the poet, implying often that be does not have the courage of his vision and does not believe that his mode of language can generate a distinctive perspective on experience. For Frost, however, and for any poet who is rooted in what I call the aesthetics of the fiction., the simile is the perfect figure of comparison, subtler even than metaphor. Its overtness becomes its virtue: in its insistence on the disparateness of the things compared (as well as their likeness) it can sustain a divided vision; can at once transmute the birches—for a brief moment nature stands humanized and the poet has transcended the scientific universe—and, at the same time, can allow the fictive world to be penetrated by the impurities of experience that resist the transmutative process of imagination.

It is at such moments as this in Frost's work that the strategies and motives of a poetry of play are revealed. There is never any intention of competing with science, and therefore, there is no problem at all (as we generally sense with many modern poets and critics) of claiming a special cognitive value for poetry. In his playful and redemptive mode, Frost's motive for poetry is not cognitive but psychological in the sense that he is willfully seeking to bathe his consciousness and, if the reader consents, his reader's as well, in a free-floating, epistemologically unsanctioned vision of the world which, even as it is undermined by the very language in which it is anchored, brings a satisfaction of relief when contemplated.

It may be argued that the satisfaction is greatest when it is autonomous: the more firmly the poet insists upon the severance of his vision from the order of things as they are and the more clearly that be makes no claim for knowledge, the emotive power of the poem may emerge uncontaminated by the morass of philosophical problems that are bound to dog him should he make claims for knowledge. Both poet and reader may submerge themselves without regret (because without epistemological pretension) in aesthetic illusion.

But I was going to say when Truth broke in
With all her matter of fact about the ice storm,
I should prefer to have some boy bend them
As he went out and in to fetch the cows—
Some boy too far from town to learn baseball,
Whose only play was what be found himself,
Summer or winter, and could play alone.

The shrewdness in Frost's strategy now surfaces. While claiming to have paid homage to the rigid standards of empirical truth in his digression on the ice-loaded branches, what he has actually done is to digress into the language of fictions. When he turns to the desired vision of the young boy swinging birches, he is not, as he says, turning from truth to fiction, but from one kind of fiction to another kind of fiction: from the fiction of cosmic change and humanized nature to the fiction of the human will riding roughshod over a pliable external world.

And the motives for all of this fooling? I think there are two: one is that Frost intends to fox his naturalistically persuaded readers; a second is that this is what his poem is all about—the thrusting of little fictions within alien, antifictive contexts.* As he evokes the image of the boy, playing in isolation, too far from the community to engage in a team kind of sport, he evokes, as well, his cherished theme of the imaginative man who, essentially alone in the world, either makes it or doesn't on the strength of his creative resources.

And now he indulges to the full the desired vision that be could not allow himself in the poem's opening lines:

One by one he subdued his father's trees
By riding them down over and over again
Until he took the stiffness out of them,
And not one but hung limp, not one was left
For him to conquer. He learned all there was
To learn about not launching out too soon
And so not carrying the tree away
Clear to the ground. He always kept his poise
To the top branches, climbing carefully
With the same pains you use to fill a cup
Up to the brim, and even above the brim.
Then be flung outward, feet first, with a swish,
Kicking his way down through the air to the ground.

One figure seems to imply another—the image of the farm youth swinging up, out, and down to earth again recalls the boyhood of the poet:

So was I once myself a swinger of birches.
And so I dream of going back to be.
It's when I'm weary of considerations,
And life is too much like a pathless wood
Where your face burns and tickles with the cobwebs
Broken across it, and one eye is weeping
From a twig's having lashed across it open.

For anyone but Frost the "pathless wood" is trite. But for him it carries a complex of meaning fashioned elsewhere. The upward swinging of the boy becomes an emblem for imagination's swing away from the tangled, dark wood; a swing away from the "straighter, darker trees"; a swing into the absolute freedom of isolation, the severing of all "considerations." This is the transcendental phase of redemptive consciousness, a game that one plays alone. The downward movement of redemptive imagination to earth, contrarily, is a movement into community, engagement, love—the games that two play together:

I'd like to get away from earth awhile
And then come back to it and begin over.

May no fate willfully misunderstand me
And half grant what I wish and snatch me away
Not to return. Earth's the right place for love:
I don't know where it's likely to go better.
I'd like to go by climbing a birch tree,
And climb black branches up a snow-white trunk,
Toward heaven, till the tree could bear no more,
But dipped its top and set me down again.
That would be good both going and coming back.
One could do worse than be a swinger of birches.

One really has no choice but to be a swinger of birches. In the moment when, catapulting upward, the poet is half-granted his wish, when transcendence is about to be complete and the self, in its disdain for earth, has lofted itself into absolute autonomy, nothing having any claim upon it, and no return possible, then, at that moment,, the blessed pull of the earth is felt again, and the apocalypse desired by a transcending imagination, which seemed so imminent, is repressed. At the end of "Birches" a precious balance has been restored between the claims of a redeeming imagination in its extreme, transcendent form, and the claims of common sense reality. To put it in another way, the psychic needs of change—supplied best by redemptive imagination—are balanced by the equally deep psychic need—supplied by skeptical ironic awareness—for the therapy of dull realities and everyday considerations.

The swings in consciousness between fictive and objective worlds are reflected in a series of perfectly placed linguistic pivots. Consider: the conjunctive "but," lines 5, 21; or the conjunctive "and," lines 42, 49, 55; or the subtle semantic ambiguity of "shed" (line 10) and "trailing" (line 18) which points us simultaneously outward (in objective reference) to the inhuman world of nature—of birches as birches—and inward (expressive reference) to the warm, ambient world of Frost's consciousness, of bent birches as girls throwing their hair before them, drying in the sun.

John C. Kemp

The philosophy articulated in "Birches" poses no threat

to popular values or beliefs, and it is so appealingly affirmative that many readers have treasured the poem as a masterpiece. Among Frost's most celebrated works, perhaps only "Stopping by Woods on a Snowy Evening" ranks ahead of it. Yet to critics like Brooks and Squires, the persona's philosophical stance in "Birches" is a serious weakness. The didactic and philosophical element that some critics have attacked strikes others as the very core of Frost's virtue.

Perhaps impartial observers can accept the notion that "Birches" is neither as bad as its harshest opponents suggest nor as good as its most adoring advocates claim. "Birches". contains three fairly lengthy descriptions that do not involve unusual perspectives. In fact, the most original and distinctive vision in the poem—the passage treating the ice on the trees (ll. 5-14)—is undercut both by the self-consciousness of its final line ("You'd think the inner dome of heaven had fallen") and by the two much more conventionally perceived environments that follow it: the rural boyhood of the swinger of birches (ll. 23-40) and the "pathless wood," which represents life's "considerations" (ll. 44-47). As a result, the poem's ardent concluding lines—its closing pronouncements on life, death, and human aspiration—do not arise from a particular experience. Instead, they are presented as doctrines that we must accept or reject on the basis of our credence in the speaker as a wise countryman whose familiarity with birch trees, ice storms, and pathless woods gives him authority as a philosopher.

Since in "Birches" the natural object—tree, ice crystal, pathless wood, etc.—functions as proof of the speaker's rusticity, Frost has no need for extraordinary perspectives, and therefore the poem does little to convince us that an "experience," to use [Robert] Langbaum's wording, "is really taking place, that the object is seen and not merely remembered from a public or abstract view of it." This is not to deny that the poem contains some brilliant descriptive passages (especially memorable are the clicking, cracking, shattering ice crystals in lines 7-11 and the boy's painstaking climb and sudden, exhilarating descent in lines 35-40), and without doubt, the closing lines offer an engaging exegesis of swinging birches as a way of life. But though we learn a great deal about this speaker's beliefs and preferences, we find at last that he has not revealed himself as profoundly as does the speaker in "After Apple-Picking." It is remarkable that the verb "to like," which does not appear in Frost's non-dramatic poetry prior to "Birches," is used three times in this poem: "I like to think" (l. 3); "I'd like to get away" (l. 48); and "I'd like to go" (l. 54).

The speaker also tells us what he would "prefer" (l. 23), "dream of" (l. 42), and "wish" (l. 51). But while his preferences are generally appealing, and while they seem intellectually justified, they are not poetically justified in the sense that Langbaum suggests when he discusses the "extraordinary perspective" as a "sign that the experience is really taking place": "The experience has validity just because it is dramatized as an event which we must accept as having taken place, rather than formulated as an idea with which we must agree or disagree" (p. 43).

"Mending Wall," "After Apple-Picking," and "The Wood-Pile" are centered on specific events that involve the speaker in dramatic conflicts and lead him to extraordinary perspectives. The act of repairing the wall and trying to reason with the crusty farmer, the termination of the harvest and the preparation for a winter's rest, the vagrant woodland ramble and the discovery of the perplexing woodpile—all these are events that we indeed "accept as having taken place."

Unlike the meditative lyrics Frost selected for North of Boston, however, "Birches" does not present a central dramatized event as a stimulus for the speaker's utterance. Although the conclusion seems sincere, and although Frost created a persuasive metaphorical context for it, the final sentiments do not grow dramatically out of the experiences alluded to. Yes, the speaker has observed ice storms that bend the birches "down to stay" (l. 4); he has "learned all there is To learn" about swinging birches (ll. 32-33); and he has struggled through the "considerations" of life's "pathless wood" (ll. 43-44). But the relationship of these experiences to his present utterance—the poem—is left unclear. We would be more willing to accept what Squires calls a "contradictory jumble" of images and ideas if we were convinced (as Eliot and Pound often convince us) that the diverse materials had coalesced in the speaker's mind.

Frost's confession that the poem was "two fragments soldered together" is revealing; the overt, affected capriciousness of the transitions between major sections of the poem (ll. 4-5, 21-22, and 41-42) indicates that instead of striving to establish the dynamics of dramatized experience, he felt he could rely on the force of his speaker's personality and rural background. In early editions, a parenthetical question, "(Now am I free to be poetical?)," followed line 22, making the transition between the ice storm and the country youth even more arbitrary.

It may seem arbitrary to press too hard the issue of honesty in this poem. Art, after all, relies on fantasy and deception. Yet there are different types of fantasy and many motives for deception. If we are confident that an artist has kept faith with some personal vision or inner self, we can accept falsification of many things. When Frost presents himself as a farm worker, for instance a mower wielding his scythe or apple picker resting his weary body—the fantasy seems sincere and convincing.

When we consider Frost's career and personal history, however, we may wonder about his motives in falsifying the character of his childhood. The resulting images lack originality and inspiration. Surely "Birches" contains some vivid and forceful passages, but when a line or phrase gives us too strong a sense of the poet's calculated effort to validate his speaker's rusticity, the spell of the poem, its incantatory charm and imaginative vision, is threatened. Fortunately, in "Birches" this threat is hardly noticeable, certainly not overwhelming or repellent, unless we want it to be.

George Montiero

SEVERAL TIMES in Robert Frost: A Living Voice, his account of the poet's talks at the Bread Loaf School of English, Reginald L. Cook quotes Frost's remarks on "Birches." Frost's words on one such occasion are given a context by Cook, who writes: In spite of his deprecatory view of explication, Frost revealed a good deal about his art. When he disclosed his feeling about certain words in "Birches," he gave a searching insight into what makes a poet's use of descriptive words stand up. And how cavalierly he did it! He offered "this little note on 'Birches' before I begin to read it. See.

The kind of explication I forbid," he said self-consciously. Then with disarming slyness, he said: "I never go down the shoreline [from Boston] to New York without watching the birches to see if they live up to what I say about them in the poem." Invariably the listener laughed, but on the double take he realized that Frost, the careful craftsman, was confirming his assertion that birches bend to left and right by verification. Getting details right was a telling responsibility. His birches, he insisted, were not the white mountain or paper birch of northern New England (Betula papyrifera); they were the gray birch (Betula populifolia).

The way in which Robert Frost came to write "Birches" is described by Elizabeth Shepley Sergeant: "As for the poet, 'who never saw New England as clearly as when he was in Old England,' he could not tie down his creative moments. It was about this time, early in 1914, while tramping the muddy yard at the Bungalow [West Midlands], that he suddenly; he says, wrote a new poem, not to be included in North of Boston. This was the now so famous and beloved 'Birches,' with its cold and crystal memories of another kind of wintry world." As this account suggests.

Frost's poem might have reflected pure, almost spontaneous invention, but if so, it was stimulated by memories of boyhood experiences of winter and summer in northern New England and sharpened by the perspective of the poet's self-imposed exile. What I would suggest, however, is that in "Birches," even though Frost saw New England most clearly when he was in Old England, he re-viewed his wintry New England scene through Thoreauvian eyes.

On December 31, 1852, a day of rain and ice in Concord, Thoreau wrote in his Journals with keen anticipation: "It is a sort of frozen rain this afternoon, which does not wet one, but makes the still bare ground slippery with a coating of ice, and stiffens your umbrella so that it cannot be shut. Will not the trees look finely in the morning?" For the next few days Thoreau described the storm's "fine" effects upon the landscape. On the first day of the new year he observed: "This morning we have something between ice and frost on the trees. What a crash of jewels as you walk!. The drooping birches along the edges of woods are the most feathery; fairy-like ostrich plumes of the trees, and the colour of their trunks increases the delusion" (436-38). The next day Thoreau continued his report:

In this clear air and bright sunlight, the ice-covered trees have a new beauty, especially the birches., bent quite to the ground in every kind of curve. At a distance, as you are approaching them endwise, they look like white tents of Indians under the edge ofthe wood. The birch is thus remarkable, perhaps, because from the feathery form of the tree, whose numerous small branches sustain so great a weight, bending it to the ground, and moreover because, from the colour of the bark, the core is less observable. The oaks not only are less pliant in the trunk, but have fewer and stiffer twigs and branches. The birches droop over in all directions, like ostrich-feathers. [440]

Thoreau's description anticipates Frost's handling of imagery. But Thoreau's entry the next day offers an interesting variation on Frost's poem. He begins by recording that day's response to the observable beauty which can be attributed to nature's transforming and creative powers and then speculates on the comparative merits of man and nature. The first paragraph is largely descriptive of this "finest show of ice" (444): "Nothing dark met the eye, but a silvery sheen, precisely as if the whole tree—trunk, boughs, and twigs—were converted into burnished silver. You exclaimed at every hedgerow. Sometimes a clump of birches £ell over every way in graceful ostrich-plumes, all raying from one centre. Suddenly all is converted to crystal. The world is a crystal palace" (445).

The next paragraph, however, moves into a new key. Stimulated by his last attempt at describing ice-laden birches, Thoreau ruminates: I love Nature partly because she is not man, but a retreat from him. None of his institutions control or pervade her. There a different kind of right prevails. In her midst I can be glad with an entire gladness. If this world were all man, I could not stretch myself, I should lose all hope. He is constraint, she is freedom to me. He makes me wish for another world. She makes me content with this.

Man, man is the devil,
The source of evil.

I have a room all to myself; it is nature. It is a place beyond the jurisdiction of human governments. There are two worlds, the post-office and nature. I know them both. I continually forget mankind and their institutions, as I do a bank. [445-46]

The conjunction of Thoreau's celebration of winter birches and his buoyant homily on man's inferiority to nature may be compared with Frost's similar conjunction of themes in "Birches." If man makes Thoreau "wish for another world " but nature makes him "content with this," to Frost it is when life most resembles nature—when "life is too much like a pathless wood"—that the poet would "like to get away from earth awhile." Frost would "climb black branches up a snow-white trunk Toward heaven," but he would come back, he quickly decides, for "Earth's the right place for love." Thoreau would undoubtedly endorse Frost's aphorism. But their initial agreement would evaporate, I suspect, if each were to explain precisely what he took the statement to mean. While Thoreau would most characteristically focus on love of nature, Frost would just as readily assert the claim of man's fundamental love for man. The distinction is notable.

In the Journal passages that I have quoted above, Thoreau (for the moment read "man") appears almost exclusively as an observer, never as a participant beyond the act of perception. It is as if in nature's pure realm man's existence were suspended. Whenever Thoreau does tell in these entries what men are doing, or what they have done, he invariably does so to admonish them. Consequently, when he "climb[s] the bank at Stow's wood-lot and come[s] upon the piles of freshly split white pine wood," he does not compliment the worker for his labour, as one might expect, but decides, rather, that the owner of the woodlot is "ruthlessly laying it waste". And in the same entry, a page or so later, he comments on the ringing of bells: "The bells are particularly sweet this morning. I hear more, methinks, than ever before.

How much more religion in their sound, than they ever call men together to! Men obey their call and go to the stove-warmed church, though God exhibits himself to the walker in a frosted bush today as much as in a burning one to Moses of old". Even when man does something well (after all, bells are a human invention), he is singularly capable of misinterpreting his own message and betraying his most noble purposes. For Thoreau the beauty and divinity which exist at this moment are in the glazed birch and the frosted bush. They are most certainly not in men. Nature and nature's workings are at the centre of creation. In these pages Thoreau reserves his approval for the landscape transformed by ice and snow and the few men who make an appearance intrude momentarily along nature's periphery.

In Frost's poem, however, values are weighted somewhat differently. Its first twenty lines are largely devoted to a description of the effect ice-storms have on birches: [quotes ll. 1-20] The details in these lines are precise and deceptively neutral. The entire passage contains nothing to suggest that nature is superior (or inferior) to man, nor are we to infer that the two are equal. As description these lines exemplify what Frost calls the "matter-of-fact" of "Truth." But Frost does not stop with the conclusion that ice storms, and not swinging boys, are the cause of birches bent "down to stay." He approaches, finally the idea that man's acts upon nature have their own meaning and beauty: approvingly Frost decides that, given a choice, he "should prefer to have some boy bend" birches. In the midst of swinging, boys are not observers of nature; they actually collaborate with nature by taking the "stiffness" out of birches.

Frost would have a bent tree signify that some boy swinging from earth, has gone beyond that "pathless wood

Where your face burns and tickles with the cobwebs Broken across it." "Birches" suggests that nature's beauty is somehow enhanced when man has worked an effect upon nature. In this sense Frost's poem may stand as a qualified reply to Thoreau's recurrent strain of illimitable nature worship.

Of course there is another side to Thoreau with which "Birches" does not conflict. A Thoreau more congenial to Frost appears in a Journal entry six months before the notable ice storm of December 31, 1852. He writes: "Nature must be viewed humanly to be viewed at all; that is, her scenes must be associated with humane affections, such as are associated with one's native place, for instance. She is most significant to a lover. A lover of Nature is preeminently a lover of man. If I have no friend, what is Nature to me? She ceases to be morally significant" For Thoreau this kind of bravely humanistic sentiment welled forth most clearly on an early summer's day. The dead of winter, we have seen, could evoke other feelings. But Frost's humanism became a harder, more durable thing in its midwinter setting of ice and snow.

As late as August 1919, in a list of poems that his friend John T Bartlett might like to read, Frost recommended "Swinging Birches." In some ways it is unfortunate that Frost stopped calling the poem by this title. I say unfortunate because the activity at the heart of the poem—the activity that generates whatever cohesion the poem has—is the boy's swinging of birches and the poet's ruminations on the possibility that the birches he sees have been bent by boys at play. He would like to think that such is the case. But since liking to think does not make it so, the poet turns to the more likely reason, the permanent bending of birches by ice storms.

You may see their trunks arching in the woods
Years afterwards, trailing their leaves on the ground
Like girls on hands and knees that throw their hair
Before them over their heads to dry in the sun.

Then, interrupting this train of thought—this "matter-of-fact" "Truth"—he returns to a consideration of the notion that by "swinging" them boys also bend trees (though not permanently, as ice storms do).

I should prefer to have some boy bend them
As he went out and in to fetch the cows—
Some boy too far from town to learn baseball,
Whose only play was what he found himself,
Summer or winter, and could play alone.

Here the poem shifts into a generalized description, a semi-dramatic account of the way such a boy proceeds:

[quotes ll. 28-40]

At this point the poet acknowledges that he, too, was once "a swinger of birches," and he admits that even now he dreams of being one again. When does he have such dreams?

It's when I'm weary of considerations,
And life is too much like a pathless wood
Where your face bums and tickles with the cobwebs
Broken across it, and one eye is weeping
From a twig's having lashed across it open.

To what sort of boyhood pleasure would the adult poet like to return? Quite simply; it is the pleasure of onanism. We do not need either Erica Jong or John Updike to remind us that "flying" is often a dream or linguistic substitute for sexual activity. But we do need to be reminded that "early orgasms at puberty induced by friction against a tree trunk" are "not an uncommon experience," to quote from a writer commenting on the following passage from the early diaries of James Boswell: "Already (age 12-13) in climbing trees, pleasure. Could not conceive what it was. Thought of heaven. Returned often, climbed, felt, allowed myself to fall from high branches in ecstasy—all natural. Spoke of it to the gardener. He, rigid, did not explain."

If physiologically there is some sort of pubescent sexuality taking place in the "swinging" of "birches," it is not surprising, then, that the boy has "subdued his father's trees" by "riding them down over and over again" until "not one was left for him to conquer" and that the orgasmic activity should be likened to "riding," which despite the "conquering" can be done time and again. One need only note that the notion of "riding," already figurative in "Birches," reappears metaphorically in Frost's conception of "Education by Poetry," wherein he writes: "Unless you are at home in the metaphor, unless you have had your proper poetical education in the metaphor, you are not safe anywhere.

Because you are not at ease with figurative values: you don't know. how far you may expect to ride it and when it may break down with you." And what is true for metaphor and poetry is true for love. Frost insisted that a poem "run. from delight to wisdom. The figure is the same as for love. Like a piece of ice on a hot stove the poem must ride on its own melting." Then it is totally appropriate within the metaphor of "swinging birches" that even the storm-bent trees should look to the adult male like "girls on hands and knees that throw their hair Before them over their heads to dry in the sun." No wonder, then, and fully appropriate it is, that when the poet thinks that his wish to get away from earth might by some fate be misunderstood such that he be snatched away never to return, his thought is that "Earth's the right place vor love." At some level of his consciousness the pleasurable activity of "swinging birches" has transformed itself into the more encompassing term "love." One might say, within the logic of this reading of the poem, that "Earth's the right place for [sexual] love," including onanistic love. The same sexual metaphor runs through the final lines of the poem as the mature poet thinks of how he would like to go but only to come back.

Guy Rotella

Although "Birches" describes a boy's game instead of a chore, it too has fact, dream, and in that intent game a commitment as deep as one of earnest love. Here Frost's comments on being at home in figurative values are most apt for his actual poetic images: knowing how to ride metaphor is analogous to knowing how to ride birches.

The facts about the ice storm in "Birches" grow the more and more figurative as the poet's imagined preference sounds real and prosaic. In the first lines, the poet associates a real scene with an image in his mind, and he deliberately distinguishes between the two. The casual assumption, "you must have seen them," makes his statements sound public and verifiable:

[quotes ll. 1-7]

What follows is by no means lifeless fact but an enchanting account. Not Just some ordinary woods, the enameled trees look as crafted and ornamental as fine glass sculpture, and the fallen ice evokes a mythical catastrophe:

[quotes ll. 7-13]

Again the poet knows metaphor's limits and implies that anyone knows them. The offhand "You'd think" shows how common it is to slip into expressions of fancy and fall back on shared myths about the heavens and earth.

The accurate description in the next lines also suggests possible metaphors:

They are dragged to the withered bracken by the load,
And they seem not to break; though once they are bowed
So low for long, they never right themselves:
You may see their trunks arching in the woods
Years afterwards, trailing their leaves on the ground.

After "withered," "bowed," and "years afterwards," I tend to picture old men bowed by life's burdens, but that is not the case. As part of our education in metaphor, we must learn that a visual image can take us in several directions. To the poet these trees are

Like girls on hands and knees that throw their hair
Before them over their hands to dry in the sun.

The poet then circles back to his first image of the boy. That turn itself suggests something about the way one habitually thinks of truth and fact:

But I was going to say when Truth broke in
With all her matter of fact about the ice storm.

"Truth" with a capital "T" is abstraction personified, a figurative value. She, a trusted absolute, it seems, and not the poet interrupts with these "facts"—"crystal shells" and "the inner dome of heaven." By implication, the poet prefers an untruth which does not deal in facts. His fancy, though, is down to earth. No idle, elvish tale here:

[quotes ll. 23-40]

Why is the game of this solitary boy so appealing and poignant? He never expresses his feelings, whether of joy, accomplishment, or adventure. His game, which leaves the birches limp, places him in no idyllic, pantheistic relation with nature, yet it redeems itself in part. The meaning of his actions is not explicit. As Frost once said, in poetry "We like to talk in parables and in hints and in indirections" ("Education by Poetry," p. 332). Here the hints and indirections tease us to make more of the parable. At the same time, something holds us back, an adherence to fact, perhaps, to orchises or apples or birches. The tease lies in the account of the boy's thoroughness and intentness in his sport. An air of dedication, purpose, and fulfillment hovers about "one by one," "over and over again," "not one. not one." The boy has power; he subdues and conquers.

He understands perfectly how to maneuver the trees and fly from branches to ground. The predicates which convey this could preface some finality. "He learned all there was" and "he always kept his poise," themselves poised at the ends of lines, evoke the mastery and freedom of one who knows "all there is" about life. But the boy's wisdom, after its fling into the air, lands on something specific: "He learned all there was To learn about not launching out too soon," "He always kept his poise To the top branches." His knowledge is valid in that context, as truth in "Mowing" is valid in terms of the sun's heat and the silence.

The swinger of birches, boy or poet, must know his own powers and know the strength of the trees and the strength of metaphor. This parable is both history and dream:

[quotes ll. 41-53]

Unlike the boy among the birches, the poet is subdued by a "pathless wood." The form of his dream of release corresponds to the boy's physical action: getting away from earth to begin "over and over again."

In the last lines, the poet clearly uses the parable for its figurative value, and another of Frost's comments comes to mind: the aim of metaphor is "to restore you to your ideas of free will" ("Education by Poetry," p. 333). The poet's imagination, with metaphors which attend to longings and to real events, restores free will without distorting the truth. The trees are not bent by the boy; thinking that he changes the woods is the fiction. However, it seems someone really has climbed the trees and enjoyed a flight from sky to earth. By using metaphors which fuse fact and dream, the poet is no longer beaten back; and he recovers the freedom of the boy who knows all there is to know and who always kept his poise:

[quotes ll. 54-61]

In the end, dividing Frost's poetic images into fact, dream and both is impossible. Frost undermines such divisions in a manner both playful and serious, exploring slippery issues about the natures of perception, interpretation, reality and truth. His poems often illustrate the mind seeking out metaphor and meaning in some rural or domestic scene, testing different possibilities. They also show with varying degrees of irony the mind, language, and familiar, perhaps inherent, myths imposing themselves on a landscape. Or maybe the landscape imposes something on the mind.

Mordecai Marcus

The discursive blank-verse meditation "Birches" does not, like "The Wood-Pile" and "An Encounter," centre on a continuously encountered and revealing nature scene; rather, it builds a mosaic of thoughts from fragments of memory and fantasy. Its vividness and genial, bittersweet speculation help make it one of Frost's most popular poems, and because its shifts of metaphor and tone invite varying interpretation it has also received much critical discussion, not always admiring.

The poem moves back and forth between two visual perspectives: birch trees as bent by boys' playful swinging and by ice storms, the thematic interweaving being somewhat puzzling. The birches bent "across the lines of straighter darker trees" subtly introduce the theme of imagination and will opposing darker realities.

Then, almost a third of the poem describes how ice storms bend these trees permanently, unlike the action of boys; this scene combines images of beauty and of distortion. Ice shells suggest radiating light and colour, and the trees bowed to the level of the bracken, suggest suffering, which is immediately lightened by the strange image of girls leaning their hair toward the sun as if in happy submission.

The fallen "inner dome of heaven" alludes to Shelley's "dome of many colored glass" (also alluded to in "The Trial By Existence") to suggest the shattering of the ideal into everyday reality. Frost's speaker then self-consciously breaks from his realistic but metaphorically fantasied digression to say he would prefer to have some boy bend the birches, which action becomes a symbol for controlled experience, as contrasted with the genial fatality of ice storms.

The boy's fancied playfulness substitutes for unavailable companionship, making for a thoughtful communion with nature, which rather than teach him wisdom allows him to learn it. Despite the insistence on the difference between ice storms' permanent damage to birches and a boy's temporary effects, the boy subdues and conquers the trees. His swinging is practice for maintaining life's difficult and precarious balances.

The third part of the poem begins with a more personal and philosophical tone. The speaker claims to have been such a youthful swinger of birches, an activity he can go back to only by dreaming. The birch trees, probably both ice-bent and boy-swung, stand for the order and control missing from ordinary experience. The "considerations" he is weary of are conflicting claims that leave him disoriented and stung. The desire to "get away from earth," importantly qualified by "awhile," shows a yearning for the ideal or perhaps for the imaginative isolation of the birch swinger.

His "I'd like to go by climbing a birch tree. Toward heaven" suggests leaving earth, but he reveals by his quick apologetic claim that he doesn't mean that. He wants to be dipped down again toward earth, but the pursuit of the ideal by going sounds like death, as his quick apology acknowledges. Frost does less in this poem than in "After Apple-Picking" to suggest a renewed pursuit of the ideal in life rather than a yielding to death. His main pursuit is continual balance between reality and ideality, but as John F. Sears and Radcliffe Squires point out, his vehicle for transcendence and his desire for nature to reinforce human intuition do not quite work.

Jeffrey Meyers

"Birches" connects poetic aspiration and physical love. It begins with a fanciful image("I like to think") of a boy swinging on and bending birches. It then shifts to a brilliant description of ice-laden branches blown by the wind that "cracks and crazes [suggesting cracked glazes] their enamel." Inspired by medieval cosmology and by a famous passage from Shelley's "Adonais" (an elegy for Keats, about poetic power cut off in mid-career by death), Frost writes of all the broken ice-glass: "You'd think the inner dome of heaven had fallen." He then returns to the swinger-of-birches theme as the boy, like the future poet, launches out at the proper time, keeps his poise and climbs carefully. Swinging himself on the branches "Toward heaven," he'd

like to get away from earth awhile
And then come back to it and begin over.
Earth's the right place for love:
I don't know where it's likely to go better.

Opposing the Platonic view of idealized love, Frost believes Earth, not Heaven, is the right place because love should be physical and tested against the realities of life.

Floyd C. Watkins

"Toward heaven" but never to, never all the way. Frost fears transcendence. Despite all the apparent moralizing ("earth's the right place for love"), this passage is one of the most skeptical in Frost. He contemplates a moment when the soul may become completely absorbed into a union with the divine. But he is earthbound, limited, afraid. No sooner does he wish to get away from earth than he thinks of "fate" - rather than God. And what might be a mystical experience turns into a fear of death, a fear that he would be snatched away "not to return." He rejects the unknown, the love of God, because he cannot know it, and he clings to the finite: "Earth's the right place for love."

George F. Bagby

The first twenty lines of "Birches" clearly hint at Promethean tendencies. The poem is set at that time of the natural year which most suggests imaginative stirrings: the springtime moment in the imagination's life when it begins to rouse itself from winter lethargy. Though immobilized by their wintry covering of ice, as the Eolian "breeze rises" the birches move "and turn many-colored As the stir cracks and crazes their enamel." "Soon," warmed by the sun, they "shed crystal shells," like the human beings of "Sand Dunes" casting off dead external coverings to take on new shapes and new vitality. The evidences of that spiritual molting, as many have noted, echo the Promethean outreach of Adonais: "Such heaps of broken glass to sweep away You'd think the inner dome of heaven had fallen." And, though the birches are permanently "bowed" by the ice storm, they remain suggestive of aspiration: "You may see their trunks arching in the woods Years afterwards," still straining toward that inner dome of heaven. In the poem's central fiction, Frost adroitly converts the birches from emblems of Promethean aspiration to emblems of natural fact conquered by that aspiration.

Rather than an ice storm, the poet "should prefer to have some boy bend" the birches; this fictive explanation represents more clearly the central presence of human activity, and human domination of the natural ("One by one he subdued his father's trees"). The comparison used to describe the care which the boy takes in climbing to the very "top branches" of the birches—"climbing carefully With the same pains you use to fill a cup Up to the brim, and even above the brim"—reminds us that this is not only a poem about trees but a celebration of spiritual thirst.

But, in the last third of the poem, where he explicitly reads in the act of swinging birches a lesson for the governance of one's imaginative life, Frost draws back from the Prometheanism implied earlier in the poem: "I'd like to get away from earth awhile And then come back to it and begin over." As that latter line suggests, the visionary assertion of "Birches" is ultimately less extreme than that of "Wild Grapes." As Richard Wilbur notes, the echoes of Shelley in this poem are ultimately used to argue against Shelley's Prometheanism: "'Birches,' taken as a whole, is in fact an answer to Shelley's kind of boundless neo-Platonic aspiration".The famous closing lines of the poem clearly move toward a reconciliation of human aspiration and earthly reality.The poet hopes that "no fate" will "willfully misunderstand" him "And half grant what I wish and snatch me away Not to return. Earth's the right place for love."

I'd like to go by climbing a birch tree,
And climb black branches up a snow-white trunk
Toward heaven, till the tree could bear no more,
But dipped its top and set me down again.
That would be good both going and coming back.

The proper role of the mind or spirit is seen here, not as a conquest of the natural, not as a transcending of earth or a "steering straight off after something into space," but as an integral part of a larger process of give and take, "launching out" and return. The young girl in "Wild Grapes," because of her "not knowing anything" about "letting go," about accommodating natural fact, is carried off by the birch in that poem like a fish caught by a fish pole.

The mature speaker of "Birches," on the other hand, knows how to use natural fact to reach its uppermost limits, to climb "Toward heaven, till the tree could bear no more," but then to accept the end of the trip and be returned by the tree in a kind of cooperative effort. The imagination here again asserts its freedom and autonomy by dominating natural fact; but then, refreshed by that flexing of imaginative muscle, it "comes back" to natural fact to "begin over," now willing to accept the different but also "almost incredible freedom," as Frost puts it elsewhere, of being "enslaved to the hard facts of experience".

Such a return or reconciliation would, for Blake or Shelley, amount to surrender. But Frost, like most other American nature writers, does not posit Blake's or Shelley's kind of inevitable struggle to the death between imaginative perception and natural fact. Like Thoreau (with certain exceptions), like Emerson in his more restrained moods, Frost believes that, in the final analysis, the two forces are capable of cooperating to achieve meaning.

Chapter 8

Study Questions and Answers

Q. Discuss Robert Frost as a Romantic Poet?

Or

Q. On whether, and in what sense, Frost was a romantic?

Although Frost once called himself a romantic, he usually used the word pejoratively. In a letter to Louis Untermeyer in 1915, for example, he referred to Edgar Lee Masters as "too romantic," by which he meant too "false-realistic". In 1938, in a letter to R. P. T. Coffin, he called Edwin Arlington Robinson a Platonist and a romantic: "By Platonist I mean one who believes that what we have here is an imperfect copy of some woman in heaven or in someone else's bed". It is hardly surprising, then, that an overwhelming majority of Frost's critics believe that, whatever else he may have been, Frost was not a romantic.

Like Lawrance Thompson they are willing to grant that he grew up in the romantic tradition. Yet, again like Thompson (43-49), they insist that Frost either greatly modified his romanticism or abandoned it altogether. Hyatt Waggoner (59) and Reginald Cook (214-15), among others, have argued that Frost's poetic vision is fundamentally different from Emerson's. Robert Langbaum (331) and Marion Montgomery (140-41) have made the same point about Frost and Wordsworth.

This view of Frost is based on two assumptions. First, Frost's critics tend to define romanticism as metaphysically naive, morally irresponsible, and epistemologically regressive. Second, most of Frost's critics see the poet as a skeptic who regarded nature as an antagonist, stoicism as a moral ideal, and visionary experience as an illusion.

To many of them, Frost saw the external world as indifferent, alien, hostile. To most, he proffered religious affirmations only equivocally or ironically. And to some, he used poetry not as a means of discovery but as a defence against nature - therapeutically and self-protectively. Of course, if romanticism is defined as a simple-minded picture of human experience that no sane and sobre adult would take seriously, then Frost was not a romantic. And if Frost's poetry shows him to be a tough-minded realist who believed that no affirmation can be more than "a momentary stay," then, once again, Frost was not a romantic. However, I believe that both of these assumptions are wrong for reasons that I hope to make clear.

Not that the case for Frost as realist and skeptic cannot be made. Frequently, as in "Spring Pools," "Reluctance," and "Nothing Gold Can Stay," his poems deal with the irreversible change of seasons and the mutability of things. The joys of summer are brief, and the losses brought about by the fall (both seasonal and theological) are experienced in winter as a kind of spiritual death. Indeed, in many poems, such as "Stars," "Design," and "Once by the Pacific," the universe is portrayed as indifferent to human needs and even destructive of human life.

The world of human beings, too, as Frost suggests in "The Bear," "Pod of the Milkweed," and "The Vanishing Red," is replete with evidence of vanity and violence. The fears that separate men from women, the miscommunications that keep them apart, and the loneliness that makes hatred harden into hostility are documented in the dramatic narratives of North of Boston and throughout Frost's poetry. In all of these poems, the realms of the real and the ideal are separated by a barrier that cannot be penetrated, transcended, or circumambulated.

Yet, although this worldview is prominent in his poetry, Frost did not always espouse it. In his letters and essays, for example, he often contradicted his own antiromantic statements. After saying in "On Emerson" that "a melancholy dualism is the only soundness," Frost added, "The question is: is soundness of the essence[?]" (Prose 112). Having defined romanticism as a futile yearning for the ideal, he said, "Many of the world's greatest - maybe all of them - have been ranged on that romantic side". In a letter to Thompson in which he called himself a dualist and questioned Arnold's enthusiasm for Emerson, he suggested that Arnold "was probably carried away by the great poetry." Frost then explained, "Wisdom doesn't matter too much".

Indeed, despite the frequency with which Frost portrays the indifference of nature and the cruelty of human beings, he just as often gives at least intimations of a monistic vision. Moments of joy are transitory, he says, but they remain occasions for celebration regardless of their brevity. Even the most trivial event can alter the poet's mood by suggesting to him the possibilities of communication and even communion between people and God, people and people, and people and things, as he suggests in "The Dust of Snow": "The way a crow Shook down on me The dust of snow From a hemlock tree Has given my heart A change of mood And saved some part Of a day I had rued".

In "Looking for a Sunset Bird in Winter," Frost indirectly laments the passing of summer into winter and realizes that the "bird with angelic gift" he saw before has abandoned the tree and left only "a single leaf" behind. But as he looks out from his vantage point on a hill, he sees something like a brushstroke across the blue sky and "a piercing little star" shining through it. Again, walking by unidentifiable flowers along the highway, in "A Passing Glimpse," he wonders, "Was something brushed across my mind That no one on earth will ever find?"

Sometimes, of course, the "glimpse" is so brief as to seem inconsequential or even questionable, as in "For Once, Then, Something." There can be little doubt, however, that the clock of "Acquainted with the Night" is really only the dark side of the moon of "Moon Compasses," in which the heavenly body "exalts" a mountain in the way that loving hands embrace a face. And the stars in Frost's poetry are not always signs of cosmic meaninglessness, as they are in "Stars" and "Bond and

Free." They are also, in "Take Something like a Star," images of steadfastness and dependability and, in "I Will Sing You One-O," intimations of eternity, "Beyond which God is". Similarly, the mowed fields that signify a change of seasons are not merely indications that the pleasures of summer are gone and the sorrows of autumn are imminent. In "The Last Mowing" and "The Tuft of Flowers," they are also occasions for communions with those who are either present to share in the tumultuousness of flowers, when "The place for the moment is ours", or, though absent, nevertheless able to send "a message from the dawn" and induce a feeling of brotherhood.

Frost offers a similar view of man and nature in three visionary poems: "Going for Water," "Two Look at Two," and "Iris by Night." The speaker in the first poem sets out with his companion to fill a pail with water from the brook in the midst of the woods. The two first hear the musical notes of the brook and then see moonlit "drops. on the pool," which look like pearls, and a sliver of moonlight running across the brook, which looks like "a silver blade".

In this poem, the momentary union of heaven and earth (represented by the light of the moon hitting the surface of the water) is not regretted because of its brevity, but celebrated, as if it were meaningful and even miraculous. Another night journey into the woods in "Two Look at Two" begins with a characteristically Frostian lament as the two travelers prepare to abandon their walk: "This is all". Yet suddenly a doe appears, unfrightened by their presence and willing to remain. Clearly the travelers' mood is full of awe at the sight. "This, then, is all. What more is there to ask?" they either think or say - as if the "all" meant "everything." Finally, they see a buck that similarly stays for a moment. "This must be all," they conclude. And the narrator comments: "It was all. Still they stood A great wave from it going over them, As if the earth in one unlooked-for favour Had made them certain earth returned their love". The final four lines of the poem serve as the culmination of a gradually escalating emotion that begins as disappointment and ends as rapture. Indeed, the narrator twice verifies the couple's perception of the event: first, by echoing their statement that the experience was "all" and, second, by confirming their sense that they have received an "unlooked-for favour."

In "Iris by Night," Frost describes another evening walk, this time down a mountainside. The hikers, acting as "one another's guide," first grope through the darkness and then come upon "a moment of confusing lights," which Frost compares to the moment before a fragmented sun "could concentrate anew and rise as one." The travelers see a "moon-made" rainbow "like a trellis gate," and as if they were entering another realm entirely they are "vouchsafed the miracle that never yet two other two befell." The "wonder" is that the rainbow did not recede as they walked toward it but "gathered [its ends] together in a ring." Frost's conclusion underscores both the sudden but momentary suspension of time and the brief but astonishing communion between friends: "And we stood in it softly circled round From all division time or foe can bring In a relation of elected friends"

As all of these poems suggest, it is difficult to prove that Frost occupied one philosophical position or another. For all his seeming accessibility, he is, as Richard Poirier has shown, an exceptionally elusive and allusive poet. In his prose works, too, in which he might be expected to be less opaque, he is too often indirect and metaphorical to be easily pinned down. And even when he seems to be speaking spontaneously and unguardedly in his lectures and interviews, he can be very misleading.

In a 1961 interview, for example, he said: "It's hard to get into this world and hard to get out of it. And what's in between doesn't make much sense" (he point seems clear enough, but when the statement is understood to be (as it may be) a paraphrase of Lord Bolingbroke, by way of Emerson's "Montaigne," it takes on a very different meaning, especially in the context of Emerson's ultimately unskeptical essay.For Emerson, Bolingbroke's sentiment is merely a stepping-stone to a broader and deeper affirmation. Statements or propositions, Emerson believed (and Frost seems to have agreed), have no meaning at all outside a poetic context. And even poems (whether in verse or prose) reveal their ultimate import only in the context of a poet's entire work.

Thus, poems like "Design" and "The Bear" must be understood in relation to the rest of Frost's oeuvre. "Pod of the Milkweed," for example, appears to be less an expression of irremediable pessimism than a meditation on Plato's view of human suffering in The Phaedrus. In answer to the question Frost asks in his poem - "why so much Should come to nothing" - Plato wrote The Phaedo as well as The Phaedrus. And perhaps in response to the same concern, Frost wrote "Trial by Existence" as well as "Pod of the Milkweed."

In Frost's visionary poems, the woods are not the abode of disillusionment that they are in "The Demiurge's Laugh." Nor are the couples in them paralyzed by their fears or trapped in their houses, as in "Storm Fear" and "Love and a Question." Like the men and women in "The Generations of Men" and "West-Running Brook," they enter a domain in which the fundamental conditions of life are mixed, even paradoxical. Yet they "trust" themselves "to go by contraries" and, in effect, transcend the conflicts and confusions that haunt Frost's couples in other poems. In a similar world of reconciled opposites, the conjunction of "love" and "truth" engenders a "fact" that is also a "dream" ("Mowing"); a ladder joining earth and heaven defines a magical sphere of half-sleep in which dream, vision, and reality are commingled ("After Apple-Picking"); and an abandoned road leads to a cellar hole and a children's playhouse where the truths of change, loss, and death merge with make-believe to create a vision "beyond confusion"

To some critics, of course, the poems of joy and communion cannot be taken seriously. They represent the regrettably sentimental Frost whose solaces are escapist and therefore unacceptable. At best, in Frost's own words, they are "momentary stays against confusion" - but only momentary and therefore negligibleTo other critics, Frost's affirmations are the willful assertions of an essentially skeptical poet who knows that order or form or meaning is imposed on nature as an expression of human need - not as a revelation of nature itself. In this view, the creation of form is either a heroic but ultimately futile act rooted in courage or a pragmatic act driven by the requirements of survivalTo a third group of critics, these poems represent the bright side of a coin that the poet tosses thoughtlessly and indifferently as the passing mood moves him. Together with poems like "Design" and "Desert Places," they add up to uncertainty and confusion. They signify Frost's inability or unwillingness to make up his mind, and they reflect the absence of any coherent vision in his poetry.

In direct response to the first group of critics, Frost said that the illuminating moments he records in "Going for Water," "Two Look at Two," and "Iris by Night" are not in fact mere moments, forgotten in the passing of time and therefore meaningless. As he explains in one of his Bread Loaf lectures in 1960, he meant much more than that in the phrase "momentary stays against confusion." "Is that all there is to it, is momentary?" he asks.

You know that kind of insults me. Do you know what the humanities are - what they call the humanities? They are the accumulation of those momentary stays that have survived. That's what the humanities are. They weren't momentary, they were good because they went on.

If Frost had made this point only in his old age, of course, it might easily be dismissed as wishful rethinking. The same theme occurs, however, in a poem from A Witness Tree (1942), "Happiness Makes up in Height What It Lacks in Length." Despite all the evidence of chaos in the universe and despite the profound ignorance of its inhabitants, Frost says, "I can but wonder whence I get the lasting sense Of so much warmth and light." Mistrusting the evidence, he says, "It may be altogether from one day's perfect weather". Ironically, then, happiness lacks nothing in "length." Somehow it endures and sustains.

Suggestively, this "fair impression" came to the poet under familiar circumstances: when the speaker and his companion "went from house to wood" - like the couple in "Going for Water" - "for change of solitude." Perhaps, then, all such experiences possessed for Frost the staying power of that "one day's perfect weather." That is, as he says in "Skeptic," these are the "times when I am apt To feel [the universe] close in tight against my sense Like a caul in which I was born and still am wrapped" (549). He implied, after all, that these moments, untranslatable though they may be, contribute to the poet's development.

In "The Poet's Next of Kin in a College" (1938), he says that "the growth of the poet is through flashes" and that poetry is made of "these flashes of light" - "sight and insight" (Poetry and Prose 374). Like Emerson, Frost seems to have believed that "faith comes in moments" and that "there is a depth in those brief moments, which constrains us to ascribe more reality to them than to all other experiences". For surely, as Frost describes them, "these moments confer," in Emerson's words, "a sort of omnipresence and omnipotence, which asks nothing of duration, but sees that the energy of the mind is commensurate with the work to be done, without time".

Frost's belief that certain experiences are cumulative and lasting is reminiscent of Wordsworth's theory of "spots of time." In Book XII of The Prelude, Wordsworth explains, "There are in our existence spots of time, That with distinct pre-eminence retain A renovating virtue". In "Tintern Abbey," he says that he receives not only pleasure and "tranquil restoration" from such memories but also moral sustenance. The two examples of "spots of time" in Book XII of The Prelude are similar in imagery and structure to several of Frost's visionary poems.

In the first, Wordsworth describes a journey down a "rough and stony moor," like the journey of the couple in "Two Look at Two," which took place after he had lost his "guide." Frightened and "stumbling on" through the field, he "came to the bottom," where he saw a gibbet on which a murderer had been hanged. After running away from the terrifying scene, he saw a pool of water under the moon and a girl carrying a pitcher and walking against the wind. Later, when he returned to the place with his "loved one at [his] side," he saw, like the couple in "Going for Water," the pool and the moon illuminated by "A spirit of pleasure and youth's golden gleam."

In the second example (11.287-335), Wordsworth describes an experience that occurred a few days before his father died. Tired and restless, he "went forth Into the fields" on an unusually dark and stormy day. Climbing to the summit of a hill, he looked out into the mist "in the deepest passion." Afterward, "all the business of the elements" and wood, water, and mist "were kindred spectacles and sounds" - to which he often returned, "and thence would drink, As at a fountain." Both "ordinary" events, these two incidents nevertheless represented "visionary" moments characterized by strong feeling. "So feeling comes in aid Of feeling," Wordsworth explains, "and diversity of strength Attends us, if but once we have been strong."

These "spots of time" occur, Wordsworth says in The Prelude, "Among those passages of life that give Profoundest knowledge to what point, and how, The mind is lord and master" (11.220-22). And they "Are scattered everywhere," he continues, "taking their date From our first childhood" (11.223-25). Among Frost's poems in which such "knowledge" is given, "In a Vale" is, appropriately, about a childhood experience. The poet recalls a time "when [he] was young" and flowers spoke to him "Of things of moment": "And thus it is I know so well Why the flower has odor, the bird has song. You have only to ask me, and I can tell". Again, the poem seems to deal with a "mere" moment (or, better, a series of moments), but one that seems in retrospect, to Frost at least, to have lasted. Despite the fact, then, of incessant change, despite the meaningless succession of "joy and grief," Frost says by way of summary in "I Could Give All to Time," some things endure:

I could give all to Time except - except What I myself have held. But why declare The things forbidden that while the Customs slept I have crossed to Safety with? For I am There. And what I would not part with I have kept.

Unlike many of Frost's visionary poems, this one implies that the speaker has not only "crossed to Safety" in the past but also that he is now, even as he announces his former triumphs over the constraints of "Time," beyond joy and grief: "I am There."

In "The Figure a Poem Makes," Frost suggests that the "forbidden" things that he has held and kept and that he refused to yield to Time presumably those timeless moments of "belief" - are "the long lost" memories that the poet remembers with "delight" when he begins to write a poem: things he "didn't know [he] knew." Frost implies that an immediate impression in some sense touches off and connects with past impressions. Then "Step by step the wonder of unexpected supply keeps growing" - that is, other lost memories are summoned. Echoing Wordsworth's "Intimations of Immortality," Frost says,

The impressions most useful to my purpose seem always those I was unaware of at the time when taken, and the conclusion is come to that like giants we are always hurling experience ahead of us to pave the future with against the day when we may want to strike a line of purpose across it for somewhere.

Frost continues, "All I would keep for myself is the freedom of my material. to summons aptly from the vast chaos of all I have lived through" (vii). For these reasons, Frost says in "A Concept Self-Conceived," "Great is the reassurance of recall".

Of course, to call Frost a romantic is to risk saying nothing at all about him or his poetry. T. S. Eliot abandoned the term in 1933 because it had become so overused as to have lost any definite meaning. And a glance at the vast number of critical treatises on the subject published in the last 50 years may only serve to justify Eliot's decision. However, if the word romantic can be taken to refer to literary works in which a moment of communion or transcendence is recounted, the experience is spiritually uplifting, and, most important, it is so emotionally powerful as to compel belief in a "higher" reality, then the term can be used to distinguish one kind of poetry from another and, in particular, one aspect of Frost's poetry from another. Frost was a romantic, then, insofar as he dramatizes in his visionary poems moments of illumination that, as he explains in "Happiness Makes up in Height," "Skeptic," and "I Could Give All to Time," he found not only consoling but also lasting. Critics have tried to prove the opposite by comparing Wordsworth's and Emerson's apples with Frost's oranges. The Wordsworth of the middle books of The Prelude and the Emerson of "Fate" and "Experience" are ignored, while the Frost of "Design" and "Desert Places" is brought to stage centre accompanied by the authors of "The Tables Turned" and "The Rhodora." The ploy is logically faulty and critically irresponsible.

Even allowing for their staying power, however, one may still wonder just what Frost's "momentary stays" ultimately mean or signify. The question asked by some of Frost's critics is not whether these visionary experiences are enduring and uplifting but whether they are real. That is, granting their capacity to console - and even inspire, like Wordsworth's "beauteous forms" in "Tintern Abbey" - one may still question their epistemological status. Are they merely solacing insofar as they satisfy the human need to believe? Are they comforting illusions resulting from the suppression of reality and the suspension of consciousness? Or are they cognitive experiences in which consciousness is fully engaged?

In this context, it is useful to remember that some poets, including Frost, have laid claim to a special mode of knowledge - in fact, a knowledge of the most profound and important kind. To Wordsworth, "poetry is the breath and finer spirit of all knowledge". To Shelley, it is "at once the centre and circumference of knowledge". One might dismiss these statements as the inevitably exaggerated beliefs of wild-eyed romantics. Yet one finds similarly large claims made for poetry in the writings of Wallace Stevens and T. S. Eliot. To Stevens, "poetic truth is factual truth, seen, it may be, by those whose range in the perception of fact - that is, whose sensibility - is greater than our own". To Eliot, simply, poetry deals with "reality" and prose only with the "ideal". Frost, equally extravagant, says in "Education by Poetry," "Poetry begins in trivial metaphors, pretty metaphors, 'grace' metaphors, and goes on to the profoundest thinking that we have"

In fact, to Frost, poetry is thinking precisely insofar as it is metaphor. Poetry is metaphor, he explains in "The Constant Symbol," in that it says "one thing in terms of another" (Prose 24). And this activity of the mind is "the height of all thinking" because it replicates the fundamental structure of the universe. The "greatest" example of metaphor is, after all, the "attempt to say matter in terms of spirit, or spirit in terms of matter" (Prose 41).

This kind of metaphor is exemplary because it is paradigmatic: It reenacts the Creation. As Frost says in "Kitty Hawk," "Spirit enters flesh And for all its worth Charges into earth In birth after birth." God himself risks "spirit In substantiation," and humankind instinctively ventures into "the material" through poetry (or any kind of labour) at a similar "risk of the spirit". In this respect, "all poems are the same old metaphor always." That is, every poem is "a symbol" or "an epitome" of the will plunging "deeper and deeper" into "commitments" or "braving alien entanglements" - again, risking substantiation. Metaphor (or form) is the "end" of these commitments ("a rounded conclusion"), a resolution of these entanglements ("the final unity"), because it is the material embodiment of spirit: "The bard has said in effect, Unto these forms do I commend the spirit" (Prose 24-25).

Thus, although "all metaphors break down somewhere" (Prose 41), there is such a thing as a "constant symbol" - an enduring metaphor. Poetry always evolves out of "the breathless swing between subject matter and form" - spirit and matter - which "embrace in the sky" (Prose 28). And the "constant symbol" that is the offspring of this embrace is also a paradigm of the meeting and marriage of all opposites: heaven and earth, male and female, play and work, delight and wisdom, sound and sense, truth and make-believe, fact and dream. "Mind you, we are Mind," Frost says in "Kitty Hawk". And when metaphor succeeds in marrying mind and matter, it does so not because it provides a solacing myth or imposes a ready-made form, but because "the mind fit[s] closely into the nature of the universe" (Prose 102). When this occurs, the poet "gives off. shimmers of eternity," and the reader receives "an immortal wound" (Prose 60-61). Thus, again, poetry is not a momentary stay, except in the most superficial sense. As metaphors, which inevitably reflect the "greatest" metaphor, poems are "the great thoughts. lasting to the end" (my emphasis). And the great poems - "the noble metaphors" - therefore constitute "the richest accumulation of the ages" (Prose 42-43).

It is important to emphasize that Frost more than suggested that he derived his beliefs from such experiences, not, as some of his critics have contended, from need. Speaking of his "four beliefs" in "Education by Poetry," he says that the first, "the personal belief," is "a knowledge that you don't want to tell other people about because you cannot prove that you know." The other beliefs are circumscribed by the same limitation: "We cannot tell some people what it is we believe, partly because they are too stupid to understand and partly because we are too proudly vague to explain." Frost's critics to the contrary, such beliefs are not made "true" because they are "believed in," as William James maintained. Rather, when they are "believed in," they are completed - that is, expressed or presented. And this occurs when the belief founded on "emotion," which is a kind of foreknowledge, is funded by more knowledge and eventuates in a work of art: "And anyway it has got to be fulfilled, and we are not talking until we know more, until we have something to show" (Prose 46).

Thus, "in his foreknowledge [the believer] has something that is going to believe itself into fulfillment, into acceptance" (Prose 44). Belief in this sense is not a willed faith in something yet to be proved. It is rather a kind of prescience that initiates a "relationship" between the knower and the known and that brings the possibility into fulfillment, the seed into bloom: "When familiar friends approach each other in the street both are apt to have this experience in feeling before knowing the pleasantry they will inflict on each other in passing"

Thus, "having a moment" is an event of some significance, for although the experience yields neither information nor explanation, it provides something more important: not consolation, but realization - a kind of feeling that is also a kind of knowing. Such moments are not, however, unambiguous and unequivocal. They cannot be verified, and they cannot be communicated, unless, perhaps, the reader shares some common ground of experience with the poet. "The great thing," Frost says in "Poetry and School" (1951), "is to know when you have one" (Poetry and Prose 413). And the challenge to Frost's readers is to know when he had one (or at least described one in his poetry). As Frost suggests in "One More Brevity," he gets, at best, "An intimation, a shot of ray".

In this poem, Frost implies that spiritual and celestial realities are embodied in material and earthly things. And when he experiences them they seem to convey "A meaning [he] was supposed to seek, And finding, wasn't disposed to speak". In a letter to Untermeyer in 1924, he said that the best kind of "belief" came from moments in which he was "rapt". Therefore, his objective was, he says in "In a Glass of Cider, "to get now and then elated". The "brevities" seem to have possessed for him, then, a meaning and a value that eludes those who do not see them for what they are - or at least what they were to Frost.

Frost makes this point even more emphatically in "All Revelation," "Take Something Like a Star," and "An Unstamped Letter in Our Rural Letter Box." In the first poem, a scientist looks into the crystal-lined cavity of a geode with a cathode ray. As (figuratively) "his head thrusts in as for the view," he asks a series of questions about the geode. The event of seeking and questioning lasts only a "moment," however. The speaker concludes that either the geode as a thing-in-itself or the scientist's presumably tentative answers to his own queries were merely a "Strange apparition of the mind" - that is, a mental projection. Yet, having said this, the speaker acknowledges that "the impervious geode Was entered," and its crystals "glowed In answer to the mental thrust." Implicitly asking the same question that is asked in "Two Look at Two," "The Most of It," and "For Once, Then, Something," the speaker answers that the glow was a response of like to like, or "mind" to "mind": "Eyes seeking the response of eyes Bring out the stars, bring out the flowers." As Frost says in a notebook he kept during the 1940s, "What life craves most" is not meaning in the ordinary sense but "signs of life." And in poems like "Two Look at Two" and "All Revelation," life gets what it wants: "The certainty of a source outside of self - original response". In other words, the scientist's observation of the geode is a special case of the quest of "life" for "life." And when the geode glows, Frost can unequivocally conclude, "All revelation has been ours"

In the same fashion, the speaker in "Take Something Like a Star" implores another object - this time, a star - to reveal its nature. He grants it the right to "obscurity" and "mystery," but he wants something: "to be wholly taciturn In your reserve is not allowed." In response, the star only says, like the geode, "I glow," an answer that does not initially satisfy the speaker. However, he claims that the star "does tell something in the end" although he neglects to say what it is. Furthermore, apparently because of its response, the speaker refers to the star as "steadfast," which, if nothing else, gives it the capacity to "stay our minds".

The letter-writing tramp in "An Unstamped Letter" similarly comes "face to face. with universal space," in which he sees two stars merge to make "the largest firedrop ever formed." Just as the speaker in "All Revelation" can elicit a response from the stars (as well as the flowers), here the coalescing stars inspire a like response in the tramp, in whose mind two memories join together. At this point he claims, "And for a moment all was plain, That men have thought about in vain". That is, he too has had a revelation that remains unexplained.

As I said earlier, the poet's flashes and insights are also moments of illumination. A "perfect moment of unbafflement," Frost says in "How Hard It Is to Keep from Being King When It's in You and in the Situation," provides the poet with an opportunity to "summons out of nowhere like a jinni" not only the words he needs to complete his thought or fulfill his vision, but also the vision itself.

The "Freedom to flash off into wild connections" is "The

freedom of [the poet's] own material" - which is, ironically, spiritual as well as material. And the experience - whether it is a poet's, a tramp's, or a scientist's - is so exhilarating that no one can help desiring it again: "Once to have had it nothing else will do". Thus, one may "blame the stars For looking and not participating," but their "detachment," their transcendence, does not preclude their accessibility, their immanence, as Frost implies in this poem and demonstrates in "Take Something Like a Star" and "An Unstamped Letter."

This view of Frost's poetry suggests yet another connection with romanticism - the belief that visionary experience is not only inspiring but redemptive. It is life-changing and lifesaving because it is not a projection of one's own needs or desires. Rather, it is actually cognitive. The spiritual reality that such experience discloses is, after all, real. And the perception of it is an intuition that is felt to be the basis for all knowledge.

This intuition is not achieved when the self-as-subject either passively perceives the other-as-object or actively imposes order and value on it. It is a mutually creative act in which subject and object open up to each other and reveal their essence, their spirit. Again, "Eyes seeking the response of eyes Bring out the stars, bring out the flowers." That is, as any Neoplatonist, Bhuddist, or Christian mystic would argue, when the self becomes spiritualized, it acquires the capacity to perceive the world spiritually. For, as it undergoes this process of self-transcendence, the cosmos is likewise liberated from its material embodiment and discloses the sacred.

If we grant that Frost portrays visionary experience as genuinely revelatory, one question remains. In the words of Frost's third group of critics, what is the relationship between his visionary poems and his poems that seem to contradict them? That is, how can the contrasting views of human experience in "The Skeptic" and "Once by the Pacific" or "I Could Give All to Time" and "Nothing Gold Can Stay" be reconciled? To understand the relationship between these opposing visions, it is useful to turn to the writings of Mircea Eliade, in which a similarly dualistic vision is presented. In

The Sacred and the Profane, Eliade describes the universe of "religious man" in a way that should sound familiar to anyone who has read Frost's "Kitty Hawk" or considered the foregoing remarks in Frost's essays:

Whatever the historical context in which he is placed, homo religiosus always believes that there is an absolute reality, the sacred, which transcends this world but manifests itself in this world, thereby sanctifying it and making it real. He further believes that life has a sacred origin and that human existence realizes all of its potentialities in proportion as it is religious that is, participates in reality.

By contrast, the world of the profane - like Frost's universe of "chaos" - is unstructured, amorphous, homogeneous, and meaningless. In it, as in Frost's poems of loss, mutability, and death, all truths are relative, and nonreligious man (who dwells in it without respite or relief) is necessarily confused and sometimes even paralyzed because his experiences are "purely subjective" and therefore illusory.

To both Frost and Eliade, this dualism is resolved in the assertion that, although the sacred and the profane (or, to use Frost's terms, the spiritual and the material) are, in one sense, merely two aspects of human experience, only the sacred (or spiritual) is ontologically "real." Religious man has access to the sacred through what Eliade calls hierophanies, or breaks in space that reveal "the fixed point, the central axis" of the cosmos - in Frost's poetry, a ladder ("After Apple-Picking" and "Directive"), a tree ("Birches" and "Sycamore"), or a pole ("The Silken Tent" and "On a Tree Fallen across the Road"), all of which represent a meeting point between heaven and earth. These "intervals of sacred time," says Eliade, occur at "the centre of the world" and at "the beginning" of time, where the hierophant "communicates with the gods" and reconnects with the "real."

For Frost, as for Thoreau, the journey to the centre must be reenacted periodically, like an annual rebirth ritual. As Frost explains in "Build Soil," periods of inner and outer awareness succeed each other: "We are always too much out or too much in." At the present time, we are "out" and must therefore go "in." We must retreat from the "market" in order to return to it strengthened and renewed. Thus, in "Directive," the return to "a time made simple," the journey under the direction of a guide "who only has at heart your getting lost," the need to be "lost enough to find yourself," and the arrival at the "source" of a brook, which is "lofty and original," are the components of an old ritual, a spiritual exercise that requires the abandonment of an old self and the acquisition of a new.

As Emerson says in "The American Scholar," "When the artist has exhausted his material," implicitly his spiritual energy, "when fancy no longer paints, when thoughts are no longer apprehended and books are a weariness - he has always the resource to live" - that is, to return to the real, the origin, the creation: "The stream retreats to its source"

To Frost, however, the journey is not made casually or easily. Indeed, to get beyond confusion, the initiate must go through it. (According to Eliade, the ritual begins with a "separation" from the quotidian world and a "retrogression. into chaos.") In "Directive," Frost invites the reader-as-initiate to embark on an arduous journey that results in the loss of the kind of consciousness Wordsworth called meddling and murderous.

That is, the "detail" of profane life, which is "too much" (and, in some respects, too little), is not simply ignored, suppressed, or forgotten, but "burned, dissolved, and broken off" in an experience that purges and purifies not only the consciousness but also the data of consciousness. Oddly enough, this end is achieved not by making the "too much" less, but by making it more - by revealing to the initiate the glacial and imperious forces of nature (11.10-19), the graveyard of all houses and metaphors (11.20-22), and the fact of ongoing and implacable change (11.23-28).

The means to the end of soul saving is thus outwalking the farthest city light and becoming acquainted with the night - that is, losing all sense of ordinary time and space. In this context, being "lost enough to find yourself" is not a platitude but another way of figuring absolute disorientation in the midst of what Frost elsewhere calls "utter chaos" and in this poem implicitly names "confusion." For the reader-as-initiate, Frost's ambiguous tone (playful and serious) and mixture of truth (in 11.10-28) and "make-believe" serve a similar purpose. He, too, is groundless, ontologically uncertain, lost.

But his descent into chaos prepares him for an ascent to "the height Of country," which is reached by a "ladder road" - the dwelling place of the gods. Following Frost's "directive," the reader leaves his present dwelling, his house, which has ceased to hold "the sacred," and, like the couple in "The Generations of Men," seeks to build a new house on an old foundation. Under these circumstances - and only then - can he "make [himself] at home" (1.39), "at home in the metaphor" (Prose 39).

At the world centre, represented in all of Frost's poetry by cellar holes (to Eliade, "initiatory graves"), brooks ("primordial waters"), trees and ladders ("cosmic pillars"), and moons (standing for the "reconciliation of contraries"), the initiate undergoes a spiritual change and acquires spiritual knowledge. And his entire journey is a reenactment of the creation of the cosmos out of chaos, the founding of the universe. The initiate's final encounter with the saddest of time's treacheries - in "Directive," the shattered debris of the children's world of make-believe - adds pity to terror and leads to his attainment (through sympathy) of childlike innocence, the final purification. In this way, says Eliade, "the work of time" is "undone," and in the ensuing "existential crisis," which is always "religious," the sacred is recovered and reintegrated.

To be sure, these revelations appear to occur randomly and fortuitously, as if they were unearned and unwarranted. In "How Hard It Is," Frost says that the causes of such moments are indeterminable: "We know not what we owe this moment to." However, all of Frost's visionary poems follow the pattern of Wordsworth's spots-of-time experiences. That is, illumination follows disappointment ("The Dust of Snow, "Two Look at Two," "The Tuft of Flowers"), a mood of despondency in response to fall or winter ("Looking for a Sunset Bird," "Going for Water," "I Will Sing You One-O"), confusion or despair induced by a vision of universal chaos ("I Could Give All to Time," "Happiness Makes Up in Height," "Iris by Night"), or a sense of futility ("One More Brevity," "All Revelation," "Take Something Like a Star"). In "Skeptic," the moment of insight follows a series of negations ("I don't believe."). In "How Hard It Is" and "Time Out," it succeeds a cessation of struggle or competition. Thus, in every case, the routine of everyday life is suspended, ordinary consciousness is abandoned, and the candidate for revelation descends into darkness - baffled, hopeless, and lost, but only for a moment.

The point is that visionary experience in Frost's poetry occurs only after intellectual exhaustion, spiritual despair, or metaphorical breakdown - that is, after the kind of experience that Frost portrays in his darker poems. And because these interludes of darkness always precede illumination, it seems reasonable to conclude that they are a precondition for it. In this respect, revelation is not just an escape from confusion and disappointment but a consequence of them. And it is not merely given, but suffered for. Under such circumstances, darkness is "precious," as one of Frost's characters says in "The Literate Farmer and the Planet Venus":

We need the interruption of the night To ease attention off when overtight, To break our logic in too long a flight, And ask us if our premises are right.

In short, the dark is not merely a contrasting backdrop against which the stars can be better seen, but the medium through or the means by which they appear - the via negativa without which vision is impossible: "The groundwork of all faith is human woe".

In Frost's poetry, darkness leads to illumination, and chaos becomes cosmos. But this can happen only when the prospective "hierophant" goes into the woods ("Birches") or returns to a cellar hole ("Directive") - that is, when the prospect of becoming "whole again beyond confusion" is made possible by a turn away from the quotidian and into darkness, chaos, or oblivion. Having entered the woods, the candidate for revelation is ready for the kind of self-transcendence that Frost found in Emerson's "Brahma": "the perfect detachment from ambition and desire that alone can rescue us from the round of existence" (Prose 97). At this new level of consciousness, the initiate is baffled, hopeless, and lost. Ultimately, however, he attains not only solace and sustenance, but also knowledge of a different - and deeper - reality.

In this context, it should be clear that poems like "Design," "Stars," and the tragic narratives of North of Boston are neither at the centre of Frost's poetic vision nor in real opposition to his more affirmative poems. Rather, they merely express the nature of the profane world, and they are subsumed in the process of illumination, which ultimately reveals the cosmos, the sacred. They are the Everlasting Nay to Frost's Everlasting Yea, the experience of alienation before the blessing of the water snakes, the expression of disillusionment that precedes the ascent of the sacred mountain. Not that these poems are trivial or incidental. Rather, although the picture they present is neither final nor absolute, it is indispensable for a thorough comprehension of human existence, and it must be accepted before understanding is actually completed by illumination.

In my view, then, Frost was not a sentimental escapist, a brooding nihilist, or a pragmatic Greek who courageously faced chaos in order to impose meaning on it. As a romantic, he did not believe that truth is simply willed into being; nor did he believe that beauty is merely created. According to his own testimony, truth and beauty are discoverable in reality. They come into being when thinker and artist transcend their ordinary selves and allow experience to complete itself. Like Emerson, Frost believed that one "sees" when the intellect is "where and what it sees" (3:26). And he agreed with Wordsworth that "the individual Mind" is "fitted" to "the external World," and vice versa, but only in the act of creation, when both Mind and World act "with blended might," as Wordsworth says in "Home at Grasmere" and "Tintern Abbey" and throughout The Prelude.

All things considered, Frost must have been amused by the responses elicited by the question in "The Oven Bird": "What [are we] to make of a diminished thing[?]". The answer, I think, is given in two poems. On the one hand, he says in

"At Woodward Gardens," "It's knowing what to do with things that counts". But, on the other hand, he adds in "Hyla Brook," "We love the things we love for what they are. What we do with them and what they are depends, of course, on what we are. And that depends on where we have been and where we are going. Creation, in Frost's view, is a matter of being and doing simultaneously and a means by which "diminished" things, subjects and objects, material things, can be seen spiritually - not only as parts, as Frost suggests in "Fragmentary Blue," but also as parts of a whole. Even a stone can be a star, Frost says in "A Star in a Stone-Boat":

Such as it is, it promises the prize Of one world complete in any size That I am like to compass, fool or wise.

Q. Discuss the similar views of Frost and Thoreau. ?

Or

Q. How Frost's extravagant theory enticed Thoreau ?

The connection between Robert Frost and Henry David Thoreau has been observed by several critics. Frost himself encouraged this association through public acknowledgment of his deep respect for Thoreau's achievement in Walden (1854): first, he listed Walden third in a list of ten books which he felt should be included in every public library; second, in a 1915 letter Frost remarks that a passage in Walden "must have had a good deal to do with the making of me," and in 1922 Frost wrote that Walden "surpasses everything we have had in America".

Still, though many critics have noted the Thoreau-Frost connection, they frequently misunderstand Thoreau by aligning his own blend of optimism and skepticism too closely with the much more positive and progressive metaphysic of Emerson-which, in turn, results in a misunderstanding of the subsequent ties between Frost and Thoreau. For instance, when Elizabeth Isaacs writes that Frost "has the practicality of Arnold, Thoreau, or Hardy; yet he is not as onesided as they are in his beliefs," she is justifiably pointing toward Frost's complexity, but she does so at the risk of underestimating a similar thematic complexity in Thoreau. Likewise, when J.

Donald Crowly writes that "although Frost found

Thoreau's modulations equal to many of his own purposes, there is in the Thoreauvian voice an ultimate confidence in the solid bottoms being everywhere, in the making snug in the limitless, that Frost often questions and goes beyond" (305), he is correctly noting Frost's "extravagant" struggle to "go beyond" the limits of this world, but his reading of Thoreau does not account for the many passages in both Walden and especially The Maine Woods where Thoreau pursues a similar "extra-vagant" quest. In fact, it is, in part, because we have poems like "For Once, Then, Something," and "The Woodpile," that we can look back at Thoreau and better understand the complex questioning of Nature that Thoreau exhibits in some of his writings.

Although Thoreau and Frost are traditionally seen as relatively optimistic in their exploration of Nature, both are in many respects dark romantics; they both question at times the optimistic and comparatively monistic vision of Emerson, and they both express a certain skepticism concerning the ability of the poet to reconcile man and Nature, or the subject and object. For instance, in his essay "On Emerson" Frost writes: "A melancholy dualism is the only soundness," and "I don't like obscurity and obfuscation, but I do like dark sayings I must leave the clearing of time to".

Moreover, writes Frost, "In practice, in nature, the circle becomes an oval. As a circle it has one centre Good. As an oval it has two centers-Good and Evil. Thence Monism verses Dualism". Aside from this dualistic interpretation of the world, Frost's "deep skepticism about the possibilities of human life" can be seen in his essay "Education by Poetry." In this essay Frost writes: "Greatest of all attempts to say one thing in terms of another is the philosophical attempt to say matter in terms of spirit, or spirit in terms of matter, to make the final unity. That is the greatest attempt that ever failed". Unlike Emerson, who likewise attempted the unification of subject and object but posited success,

Frost sees attempts at such a unification at once heroic, and doomed.l Thus, while Frost's theory of "symbol" and "metaphor" seems Emersonian in theory, in practice Frost's uses of symbol and metaphor resemble those of the dark romantics, particularly Hawthorne, Melville, and the Thoreau of The Maine Woods. Frost's symbolism and metaphor tend not toward Emerson's revelatory union with Nature, but tend toward multiple interpretation, indirection, and ambiguity.

Roberts French, in "Robert Frost and the Darkness of Nature," is one of a few critics who has seen the dark romantic within Frost. He writes: "While Frost has written poems that express a certain joy in nature. he is far from being a lover of nature; reading through his works, one finds that a major tone involves feelings of profound uneasiness, even of fear, toward nature". Victor Strandberg sees Frost's "profound uneasiness" akin to a similar unease in Melville:

Beneath [Frost's and Melville's] surface differences, the two writer's affinities rested upon fundamental parallels in theme and technique. In theme, the poet and the novelist shared a lifelong fixation upon the most significant issue in Western literature since the Romantic period-that Crisis of Belief, or search for beliefs to live (and die) by. Strandberg notices that both Melville and Frost share a characteristic typically associated with dark romanticism: the epistemological crisis of belief. While epistemological concerns are indeed central to Melville's fiction, as I see it, the link between Frost and the dark romantics may not be primarily through Melville, but through Thoreau.

One way to approach the Frost Thoreau connection is through the "Extravagance" theme. As Richard Poirier has noted, Frost makes significant use of the conclusion to Walden where Thoreau writes:

I fear chiefly lest my expression may not be extravagant enough, may not wander far enough beyond the narrow limits of my daily experience, so as to be adequate to the truth of which I have been convinced. Extravagance!. I desire to speak somewhere without bounds; like a man in a waking moment, to men in their waking moments; for I am convinced that I cannot exaggerate enough even to lay the foundation of a true expression.

The key to Extravagance is the attempt on the part of the

poet to journey beyond conventional boundaries in an attempt to uncover hidden truth. It is both a literal wandering, and a figurative questing; it is an attempt, in Frost's words, to say "spirit in terms of matter." In the works of Thoreau and Frost, Extravagance is used both as a structural device-in which the poet actually sets forth on a quest, or a wandering-and as a thematic device in which the poet attempts, by pushing beyond conventional boundaries, to reconcile the subject and object, to unify man and Nature, to find "a true expression." As French has suggested, for Frost and Thoreau the object is not to "go into nature, but to go beyond nature". For both Frost and Thoreau, however, the quest beyond Nature results in an epistemological "crisis of belief" and ultimately fails.

Although Thoreau introduces the irreconcilability of man and Nature in Walden, in The Maine Woods (1864) he gives the inscrutability of Nature its fullest treatment. In each of Thoreau's three quests into the forest of Maine he foregrounds an epistemological crisis which ultimately reveals the inscrutability of Nature, and the inability of man, as Melville might suggest, to pierce through the "pasteboard mask" of Nature.

Frost develops these same themes in many of his poems. Each of the three sections that follow explores first Thoreau's Extra-vagant quest for subjectobject reconciliation in The Maine Woods, followed by a detailed examination of Frost's poetry, demonstrating how Frost uses, manipulates, and reconfigures similar themes in many of his poems.

The Negative Ascent: "Ktaadn" and "The Mountain"

In "Ktaadn" Thoreau introduces the epistemological themes that he will develop further in "Chesuncook" and "Allegash and East Branch." Each of these three excursions is an Extra-vagant wandering from civilization out into the wild interior of Maine, and then back to civilization (although it must be noted that none of the three excursions is completely circular: in the first and third journeys Thoreau and his companions leave from Boston, but only return as far as Bangor; in the second journey Thoreau leaves from Boston and returns to Oldtown, just a bit past Bangor). The central opposition at work in all three excursions is the contrast between civilization and Nature, the tamed and the primitive. The hallmarks of civilization are money, property, politics, and machines, such as the railroad and steamboat; the wilderness features wild animals, tangled plants, bugs, mountains, rivers, and Mount Ktaadn.

"Ktaadn," the first excursion, takes place in 1846. The themes of "Ktaadn" are grounded in the relationship between civilized man and primitive Nature. Thoreau sets out from Boston into the wilderness of Maine in order to ascend Mount Ktaadn in an effort to re-establish an original relation with Nature, to push beyond boundaries into the realm of the Indian storm-bird Pomola-who, according to Penobscot legend, lives on Mount Ktaadn3-where man and Nature unite and ultimate truths are revealed. He never reaches the summit of Mount Ktaadn, however, and Thoreau makes it clear that Nature remains ultimately inscrutable. Speaking of Ktaadn, Thoreau writes:

It was vast, Titanic, and such as man never inhabits. Some part of the beholder, even some vital part, seems to escape through the loose grating of his ribs as he ascends. He is more alone than you can imagine. There is less of substantial thought and fair understanding in him than in the plains where men inhabit. His reason is dispersed and shadowy, more thin and subtle, like the air. Vast, Titanic, inhuman Nature has got him at disadvantage, caught him alone and pilfers him of some of his divine faculty. She does not smile on him as in the plains. She seems to say sternly, Why came ye here before your time. This ground is not prepared for you.

This confrontation with Nature comes to a crisis near the end of the chapter. Thoreau writes: "Talk of mysteries! Think of our life in nature,daily to be shown matter, to come in contact with it,-rocks, trees, wind on our cheeks! the solid earth! the actual world! the common sense! Contact! Contact! Who are we? where are we?". Without answer, Thoreau turns from Ktaadn and begins the journey homeward, having sought the unification of man and Nature, and failed.

One can see much of "Ktaadn" in several of Frost's poems. The antagonism between Pomola and Thoreau can be read into "Not All There," and the ultimate return from the "dark and deep" woods to civilization is the central concern of "Stopping by Woods on a Snowy Evening." But the two poems which both illuminate, and are illuminated by, "Ktaadn" in suggestive ways are "Mountain" and "Birches." Like Ktaadn, the "Mountain" is daunting and sublime, holding "the town as in a shadow". The narrator learns from a "man who moved so slow" that "There's a brook That starts up on it somewhere-I've heard say Right on the top; tip-top-a curious thing". But,just as Thoreau fails to reach the top of Ktaadn, none have gone high enough up the mountain to find the origin of the spring. In "The Mountain" Frost leaves the narrator's questions unanswered: Frost does not reveal the location of the brook, or confirm that the brook even exists, nor does he reveal if the winter-warmth and summer-coldness of the spring is natural or preternatural in origin.

This ambiguity is playfully undercut in the Frost poem with the possibility developed at the end of the poem that the Old Man's account of the brook on the mountain-a brook none, apparently, may have ever seen-may indeed be only, as Richard Poirier notes, a country tall-tale. The Old Man's admission that "all the fun's in how you say a thing" may or may not explain the mysteries of the brook and mountain, but it does point to Frost's thematic exploration of the subjectivity of experience, which both looks back to earlier models in Thoreau and the dark romantics, and forward to the high modernists who were intimately concerned with subjective experience, the psychology of the human mind, and the role of language as a filter for experience.

"Birches" develops some of the thematics of "Ktaadn" but in provocatively different ways. The dramatic situation in "Ktaadn" and "Birches" is remarkably similar: in both there is an Extra-vagant ascent into Nature, and a subsequent return to earth, a going-forth and a coming-back, an expansion and recoil. In "Ktaadn" Thoreau seeks the realm of the god Pomola; in "Birches" the poet climbs "Toward heaven, till the tree could bear no more". In both the object of the quest is ultimately unreachable-Thoreau does not reach the summit of Ktaadn, and the birch eventually bends back toward the earth under the weight of the climber. Both wanderings are from civilization into Nature and toward heaven, and both end with a return to civilization. Finally, both quests feature an isolated figure: Thoreau ascends Ktaadn alone; Frost's boy lives "too far from town to learn baseball, Whose only play was what he found himself".

The basic difference between "Ktaadn" and "Birches" is in the relationship between the human and Nature. Frost's narrator seems satisfied in the return to earth, and, in fact, would be disappointed if the journey was not circular. Frost writes, "I'd like to get away from earth awhile And then come back to it and begin over. May no fate willfully misunderstand me And half grant what I wish and snatch me awayNot to return. Earth's the right place for love: I don't know where it's likely to go better". The ascent in "Birches," therefore, is, as Richard Poirier writes, "safely controlled by the recognition that birch trees will only bear so much climbing before returning you, under the pressure of human weight, back home". Thus, while Thoreau seems awed at the terrible and sublime crisis of belief that he experiences at Mount Ktaadn, Frost seems to find satisfaction in the circularity of the voyage: there is a mutual complicity between the climber of birches and Nature in the Frost poem.

Both "Ktaadn" and "Birches" are negated ascents-both personas wander beyond the boundary of civilization and ultimately return to it, but while Thoreau laments the inability to penetrate fully into the realm of Pomola, the narrator in "Birches" takes comfort in the fact that Nature herself will not allow man to remain in the heavenly realm, but will bend the branches of the birch earthward-to remain in the realm of the beyond is an extreme the Frost narrator actively avoids.

Indiscriminate Hunters: "Chesuncook" and "A Minor Bird"

Thoreau's secondjourney into the wilderness of Maine occurs in 1853. In this central chapter Thoreau more fully develops a series of oppositions introduced in "Ktaadn." In "Chesuncook" Thoreau explores the contrast between civilization and wilderness, the civilized and the primitive, the present and the past, lower uses of Nature and higher laws, the indiscriminate hunter and the poet, and commodity and discipline. In his excursion, Thoreau wishes to recapture the past-to relive what the Jesuit missionaries experienced when traveling through the primitive wilderness untouched by civilized man-but he is unable to: he is tainted by the corrosive effect of civilization.

Thoreau makes this clear in the chapter's central crisis: the destruction of the moose by Thoreau's band of indiscriminate hunters. Framed by suggestive allusions to Mount Ktaadn, Thoreau's participation in the killing of the moose provokes the wrath of Nature against Thoreau, thereby cutting off any chance Thoreau may have had of succeeding where he failed in "Ktaadn": to establish an original relation with Nature, to go beyond boundaries and express truth.

Read in light of "Chesuncook," Frost's "A Minor Bird" becomes an intriguing exploration of the complicated relationship between man and Nature. In "Chesuncook" Thoreau laments his only half-willed participation in the destruction of Nature; in "A Minor Bird" the narrator tries to understand what there is within man that would cause him to "silence any song" of Nature, whether that song be in-or-out of key. The suggestion in "A Minor Bird" is that there is some mysterious separation between man and Nature, a disharmony. The killing of the moose in "Chesuncook" acts as symbol for one of the major themes of the chapter: the gradual destruction of the primitive wilderness through the progress of civilization. At the end of the chapter Thoreau reflects on the relentless, inevitable advance of civilization, and the destruction of Nature which this advance brings with it.

This poses a serious problem, for the Poet, notes Thoreau, draws power and inspiration from contact with primitive Nature. In the end Thoreau suggests that perhaps man can preserve some of the raw wilderness left in America (through some form of park system or similar venture). This solution is

Thoreau's problematic attempt at a mediating compromise between the relentless progress of civilization and the need of the Poet to tap into the inscrutable power within Nature, the Poet's muse. In the past, Nature was untouched and available to the Poet; in the present, Nature is quickly receding.

Something similar to Thoreau's valorization of the primitive past over the decay of the civilized present can be seen in Frost's poems "Nothing Gold Can Stay" and "The Oven Bird." In "Nothing Gold Can Stay" the narrator, like Thoreau, valorizes the Edenic, pristine past; and, as in "Chesuncook," the narrator notes how this golden "first green" vanishes in a brief hour and gives way to the fallen present,just as "Eden sank to grief". This process, as Thoreau makes clear in "Chesuncook," is inevitable, and carries with it spiritual implications, for just as the fall of man in Eden separated man from God, so the destruction of Nature in "Chesuncook" separates Thoreau from communion with Nature.

Frost takes this theme and develops it in a slightly different manner, for he casts the descent from the pristine past metaphorically in the circularity of the seasons, taking the early flowers of spring which give way to the leaves of summer as symbol for the sinking of Eden. In this way Frost conflates a linear, Judeo-Christian historiography with a circular historiography-a formulation that finds modernist analogues in, for instance, Eliot's Four Quartets and the use of fertility myth in "The Waste Land." "The Oven Bird" explores similar themes. Again there is the passage of time, from the valorized past when "pear and cherry bloom went down in showers" to the present when "the highway dust is over all". In the end, the question that the bird "frames in all but words Is what to make of a diminished thing". Therefore, like Thoreau at the end of "Chesuncook," the Oven Bird is left wondering what can be salvaged from the decay of the present. This "decay" will become a major theme in the remaining chapter of The Maine Woods.

For Once, Then, Something: "Allegash" and "The Woodpile"

The themes developed in "Ktaadn" and "Chesuncook"

reach a climax in "Allegash and East Branch." This Extravagant excursion takes place in 1857, and civilization has pushed far into the forests of Maine. Thoreau writes: "Things are quite changed since I was here eleven years ago. Where there were but one or two houses, I now found quite a village". The central crisis of this chapter, and of the entire book, comes near the beginning of the excursion. Thoreau, getting up in the middle of the night in the pitch-blackness, sees a white, glowing ring of phosphorescent wood sticking partially out of the fire.

He gathers the glowing wood chips together, remarking that Nature was using the moment to communicate something significant: "I little thought that there was such a light shining in the darkness of the wilderness for me". This light was beyond the realm of simple scientific explanation; instead, "It suggested to me that there was something to be seen if one had eyes" -the eyes of a Poet, presumably, the transparent"eyes" of Emerson, the "I" of Whitman. Significantly, however, at the end of the section Thoreau notes that he is unable to reproduce the experience: "I kept those little chips and wet them again the next night, but they emitted no light" (248). Thus, instead of a unification with Nature, Thoreau experiences little more than a Poe-esque momentary glimpse of the supernal; communion and communication with Nature seems impossible-the ties between civilization and the wilderness have been severed.

Thoreau explores further the reasons for this separation later in the chapter. He notes that he has been so altered by civilization that he cannot observe Nature on its own terms; instead he sees it through the subjective lens of civilization: Wild as it was, it was hard for me to get rid of the associations of the settlements. Any steady and monotonous sound, to which I did not distinctly attend, passed for a sound of human industry. The waterfalls which I heard were not without their dams and mills to my imagination. While Thoreau introduces the idea of Nature as Muse in "Chesuncook," he brings it to a crisis in "Allegash":

The Anglo-American can indeed cut down, and grub up

all this waving forest, and make a stump speech, and vote for Buchanan on its ruins, but he cannot converse with the spirit of the tree he fells, he cannot read the poetry and mythology which retire as he advances. He ignorantly erases mythological tablets in order to print his handbills and town-meeting warrants on them.

Thus, Thoreau is doubly-damned: the mythological tablets that only the poet can read are being destroyed by civilization, and the poet himself has been so corrupted by civilization that even he can no longer read the few glowing wood chips that remain. The poet yearns for communication with Nature, but he cannot bridge the gulf which separates them. In the end, Thoreau symbolically resigns himself to his fate: when he and Indian Joe pass by Ktaadn on their way back home, they do not even attempt to climb. Indeed, this passage at the end of "Allegash," where Thoreau and his companion excuse themselves from a second attempt at climbing Mount Ktaadn by claiming that they need a new pair of moccasins, resonates in "The Mountain." Frost's narrator thinks of ascending the mountain, but does not: "Is that the way to reach the top from here? " he asks the "man who moved so slow," "Not for this morning, but some other time: I must be getting back to breakfast now".

Frost explores the inability of man to fully communicate with Nature in several of his poems. Roberts French writes: "If Frost's poetry insists on anything. it insists on the impenetrable barrier between man and Nature: we live in a world that we cannot know, for it will not reveal itself; and yet we yearn for some sort of communion". This "failed" communication-such as Thoreau experiences with the decaying wood chips-is central to Frost's "The Woodpile," "For Once, Then, Something," and "The Most of It."

Frost develops many of the themes explored by Thoreau in "Allegash" in his poem "The Woodpile." The poem begins with a dramatization of the Extra-vagant motif. Frost writes: "Out walking in the frozen swamp one grey day, I paused and said, 'I will turn back from here. No, I will go on farther-and we shall see"'). The poet wanders "far from home" where he eventually comes upon "A small bird." The bird is "careful To put a tree between us when he lighted, And say no word to tell me who he was Who was so foolish as to think what he thought" (100). In this episode with the bird, four ideas are developed: first, as in The Maine Woods, the poet recognizes a separation between the poet and Nature (the tree which separates poet from bird); second, the poet points out that Nature seems to withhold communication from the poet ("say no word to tell me who he was"); third, this lack of communication forces the poet to try to guess at what the bird is thinking (if anything at all).

And finally, Frost carefully builds an ambiguity into the italicized "he" in the line "Who was so foolish as to think what he thought": the reference could either point back to the narrator, which would imply a self-recognition upon the narrator's part that his trying to read thoughts onto the bird is a foolish gesture, or the reference could point forward to the line "He thought that I was after him for a feather-" which would suggest that the narrator thinks the bird foolish for fearing him.

Frost uses this ambiguity to explore the breakdown in communication between man and Nature in away which foregrounds the subjectivity of experience and the psychology of the human mind, for if the bird is foolish for fearing the narrator, then Nature has failed to interpret man correctly-on the other hand, if the narrator is foolish for projecting thoughts onto the bird, then Frost is exposing the way in which experience is filtered through a lens of subjectivity. In this way, the bird episode is not so much a "parody" of romantic associations, as Richard Poirier suggests, but an ironic foregrounding of epistemological concerns that call into question the romantic associationism of Emerson and other light romantics.

The bird seems to direct the poet to a decaying woodpile, abandoned in the wood long ago. Like the decaying phosphorescent wood chips which suggest communication, but leave Thoreau with only an ambiguous sense of the separation of man and Nature, so the woodpile is suggestive, but ultimately does not reveal its mysteries to the poet. In the end the poet, like the one who created the woodpile, leaves the woodpile "To warm the frozen swamp as best it could With the slow smokeless burning of decay". Poirier writes: the "slow smokeless burning of decay," "induces a kind of awe because it is the acknowledgment of nature as a realm wholly independent of human need or even human perception". And in this way "The Woodpile" stands in dialogical relationship with a poem like "The Tuft of Flowers" where a Whitman-esque unity of past and present experience is valorized in the concluding lines: "'Men work together,' I told him from the heart, 'Whether they work together or apart'"

As in "The Woodpile," in "The Most of It" the isolated individual who "thought he kept the universe alone" yearns for communication with Nature, but all he receives is a momentary stumbling "through the rocks with horny tread". The individual seeks not mere echoes from Nature, but "counter-love, original response". Nothing ever comes of his cry, except for once, when, like Thoreau's brief and ambiguous communion with the decaying wood chips, Nature sends a reply. But "Instead of proving human when it neared And someone else additional to him, As a great buck it powerfully appeared" pushing its way through the rocks and underbrush, "and that was all". Like Thoreau, the individual in Frost's poem seeks the unification of man and Nature, the harmony of subject and object, but he is left with a mysterious and ambiguous response.

Even more so than "The Woodpile" and "The Most of It," "For Once, Then, Something" reconfigures the central epistemological crisis of "Allegash and East Branch," and of The Maine Woods as a whole. In this poem, the narrator, another isolated individual, subject to the taunts of others, has the curious habit of always looking down the shaft of a well "wrong to the light". In this way the narrator never sees "Deeper down in the well than where the water Gives me back in a shining surface picture Me myself in the summer heaven, godlike". On one occasion, with the emphasis on Once, the narrator "discerned, as I thought, beyond the picture, Through the picture, a something white, uncertain, Something more of the depthsand then I lost it". During that one brief moment-just like Thoreau's moment of wonder at the glow of the decaying wood chips-the narrator saw through the reflective barrier of the water's surface and received a glimpse of what lay beyond. It was but a mere moment, however, and the meaning of the narrator's vision remains unclear. "What was that whiteness?" the narrator asks, "Truth? A pebble of quartz? For once, then, something".

In this poem Frost changes Thoreau's equation significantly. Thoreau actively seeks to pierce through the pasteboard masks of nature, and the vision of phosphorescent wood chips is hailed as a wonderful moment of communication-when the chips fail to glow on the second night Thoreau laments his failure to establish that extra-vagant original relation with Nature. The Frost narrator, however, like the climber of birches who finds a satisfaction in his grounding, only looks beneath the surface of Nature once. There is no explicit reason given to suggest that the narrator could not repeat the action virtually at will-and so the fact that the action was taken only once is significant. The narrator remains content to stare at "Me myself in the summer heaven godlike," which takes on a further irony in relation to the fact that the narrator is taunted by others-do they mock the narrator's timidity at confronting the reality beneath Nature's surface? This would certainly make the narrator's "godlike" selfprojection ironic.

Q. Discuss the secretive and playful epiphanies of Frost ?

Or

Q. Write any Essay on the writing style of Robert Frost ?

Surprisingly, no one has yet tried to find a pattern that can unify the major epiphanies in the poems of Robert Frost; no study of the poet in the last thirty-five years even contains any variant of "epiphany" in its title (though Robert F. Fleissner invokes the related "spot of time"1). I seek here to identify the pattern of thematic focuses, recurrent formal features, and psychological implications unique to Frost's epiphanic style or "signature," his distinctive manner of epiphany-making.2 Two thematic concerns distinguish the strongest poetic epiphanies of Robert Frost: playfulness3 and interpersonality. A playful epiphany is an ambivalent one. Because epiphanic moments convey a discovery with deep implications, a playful epiphany creates a conceptual tension, an emotional ambivalence: is the episode a revelation or a mere frivolity? Equally fraught with tension is Frost's awareness that the solitude often required for epiphanic experience must define itself in relation to one's need for social validation. Frost presents his doubly ambivalent epiphanies of playfulness in the conflictual4 context of the "relational self".

In The Ambiguity of Play, Brian Sutton-Smith distinguishes seven thematic focuses that have helped theorists organize discussions of play: Progress, Fate, Power, Identity, the Imaginary, Self, and Frivolity5. These categories have enabled investigators to clarify, respectively, ludic activities as diverse as children's play, games of chance, contests of skill and strategy, festivals and parades, theatrical fantasy, leisure, and humorous nonsense. Every one of Sutton-Smith's seven rubrics illuminates the playful epiphanies of Robert Frost. Progress, Fate, Power, and Frivolity are important but subsidiary. Some of Frost's visions recall stages in the developmental progress whereby a child learns to balance the demands of self and other. Frostian solitaries love to challenge fate and to assert their hard-won visionary power while deprecating their epiphanic achievement with comic whimsy.

But the categories that shed most light on the psychology of Frost's playful epiphanies are the ones Sutton-Smith calls Identity, Self, and the Imaginary. Sutton-Smith sees Identity (what I will call Companionship or Commmunity) as rooted in tradition, community feeling (or communitas) and cooperation, forces that validate one's identity or respectability in a social context. Because Sutton-Smith identifies Selfwith the drive that seeks out individual "peak experiences," I rename it Solitude to emphasize that it empowers Frostian characters' lonely epiphanic searches. And Sutton-Smith's idea of the Imaginary (I call it Imagination) is highly apposite to Frost's playful epiphanic practice.

Frost's playfulness is bound up with the quest for imaginative epiphanies, and Sutton-Smith shows how seriousness and play have been historically linked through Imagination. He connects Imagination to the poetic exuberance of Romanticism and to the satirical dialogism of Bakhtinian carnival, both of which blend seriousness with play: for the philosophic Romanticist Schiller, serious imaginative art was at the same time the most human form of play; obversely, Bakhtin finds the satiric-dialogic mood of carnival gaiety at the root of much serious literary protest.

It is not surprising that Frost, well grounded in Romantic tradition, would blend seriousness and play in the epiphanic quest. But to this I would add that, for Frost, the drive toward Solitude and the equally irresistible need for a sense of communitas, like seriousness and play, encounter each other in the realm of Imagination. This psychologically crucial encounter, in a Frostian epiphany, is likely to be as anxiously ambivalent as it is intense, mysterious, and resonant.

To analyse the ambivalent interpersonal play-epiphanies of Frost I will identify both their subjective and objective features.6 I define a literary epiphany as an experience felt by the reader to be intense, mysterious, and expansive in meaning-signifying more than such a brief moment would normally have any right to mean. Using this definition of epiphany based on its subjective effects on the reader, I then identify, as objective criteria, recurrent formal features that, taken together, constitute a recognizable pattern unifying a given writer's epiphanic oeuvre.

These formal indicators, derived from the thinking of phenomenologist Gaston Bachelard, include (1) patterns of motion, (2) elements-in the ancient sense of earth, water, air, and fire, (3) shapes-often linked to elements, as trees are associated with earth or birds with air, (4) colors, including black and white, and (5) sounds and silences. After specifying the component features of Frost's epiphanic pattern, I locate and describe in detail his paradigm epiphany, the one privileged moment where the formal features of the pattern are most vividly presented and clearly developed. I devote the remainder of the analysis to more fragmentary or attenuated variants of Frost's paradigm, unfolding their implicit social psychology of epiphanic questing as ambivalent, conflicted play.

The strongest epiphanies of Robert Frost manifest a readily recognizable pattern of motions, shapes, elements, colors, sounds, and silences. The motion pattern features two contrasting types of movement frequently appearing together, as if to symbolize the necessary coexistence and interdependence of the two contrasting attitudes they express: solitary questing and community tradition, imaginative loneliness and companionship.8 There is, first, the motion of the solitary seeker toward an undefined imaginative goal. In contrast, the person or entity embodying the values of communitas or would-be companionship in Frostian epiphanies has three choices: (1) not to move, (2) to move in a direction opposite or contrasting to that of the Solitary, and (3) to pursue the Solitary in a game of hide-and-seek, a frequent and favored motion scenario.

No type of Frostian epiphanic movement or immobility can attain its meaning except in contrast with its actual or implicit contrary. The solitary seeker and the collectivity, individual and community, confirm and define each other, though tensions are palpable. Frostian players of hide-and-seek are never "caught" except on their own terms or by their own consent. Yet solitude and companionship, the reclusive independence of the poetic wanderer (option A) and the conventional security of communitas (option B), need not be embodied in distinct persons in a Frostian epiphany. Instead, the two tendencies or "voices" often compete within the mind of a single epiphanist-persona who hovers playfully and guiltily between them-like "voices" of rebellious independence and parental caution in the mind of a growing child.

Frostian epiphanic shapes can be quasi-geometrical, natural forms, or barely definable flashings, flutters, or gleams. The predominant geometric shape in a Frostian epiphany is a rounded, circular, or cylindrical enclosure, formed by a tunnel, a well, a dark pool, a fern wreath, or trees in a forest. At times the dark enclosure may take a squarish outline, such as a dark house, or even a grey woodpile felt to contain a hidden, slow-burning fire. Among natural and nature-like forms, Frost favors trees and birds, or a birdlike white wave or fluttering book page. A single tree may be the locus or agent of a revelation, or a group of trees may be the epiphanic site. Birds, associated with trees, are central to Frostian epiphany; Frost makes the two images evoke each other, and he links birds and trees to music. Lastly, Frost favors sudden flashings, flutters, or gleams of whiteness, often in dark enclosures or on dark backgrounds, and often related to his birds and waves.

Fascinated by the indefinable or ambivalent, Frost may blend sound with silence in his epiphanies. As just noted, birds and trees suggest music: panpipes appear as a forest emblem or "sylvan sign," and even morning-glory vines, a diminutive thicket, recall harp strings. Yet, paradoxically, silence-or the muffling of sound-may be as crucial to these epiphanies as music. The poet's song may be "swallowed up" by a throatlike enclosure of trees, or a distant violin may be heard, or a woman may have "on her lips" a song "only to herself," or pipes may be muted as a new music is pondered. We hear enigmatic or conflicted combinations or blendings of song and silence. Frost may use white noise-the rushing of leaves-to bridge sound and silence, music and tonelessness. Indefinability, indeterminacy, and the linking of opposite ideas open an area where limits are questioned, an ambivalent liminal zone or epiphanic border-realm.

The elements of earth, air, water, and fire interrelate in Frostian epiphanies. Earth predominates because of the sylvan emphasis; woods are abundant. Air is associated with birds, with the rustling music of tree branches, with the breath of song, or with the breath of spirit, of silence. An eddy in a pool may take on a strangely aery, birdlike epiphanic shape. And an abandoned woodpile may seem to burn, warming the forest with its hidden Heraclitean fire of decay. So all four elements contribute to the revelation of the Frostian reclusive seeker.

Just as Frost juxtaposes sound and silence in the ambivalent enclosure of his epiphanies, so, too, he shows a kind of elemental ambiguity embodied in glass, seemingly a solid but really a liquid in suspension. Combining brightness and colorlessness, transparency and reflected light, glass embodies a questioning of categorical limits, a material ambivalence. Frost varies the epiphanic theme of glass as water-mirror, crystal, and quartz, or-audibly-in the crystalline timbre of bells.

Frost, who loves indefinability, can question the limits of tonal and elemental categories, respectively, through the use of a sonar border-concept suggesting indeterminacy (the white noise or pitchless tones of rustling leaves) and by the ambivalent combination of vivid brightness and empty transparency in the solid-liquid anomaly of glass. He similarly questions colour categories by making his epiphanic moments chiefly a matter of black, the non-colour, andor white, the all-colour. (Sometimes the more indeterminate idea of invisibility may substitute for the negative notion of darkness or blackness.) An indeterminate, fluttering or vacillating, birdlike or wavelike white object may appear in a black enclosure, a tunnel, a well, a dark pool. Or a black enclosure may be starkly contrasted with a surrounding or adjacent whiteness (woods on a snowy evening). The category— questioning, the indeterminate, the all-or-nothing, the all-andnothing-such is the focus of a Frostian ambivalent epiphany of blackness or invisibility, andor blank, riddling whiteness.

I have stressed that Frostian solitary epiphanic seeking and community tradition, loneliness and sociability, define each other and thus imply each other by vivid contrast. But we also find in Frost a kind of attempted epiphanic compromise, a shared epiphany that is Solitary- or recluse-friendly, experienced by a select group-sometimes of three persons, like a nuclear family. In such revelatory if transient, always ambivalent compromise between the demands of solitude and society, a black-white contrast may no longer be required: a suspensefully irresolute, erect white "leaf" of an open book may be observed in a lighted room. Shared recluse-friendly epiphanies may show large areas of light: a silver cloud approaches a refulgent moon.

The ambivalent playfulness of the poetic seeker in a Frostian epiphany may involve willfulness, whimsy, mockery, caprice, or teasing-often a teasing secretiveness. Though we find in Frost a few privileged moments of relaxed and playful love, the playfulness in his epiphanies is more commonly of a troubled and troubling kind: it may be prankish, mischievous,10 defiant, ironic, sarcastic, irresponsible, dangerous, even seemingly cruel. It may include feelings of guilt or profanation, at times engendering a twinge-or surge-of regret, an impulse to repent. Frost embodies the playful-epiphanic intermixture of disturbing ironies with appealing imaginative daring in variants of the myth of the willful or mischievous poet-child-god: satire-satyr Pan, self-enwreathed Narcissus.

"A Dream Pang," Frost's playful, interpersonal epiphanic paradigm, displays-in a characteristic mood of intense ambivalence and uneasy equivocation-his recurrent motion pattern (hide-and-seek), shape (enclosure of trees), and interactive elements (woods and wind), his ambivalent blendings of sound and silence (muffled song, white noise of leaves), and the equally central related theme of invisibility. The oneiric power of this oddly unregarded11 dialogic dream sonnet is exemplary, as is the Frostian dialogue between the perspectives of the wouldbe Companion in the opening octet and the would-be Solitary in the sestet's antiphonal response. The two-part epiphany is a play scenario involving secretiveness and pursuit, hide-and-seek:

I had withdrawn in forest, and my song
Was swallowed up in leaves that blew always
And to the forest edge you came one day
(This was my dream) and looked and pondered long
But did not enter, though the wish was strong.
You shook your pensive head as who should say,
"I dare not-too far in his footsteps stray—
He must seek me would he undo the wrong." (1-8)12

The dream game is by no means pure pleasure. It may be narcissistically gratifying that the Companion purportedly has such a strong wish to enter the forest where the Solitary is hiding. But this powerful desire of the Companion may be merely fantasized, while the enunciated reproach is all too real.

The Companion's reluctance to "dare" to enter the forest may seem timid, but the reproof is bold: the Solitary has strayed from the true path and must "undo" such a "wrong." This accusation may be a spouse's or a lover's, but it sounds more like a parent's reprimand stipulating how the child must rectify the offense he has committed; one readily imagines the early childhood origin of the tense dream scenario.13 Not only is the Solitary made to feel guilty in relation to an authoritative Companion, but even the poetic achievement he has effected through his solitude is highly equivocal: the swallowing of his song in leaves, as if in the dark cylindrical throat of the forest, threateningly renders the poet mute. But perpetually blowing leaves can magically make a lovely, quasi-musical rushing sound, and the Solitary may well feel comfortable surrounded by this waterlike white noise, auditory insulation from unwelcome human company. In the sestet we hear his revealingly equivocal reply to the proffered charge of aloofness:

Not far, but near, I stood and saw it all:
Behind low boughs the trees let down outside;
And the sweet pang it cost me not to call
And tell you that I saw does still abide.
But 'tis not true that thus I dwelt aloof,
For the wood wakes, and you are here for proof. (9-14)

The singer admits a continuing sense of guilt, or at least regret. Yet he rejects the imputation of willful coldness. The waking of the wood may mean that the slumbrous dream was not real anyway, that daytime reality has now supervened, replacing defiance with pleasant companionship. Yet the waking of the dream-wood may equally well mean that the nocturnal rebellion was real and that its reality survives into daytime-that the poet's triumphant, secretive defiance in the dream was real then and is real now. The guiltily playful epiphanist-persona, like a rebellious growing child, is torn between apology and apologia.

Everything about this playful-disturbing paradigmatic

dream epiphany is uneasily ambivalent. The enclosure of trees muting the poet's voice is potentially incapacitating but reassuringly protective, too, of the Solitary's fragile independence. The kind of movement in Option A is bolder, more exploratory, than that of option B; the Solitary dares to venture into the dark enclosure, while the Companion does not. The Solitary will not allow himself to be caught except by his own consent, and only in the fantasy context of a concluded dream. His song may be silenced for a while, but the white noise of rustling boughs may well betoken an initiatory entry into a privileged oneiric if ambiguous realm of subtler, more puzzling poetic music.14 Yet when the dream forest awakens, the rebellious quester, too, will awake to a sobering realization: no Solitary can be a poet without help of a hearer. In his conflicted epiphany scenario, the maturing singer demands respect yet feels partly culpable, not wholly secure. Using the categories of Sutton-Smith, we may say that in his playfulness the Solitary has shown Progress toward independence, has asserted Power, has dared Fate, and has courted the charge of Frivolity. Most important, Imagination has produced an epiphany of mysterious, intense if unstable power by playing Solitude against Companionship or communitas. The dream ritual has tested the Solitary's power to tease out or provoke the acceptance, or love, of his importunate, baffled Companion.

Six subtly balanced, conflicted epiphanies-"Pan With Us," "The Good Hours," "For Once, Then, Something," "Stopping by Woods on a Snowy Evening," "The Hill Wife," and "The WoodPile"- show the role options of Solitary and Companion (or Community) competing within the mind of the epiphanist, with results ambivalently varying the play-impulse. Pan, a sylvan poet-child- god, is both older and younger than we might have thought. "His skin and his hair and his eyes were gray, The gray of the moss of walls" (2-3); fearing he may be a superannuated ludic deity, he no longer knows what to do with his classical "pipes of pagan mirth" (26). But as "Pan With Us," the new era's newborn child, he becomes sufficiently Judeo-Christian to suit a more modern world ("Immanuel" means "God with us" [Isaiah 7.14; Matthew 1.23]). As Pan looks "At wooded valley and wooded hill," his heart knows "peace, for none came here"-with a few exceptions, kindred playful "children" who "tell no tales" (5, 11, 14-15)-so he is ready for a solitary sylvan epiphany, less peaceful than ambivalent:

He tossed his pipes, too hard to teach
A new-world song, far out of reach,
For a sylvan sign that the blue-jay's screech
And the whimper of hawks beside the sun
Were music enough for him, for one. (16-20)

Looking away from sun toward the darkened earth, Pan, enclosed now within his own thoughts, poses a question but may well experience it as an ambivalent inward illumination, problematic for a poet: how can any kind of communally shareable music now express, or equal, the deep silence of a newly learned solitary inwardness of spirit? In "Good Hours" the companionable and solitary ways of life confront each other more schematically but with comparable ambivalent playfulness and epiphanic mysteriousness. The twopart epiphany affords equal physical space first to solitary motion outward (option A), and then to the reverse motion back to communitas (option B). In part one the Solitary moves away:

I had for my winter evening walk—
No one at all with whom to talk,
But I had the cottages in a row
Up to their shining eyes in snow.
And I thought I had the folk within;
I had the sound of a violin;
I had a glimpse through curtain laces
Of youthful forms and youthful faces. (1-8)

A poet like every Frostian epiphanist, the Solitary strolls into the realm of fanciful imagination, where cottages, in fairy tale fashion, seem buried up to their "shining," magically bright glassy eyes in the customary Frostian epiphanic enclosures— here, vertical tunnels of snow (though these are, atypically, white enclosures, not dark ones). Music is distant and enclosed, while the human forms can be only glimpsed, barely perceived, so both sounds and shapes must be mostly imagined. That is the joyful prospect of the solitary venture. But, as the homeward journey shows, the hazard-and the unmistakable thrill-is ambivalence:

I had such company outward bound.
I went till there were no cottages found.
I turned and repented, but coming back
I saw no window but that was black.
Over the snow my creaking feet
Disturbed the slumbering village street
Like profanation, by your leave,
At ten o' clock of a winter eve. (9-16)

The Solitary's imaginative acquaintance with the black-andwhite emptiness of a snowy night is felt as if it were a kind of sin, his pleasantly guilt-ridden return to the sacred precincts of community life having the effect of a "profanation"-even after he has "turned and repented"! But the remorse is partly playful, hardly moralistic: it partakes of the guiltily stimulating epiphanic mystery of a child's risky play.15 There can be no true "turning," no conversio, from the "sweet pang" that must arise from this delightfully ambivalent, stealthy joy. The sense of having "[d]isturbed" the torpid repose of a conventional (parental?) communitas by one's lonely boldness offers the indispensable defining context for an epiphany of solitary imaginings. Even if the shining eyes of the windows are now all black, the "good hours"-also the testing, trying hours- of the poem's title are those of departure and return.

The last three exhibits in this group of unresolved confrontational epiphanies wherein solitude encounters community in a context of varied types of playful caprice all feature the motif of glass or mirror (as in the shining window-eyes of the mostly— buried houses we just viewed), a theme that heightens ambivalence through its mutually contrasting reflectiveness and transparency. "For Once, Then, Something" opens with the voice of the community taunting the boy as he plays his mirror-game:

Others taunt me with having knelt at well-curbs
Always wrong to the light, so never seeing
Deeper down in the well than where the water

Gives me back in a shining surface picture
Me with myself in the summer heaven, godlike,
Looking out a wreath of the fern and cloud puffs. (1-6)

The community-voice within the mind of the solitary epiphanic persona decries his desire to see himself reflected in a watery mirror as playful childlike Narcissus, so flatteringly enclosed in an epiphanic circular poet-praising wreath uniting the natural beauties of earth and heaven. (The classical hendecasyllabic meter chosen for this lyric melodiously prompts us to seek ancient mythic analogues.) But the reflectiveness of solitude has deeper resources, revealed in a category-defying epiphanic game of hide-and-seek:

Once, when trying chin against a well-curb,
I discerned, as I thought, beyond the picture,
Through the picture, a something white, uncertain,
Something more of the depths-and then I lost it.
Water came to rebuke the too clear water.
One drop fell from a fern, and lo, a ripple
Shook whatever it was lay there at bottom,
Blurred it, blotted it out. What was that whiteness?
Truth? A pebble of quartz? For once, then, something. (7-16)

Quartz, which can be both crystalline-mirrorlike and white (the inclusive all-colour), now seemingly appears at the bottom of the deep, dark well, the Frostian cylindrical epiphanic enclosure, to create a black-and-white epiphany of the ambivalences of poetic solitude: narcissism-transcending yet resolutely independent, reflection-penetrating yet reflective, questionable yet possibly, strangely, truth-telling. The epiphany is indeterminate, its meaning undecidable (only a seeming white "something" amid a dark nothing), a tantalizing perceptual and ontological hide-and-seek game.

In "Stopping by Woods on a Snowy Evening," where the colour-transcending interrelated opposites black and white are starkly contrasted as a Solitary watches woods "fill up with snow" on the "darkest evening of the year" (14,8), the Frostian epiphanic motifs of music and glass together signal the Solitary's ambivalently capricious-but-privileged moment.

When the horse gives its "harness bells a shake To ask if there is some mistake," playfully16 dramatizing what seems the traveler's highly capricious choice to stop suddenly at the forest's border, we note in this signal a musical, crystalline token of an ambivalent revelation-to-come from a Frostian dark enclosure: "The woods are lovely, dark, and deep" (9-10, 13). "But I have promises to keep, And miles to go before I sleep, And miles to go before I sleep" (14-16)-the voice of communitas tells of social responsibilities to be heeded, promises to be honored. Communitas directs the pattern of motion (along the social road of duty, not into the solitary wood of desire), yet it hardly has the last word. That final word, "sleep," belongs instead to the delights of the beckoning, re-echoing, dark sylvan enclosure, to the ominous deeps of ever— ambivalent solitary inwardness with its riddlingly two-sided closure-and-opening into unconscious sources of death-and-life.

Q. Draw a character sketch of Robert Frost ?

Or

Q. Discuss the life and works of Robert Frost ?

Robert Frost is one of the few twentieth century poets to receive critical acclaim and popular acceptance. His simplistic style appeals to the novice and expert poetry reader alike. Robert Frost's understated emotional appeal attracts readers of all literary levels. Frost develops subtly stated emotions and a clever use of imagery in his poetry. Influences on his poetry include his family, work, and other life experiences. Frost also works to develop iambic pentameter using simple language, in an attempt to effectively portray the New England lifestyle.

Frost successfully blends classic poetry and a modern simplicity to create a new generation of poetry lovers. Frost's poetry is greatly influenced by his life experiences. To understand his poetry, it seems necessary to understand the man himself. Ironically enough, the famed New England poet is born on the West Coast and named for a Confederate general. Robert Lee Frost is born on March 26, 1874 in San Francisco. He is the first child of Isabelle and William Prescott Frost Jr. His father dies when he is eleven, prompting him to move to Lawrence, MA to live with his grandparents. Although he seems bright, young Frost dislikes academics and drops out of school in each of his first three years (Poirier).

Frost eventually graduates second in his high school class and attends, and later teaches at prestigious colleges and universities, such as Dartmouth and Harvard. However, unwilling to commit his life solely to academic pursuits, Frost seeks a simpler lifestyle, working at such jobs as bobbin boy at a mill, making shoes, editing, teaching, and farming. This craftsmanship affects his writing. Frost seeks to put complex meaning into each of his poems, while each verse remains "as simple and honest as an axe or hoe." Frost uses this simple writing style throughout his poetic career. Frost combines this unadorned style with an ability to blend common language with artistic expressions. Frost first learns the beauty of the straightforward, manner of speech from the rural people of New England: "On his New Hampshire farm he discovered this in the character of a man with whom he used to drive along the country roads,". His first books, A Boy's Will and North of Boston, which reflect this discovery are published in 1914 and gain him instant status as a unique and talented poet. Frost wrote these books after he had moved to England in 1912 to pursue a full time writing career and upon his return to America in 1915.

He is pleasantly surprised to find his poetry gaining popularity among poetry readers. Many critics also delight in this promising young poet. Poetic scholars marvel at his exceptional ability to learn from the best English and American poets, while at the same time retaining his own identity. Robert Frost studies poetry for years, practicing and refining his own style. He assumes the qualities of each poet that he enjoys most, and fuses them with his own. For example, much of Frost's poetry is written in iambic pentameter. He attempts to listen to New Englanders' naturally iambic rhythm and adopt it into his poetry.

By using iambic pentameter, Frost shows that ordinary people can talk and argue within a medium that William Shakespeare and John Milton in the 16th and 17th Centuries had reserved for aristocrats and angels (Thompson 142). Such authors and poets as Shelley, Wordsworth, and Emerson also influence Frost. However, by far the most influential writer on Frost's is another famous New England naturalist, Henry David Thoreau. Many critics have discussed the connection between Frost and Thoreau. Frost read Thoreau's Walden several times during the course of his life. The subject matter that each writer addresses often concerns Mother Nature.

It cannot be denied that Frost and Thoreau are great admirers of Nature. Each writer uses nature as a prevalent subject in his or her works. Frost and Thoreau share great optimism for nature in their writing, yet they are also aware of the complexity nature brings upon them. Frost and Thoreau both partake in nature in their lives and writings, and their works are filled with natural imagery. Both feel a strong relationship with nature. Frost's connection with nature is unambiguous. In the poem Trees at My Window the narrator respects nature for what it is, as Frost writes: "Tree at my window, window tree My sash is lowered when night comes on; But let there never be curtain drawn Between you and me." It is clear that that the narrator recognizes that man is separate from nature, yet at the same time has a longing to connect. In much of Frosts' poetry, imagery of nature is both revered and feared. Frost seems aware of a connection between man and nature, yet restricted by an inability to fully connect.

This feeling is also very clearly displayed in the writings of Thoreau. True-life tragedies also manifest themselves in Frost's poetry. At a young age Robert Frost witnesses his father's excessive drinking, as well as his illness and death of consumption. This matter is only the beginning of his problems. In the year 1899 Frost's four-year-old son Elliot dies of cholera. The same year his mother is diagnosed with advanced cancer, institutionalized, and dies as a result of her illness (Poirier). Eight years later, Frost's daughter Elinor is born, but dies only three days afterwards. In 1920, his sister's insanity forces him to commit her to an institution. Some time later, his daughter Irma suffers a similar fate and is confined for mental disorder.

Other events that rock Frost's life include his son Carol's suicide, his daughter Marjorie's death of puerperal fever in 1934, and his wife Elinor's death of heart failure in 1938. All of these tragic events influenced Frost's poetry. Much of Frost's poetry reflects these dark emotions that result. Frost expresses these emotions through imagery of nature. The author Robert French, who wrote a critical essay about Frost, points out that Frost's narrator feels a fear of darkness in nauture. Even though Frost writes with a certain joy about nature he also expresses a tone of uneasiness and even fear towards nature. This fear is expressed more often in Frost's later poetry, as his life became more and more difficult. Because of this more somber tone Frost loses some of his critical appeal, but his following is larger than ever. Throughout and following his career, Frost enjoys the respect of most critics. However, some criticize him for his over simplicity. The problem with over simplifying his statement poetry is that many interpretations can be taken from a given poem. Without detail, "the reader is left to interpret meaning, which often results in over interpretation. Few critics argue, however, that Frost is a master of rhyming and rhythm. His poem "Departmental" is noted for its clever rhyme scheme.

Frost's ability in this particular field aids him in becoming one of the most well recognized and rewarded writers in American history. In addition to several other awards, Frost becomes the first writer to receive four Pulitzer Prizes in 1924, 1931, 1937, and 1943. However, the most impressive evidence of Frost's influence relate to his social impact. By the year 1950, Frost is much more than a masterful poet; he is an icon. The United States Congress adopts a resolution in that year to honour Frost's seventy-fifth birthday (it is actually his seventy-sixth, but Frost believes that he was born in 1875). The Vermont State Legislature names a mountain for Frost (Poirier). Eisenhower invites Frost to the White House in 1958. President John F.

Kennedy invites Frost to read at his inauguration, and then asks the aging poet to serve on several goodwill missions to the Soviet Union. These far-reaching social impacts are evidence of Frost's influence. Frost gains such influence because of his critical and popular appeal. His simple writing style invites readers of all levels and ages to read his work. Many of Frost's contemporaries, as well as poets that follow in his wake, try to emulate this simple writing style. His ingenious rhythmic patterns are now taught in nearly every advanced poetry class. Frost's poetry expands poetry into a new era, in which any given poem can be read and enjoyed by readers of all literary levels. Frost's poetry is appreciated in mainstream social circles, as well as societies of the critical elite.

Frost introduces a new generation of poetry readers and writers. His unique style has encouraged the likes of Maya Angelou and others to blend classical styles with their own individual flare. Robert Frost is a unique and influential author. His poetry merges the rhyming schemes of old with an unsophisticated manner of speech, accomplishing unparalleled success. Frost has accumulated numerous awards and honorary recognitions. Novice poetry readers and poetic experts alike respect his work. His poetry about the rural New England individualists contains beautifully subtle emotions and feelings. Frost's poetry reaches to the far ends of the social spectrum, initiating a new brand of poetic enthusiasts and rhymesters.

Q. Write a Passage on the Nature Imagery in the Works of Robert Frost ?

Or

Q. What is the significance of Nature Imagery in Poems of Robert Frost ?

Many of Robert Frost's poems explore the splendor of the outdoors. In poems such as "A Prayer in Spring" and "To the Thawing Wind," the speakers show appreciation of nature's beauty surrounding them. However, "A Servant to Servants" is a contrast to the typical Frostian nature poem. The poem's speaker, the wife of a hard-working farmer, no longer takes pleasure in her beautiful surroundings. She feels trapped in a life that, to her, seems meaningless, under appreciated by her husband and the hired hands she cooks for. She explains her monotonous daily routine and subtly reveals her desperation. The speaker knows she is falling victim to the insanity that runs in her family, but although she perceives what is happening, she is unable to change her situation.

Frost wrote "A Servant to Servants" using iambic pentameter, although he varies the meter, such as in line 20, "Like a deep piece of some old running river." This, aided by his frequent use of enjambed lines, makes the poem sound more conversational, rather than following a rigid meter. He includes colloquialisms in the woman's speech so that the reader hears a realistic farm woman. There is no apparent rhyme scheme, also adding to the conversational flavour of the dramatic monologue. A rhyme in a serious poem like "A Servant to Servants" would run the risk of de-emphasizing the poem's content while calling more attention to the rhyme. This is evident in "Blueberries", where Frost writes rhymed couplets throughout the poem and cannot help but create a lighter tone.

At the start of "A Servant to Servants," the speaker is conversing with a man who has been camping on her land. She reveals her happiness that he is there and mentions that she had meant to visit him. "I promised myself to get down some day And see the way you livedŠ With a houseful of hungry men to feed I guess you'd findŠ" Although she wanted to see how her guest was living, she is trapped by the routine of her endless cooking duties. She didn't take the initiative to visit him, which reveals that she does not see the possibility of change in her monotonous life. Even a disruption in her schedule for a quick visit was impossible.

Then the speaker explains that she no longer feels emotion and has trouble expressing herself, foreshadowing the inevitability of her fate. "I can't express my feelings any more," she says. "It's got so I don't even know for sure Whether I am glad, sorry, or anything." She goes on to describe the lake outside her window as an example. It's evidently a beautiful thing to look at, but she no longer enjoys it. Perhaps the lake represents the freedom that exists in nature‹a freedom the speaker cannot have in her role as an under-appreciated wife and cook.

She has to "make [her]self repeat out loud The advantages it has." (18-19) This refers back to her statement that because she doesn't feel emotion, she has to tell herself "how I ought to feel." She wants to conform to her role, but although she knows what she "should" think and what she "should" feel, she cannot think or feel these things. The lake, just like her life, has lost its beauty.

Then, she asks the man how he had heard of their land. Frost does not write the camper's responses in the poem, unlike conversational poems such as "The Generations of Men" or "The Fear." There is no need to break up the woman's monologue with insignificant words of an outsider. "A Servant to Servants" focuses entirely on the speaker's rambling speech to the camper, who merely provides the audience she needs. Interrupting her stream of consciousness would only disrupt the poem's flow. However, the woman repeats the man's answer, making it known that he heard of her land in a fern book. "In a book about ferns? Listen to that! You let things more like feathers regulate Your going and coming," she says, amazed at her guest's whimsical behaviour. (35-7) Again, nature represents freedom. The speaker wishes that she could come and go as she pleased, living in the simplicity of nature, but she is chained to her daily routine.

The speaker then reveals some characteristics of her husband, Len. He is an optimist, totally absorbed in his work, believing that their land will be worth something with time, and that his wife will "be all right With doctoring." However, just as no one appreciates the land, the speaker is likewise unappreciated. She knows that living such a mundane, meaningless life is slowly driving her insane, yet she accepts this. She needs a break "From cooking meals for hungry hired men And washing dishes after them‹from doing Things over and over that just won't stay done," yet the speaker takes Len's advice that "the best way out is always through." (50-2, 56) She knows that there is no escaping her destiny. "As that I can see no way out but through‹ Leastways for me‹and then they'll be convinced." She knows that she is beyond the help of doctors and their medicine, but Len is so caught up with his work, "from sun to sun," that he doesn't notice his wife's deteriorating situation.

She tells the camper about the indolent hired hands that take advantage of her absorbed husband. The woman resents that she has to continuously cook and clean up after these lazy men, "great good-for-nothings, Sprawling about the kitchen with their talk While I fry their bacon." (76-8) Although she works as hard as her husband, even the hired men don't appreciate her efforts. She is a "servant to servants."

The speaker then describes the insanity that runs in her family. She had been put into the State Asylum at one point in her life, but feels that the state institution is better than being kept at home. It was the common belief that the asylum was the "poorhouse," and those who could afford it should care for mentally ill family members. She argues that at the asylum, "they have every means proper to do with, And you aren't darkening other people's lives‹ Worse than no good to them." (98-100) Perhaps this is foreshadowing her own situation‹she already feels unnoticed in her work. Also, the speaker comments that "You can't know Affection or the want of it in that state," referring back to her remark that she no longer feels emotion. She seems unable to avoid her progressing insanity.

The woman's uncle had been mentally ill, kept in a cage of hickory poles built by his family. Because he would tear up any furniture they tried to give him, "they made the place comfortable with straw, Like a beast's stall, to ease their consciences." This physical cage may be symbolic of the speaker's own cage‹her unsatisfying life and unbreakable routine. Though the family meant well by caring for the speaker's uncle, they reduced him to the state of an animal. This experience is probably why the woman is in favour of the State Asylum. "I've heard too much of the old-fashioned way," she admits. Her uncle would yell at night, keeping her mother awake. "She had to lie and hear love things made dreadful By his shouts in the night," the speaker describes. She goes on to say that "they found a way to put a stop to it." This "way" is not revealed, allowing the reader to imagine what they could have done to quiet the caged man.

Although the uncle died before the speaker was born, the cage remained upstairs‹a constant lurking presence of madness. The woman would joke, "It's time I took my turn upstairs in jail," again foreshadowing her own insanity. When she finally moved away with Len, she thought the change would make her happy. However, she had merely escaped from one unfavorable set of circumstances to the next. She had her attractive natural surroundings, but "the change wore out like a prescription," she states ironically. (161) The beauties of nature couldn't mask unhappiness caused by her situation. However, she seems to accept her impending insanity, speaking in a matter-of-fact tone about such subjects. She says, "I'm past such help‹ Unless Len took the notion, which he won't, And I won't ask himŠ I s'pose I've got to go the road I'm going." (163-6)

Then, she seems to remember that the camper is listening to her soliloquy. She mentions that she wishes she could live as he does‹to "drop everything and live out on the ground." She quickly changes her mind, saying that she may not like the night in the outdoors, or the rain. Although her mundane life behind kitchen walls constrains her, she is drawn towards it. There is no escaping the inevitable. She sees herself too weak to live as the camper does. "I haven't courage for a risk like that," she explains. She knows the only way out of her seemingly meaningless existence is to break the routine that imprisons her, but she is unable to do it. She knows that she is destined to insanity, yet accepts this without a battle. She even jokes about it when speaking of the hired hands, saying, "I'm not afraid of them, though, if they're not Afraid of me." (85-6) She tells the camper, "The worst that you can do Is set me back a little more behind. I sha'n't catch up in this world, anyway." (182-4)

Finally, the speaker answers the question that the camper had most likely come to ask. "I'd rather you'd not go unless you must." She wants to see an example of someone living freely‹someone who can travel from place to place, based on locations he reads about in fern books. The camper is a foil to the speaker. While he is capricious, taking what nature gives him, the woman is trapped by routine and looming insanity, unable to change her fate. Because she has no hope for herself, she enjoys thinking about and watching this man taking pleasure in nature that she no longer finds beautiful.

A constant symbol in this poem is nature representing freedom. Like her tragic uncle, the speaker is trapped in a cage‹the endless job of cooking for her husband's hired men. This task will never bring her satisfaction, and yet she has no other options. She is the wife of a farmer, with limited finances and limited opportunity. Although she appreciates the idea of living in freedom like the camper, she knows that for her, this is impossible. Nature has lost its beauty because she knows she will never be the recipient of the freedom it represents. The outdoors used to take "[her] mind off doughnuts and soda biscuit To step outdoors and take the water dazzle A sunny morning," but it no longer has this effect. She has accepted her fate as the wife of a man too absorbed in his work to notice her, and as an unappreciated cook for hired men, a servant to servants.

Chapter 9

Critical Essays on Robert Frost's Poetry

Learning to Hover: Robert Frost, Robert Francis, and the Poetry of Detached Engagement

In Robert Francis's reminiscence of Robert Frost, A Time to Talk, the entry dated April 4, 1932, contains a poem published the day before in the Springfield Republican and Union. Francis wrote the poem to commemorate Frost's arrival at Amherst. Here are its final stanzas:

Best of all—you've heard?—he comes to stay.
This is his home now. He is here for good.
To leave us now would be running away.
(I too would stay forever if I could.)
While he stays, life that breathless fugitive,
Will stay. While he lives, some things here won't die.
And we, breathing his air, may learn to live
Close to the earth, like him, and near the sky.

An example of Francis's exuberant juvenilia, the lyric was, in his words, "the first pop gun fired in my private campaign to establish a significant relation with this most significant man in town" (48-49). The following January, he befriended Frost in his home on Sunset Avenue in Amherst; thereafter blossomed a relationship in which the younger poet found in Frost a mentor. In fact, he recalled, when he made Frost's acquaintance, he "was still unpublished in book form, a young poet looking for guidance. So Frost took the role of mentor, and much that he said had to do with my own poems and my problems as a poet".

After his second book, Valhalla and Other Poems, was published in 1938, the volume "made no stir anywhere", Francis wrote in his autobiography, The Trouble with Francis. But if the book failed to excite critical notice, it brought "some quiet rewards", one of which was a letter from Robert Frost:

I am swept off my feet by the goodness of your poems this time. Ten or a dozen of them are my idea of perfection. A new poet swims into my ken. I can refrain from strong praise no longer. You are achieving what you live for. You have not only the feeling of a true lyric poet, but the variety of a man with a mind.

Francis's mention of Frost's letter is important because Frost's praise was a formal recognition of his poetry. The letter also provided evidence of Frost's influence on Francis: note that his praise of Francis's poems is reserved for those that are "[his] idea of perfection". Not surprisingly, then, there is a sort of Frost static everywhere in this volume. Compare a passage from Francis's "Valhalla"-

The valley sees the pasture on the hill.
Below the pasture and above are woods
Up to the wooded peak up to the sky.
The valley sees the darkness of evergreens
Waiting above the pasture to come down
As other evergreens have come or wait
To come to darken pastures on other hills.

—to an excerpt from Frost's poem, "The Mountain":

The mountain stood there to be pointed at.
Pasture ran up the side a little way,
And then there was a wall of trees with trunks;
After that only tops of trees, and cliffs
Imperfectly concealed among the leaves.

As David Graham observes, the echoes of Frost in Francis's early poems helped shape a critical view that Francis was "a minor lyricist perpetually standing in Frost's broad shadow". Reviews of Francis's early volumes focused on the thematic resemblance of his writing to Frost's. Consider, for instance, Louis Untermeyer's critique of Francis's third book,

The Sound I Listened For, whose poems accentuate what he asserts is Francis's "gift for seeing minutiae which are anything but trivial." "In this," Untermeyer animadverts, "he reminds the reader of his more illustrious forerunners, especially of one whose background is contiguous. It is nothing against Robert Francis that he often resembles Robert Frost." And though Untermeyer admires Francis's lyrics for the way in which "they blend observation with imagination," he adds, finally, "[b]ut we know who wrote them first".

Untermeyer's praise of Francis's perceptiveness provides a critical basis for a comparison of Frost's and Francis's poetry. Like Frost, Francis sees nature emblematically; he reads meaning in the things and creatures of the world. He also approaches Frost in translating his perception of nature's moral significance into a code of conduct. This way of seeing traces back to Emerson, Thoreau, and the influence on them of classical Stoicism, which emphasizes, as Robert D. Richardson Jr. argues, turning to nature for instruction as to "how one's life should be lived".

However, Francis and Frost depart from Emerson and Thoreau in their willingness to probe nature's dark design, and move even further from them in their readiness to explore a corresponding experiential darkness, which expresses itself as psychological loneliness. While both poets exhibit wariness at entering the darkness they describe, they differ in the stances they take up in relation to it. In Frost's case, this state of m ind is defined by Richard Poirier as "a sense of 'nothingness' or a condition of vacancy", which he argues Frost contrives in order that he may resist it. When Frost adopts a posture of resistance, he becomes his own ideal version of himself. He then extends his self-idealization from the poems to the fictions he creates about how easily he composed them.

In Francis's case, the stance he takes up in the face of loneliness is one of detachment, a detachment that is paradoxically an engagement in that he displays (to borrow Poirier's phrase) a "contemplative receptivity" rather than a resistance to his "vacant" condition. Ironically, Francis adopted this stance on the advice of Frost, whose words are invoked in the poem "For the Ghost of Robert Frost." Here, Francis pictures detached engagement as the hovering of a hummingbird over a flower, defining, in the process, an important way in which he has outgrown Frost:

"You've got to learn to hover,"
He said. The way a hummingbird
Hovers over a flower, the way
The flower's fragrance hovers over it.
Not to move on, not to
Keep jumping like a nervous grasshopper
But to hover there until you
Have gathered all that is there
For you or anyone to gather.
"You've got to learn to hover."

The motif of detachment persists throughout Francis's career, but early on reveals itself amid stylistic echoes of Frost. For example, in "Blue Winter," from Valhalla and Other Poems, his painterly description of a landscape that recedes into the distance and converges at a starry point in the horizon showcases, as Francis records in A Time to Talk, what Frost calls his "ability to fit sentences and lines together". In its concision of expression, its use of conversational language, its shifting of stresses in a line for flexibility and variety, and its blending of sounds (as in "shade" into "shadows"), Francis's poem bears a strong affinity with Frost's writing:

Winter uses all the blues there are.
One shade of blue for water, one for ice.
Another blue for shadows over snow.
The clear or cloudy sky uses blue twice-
Both different blues. And hills row after row
Are colored blue according to how far.
You know the bluejay's double blue device
Shows best when there are no green leaves to show.
And Sirius is a winterbluegreen star.

Indeed, when Frost showed the lyric to Untermeyer, hoping to persuade him to publish Francis's poetry, Untermeyer replied that Francis's "lyric style, casual yet compact, reminded me so much of Robert's that until I learned better, I thought my leg was being pulled and that Robert Francis was an alter ego Robert Frost had invented by slightly altering his last name". As "Blue Winter" illustrates, Francis's colloquial idiom and "casual yet compact" style are directed toward a clear perception of nature.

To understand the role that perception plays in Francis's work is to explore the ways in which his poetry most importantly resembles Frost's. Untermeyer's observation that Francis shares Frost's "gift for seeing minutiae which are anything but trivial" suggests that Francis displays in his poems a penchant for perceiving nature "less for itself and more for what it represents". While the natural objects he describes reflect a perception decidedly pastoral as far as their literal preoccupations are concerned, his poems, like Frost's, translate nature's forms into emblems of moral values; the things and creatures of the world become metaphors for human conduct. Take, for instance, another passage from "Valhalla," in which spruce trees serve as an image of endurance:

The dark trees on the peak, the pointed spruces,
Seem to those who see them always the same-
Dark in summer, dark in winter, dark
And undisturbed from year to year by fall
Or wind or rain or frost or snow or spring.
They keep the peak, holding and held by rock,
Holding and fed by soil once tree and rock.
So they endure.

Similarly, in Frost's "Blueberries," the thriving of these fruits in a pasture ravaged by fire is, as the speaker suggests, evidence of their perseverance and hardiness:

There may not have been the ghost of a sign
Of them anywhere under the shade of a pine,
But get the pine out of the way, you may burn
The pasture all over until not a fern
Or grass-blade is left, not to mention a stick,
And presto, they're up all around you as thick
And hard to explain as a conjuror's trick.

The idea of perceiving commonplace natural forms as

metaphors for conduct derives from the transcendentalists, in particular from Emerson and Thoreau, in works such as "Nature" and Walden. Emerson set forth the notion of a radical correspondence between humans and nature—what he termed "an occult relation"—in which the "laws of moral nature answer to those of matter as face to face in a glass" (18). Or, as he puts it later in "Nature," "every natural process is a version of a moral sentence".

Echoing Emerson, Thoreau writes in his journal, "the perception of beauty is a moral test" (10:126). As Richardson points Out in Henry Thoreau, Thoreau and Emerson turned to classical Stoicism (among other philosophical traditions) for their ideas about seeing nature as an emblem of values. Drawing on the Stoic perception of nature as a "source of trustworthy moral principles" from which one can develop a basis for ethical conduct, Thoreau and Emerson work out, in their writings, "the meaning of the Stoic idea th at the laws ruling nature rule men as well".

To the extent that Frost and Francis perceive moral values in nature, they follow the philosophical lead of their literary forebears. For example, consider Frost's poems that celebrate the virtue of letting nature take its course, a stance that correlates, as he once told Francis, with his "laissez-faire" inclination to "let the world come as it would, only giving it now and then 'a kick and a touch'". To illustrate Frost's inclination, Francis cites two of his poems in A Time to Talk. Francis summarizes the argument of "In Time of Cloudburst" as follows:

[Y]ou wait a geological age for your eroded farm to sink out of sight and for a new farm of rich alluvial soil to rise from the sea. If you protest that this is too long a time, Frost might reply that this is what will actually happen, whether you wait or not.

In "Something for Hope," the political implication of the doctrine of laissez-faire is explicit. Here Frost preaches patience if a rocky meadow becomes overgrown with weeds that have "crowded out the edible grass." Instead of plowing out the weeds, he advises us to do nothing at all. Wait for the trees to "put on their wooden rings," Frost writes, and come in on their own. Once they are mature,

Then cut down the trees when lumber grown,
And there's your pristine earth all freed
From lovely blooming but wasteful weed
And ready again for the grass to own.
A cycle we'll say of a hundred years.
Thus foresight does it and laissez-faire.
A virtue in which we all may share
Unless a government interferes.
Patience and looking away ahead,
And leaving some things to take their course.
Hope may not nourish a cow or horse,
But spes alit agricolam 'tis said.

Perhaps less obvious than the way in which Frost's poetics reflect his conservative politics is the attitude toward nature that his inclination implies. To let nature take its course and allow things to grow as they please is to assume a passive attitude, one which, at least in these poems, presupposes that nature's processes are benign. This inclination thus constitutes one aspect of Frost's doubleness in that it contrasts with his stance of resistance discussed later in this essay.

This doctrine is also explicit in what Frost has to say concerning his career, art, and method of poetic composition. About his own success, Frost remarked to Francis, "he had never lifted a finger to advance his career and that what had come to him had just come to him". (This statement, as I point out later on, proves to be disingenuous.) As in his career, so in his theory for writing poetry.

In a comment he made to Francis that was recorded in A Time to Talk, he was adamant that "a poem not only should but must be written in a single free-flowing run". "Like a piece of ice on a hot stove," he wrote in "The Figure a Poem Makes," "the poem must ride on its own melting" (Selected Poems 4). In his writing, especially in the longer blank-verse poems, as well as the eclogues and dialogues, Frost's "custom of composing in a free flow" (A Time to Talk is skillfully fitted to open poetic forms that accommo date the flexible iambic rhythms of common speech, an d so provide the feel of language spontaneously uttered.

Francis, too, celebrates the virtues represented by nature, but he lives the life in art that Frost only says he will live. A good example of Francis's habit of seeing natural objects as metaphors for conduct is a short poem called "Mountain Blueberries." Part exposition and part description, it takes as its starting point the poet's response to the appearance of blueberries that he encounters during a solitary mountain walk. After the first stanza, in which he tries to account for his discovery of the berries in so remote a terrain, he uses description in the second stanza to suggest that they represent qualities rich in meaning, qualities similar to those hinted at in Frost's "Blueberries":

These blueberries belong to birds
If they belong to anyone.
Who else could have planted them but birds
Three thousand feet up towards the sun?
They live on sunshine, dust of granite,
A little rain, a little dew.
In shape a miniature moon or planet,
In colour distant-mountain blue.

Writing about "Mountain Blueberries" in "Two Poets Named Robert," Donald Hail observes that it is "a poem about making do on little". As it pertains to Francis's own life, the poem has a special significance. After the poet moved into his own home, Fort Juniper, in 1940, he lived deliberately, along Thoreauvian lines. Determined to "cultivate the art of living without money" (The Trouble with Francis, he got rid of his old car and decided not to keep a telephone; he made "full use of everything [he] possessed" and threw out "everything [he] didn't need"; he cultivated a modest garden and grew his own vegetables, herbs, and small fruits; and in a letter addressed to Thoreau that is included in his autobiography, Francis espoused, in Hall's words, "the pleasures and virtues of eating soybeans". As it reflects a life based on principles of strict economy, "Mountain Blueberries" is a model of resourcefulness, combining brevity of structure with richness of meaning, while satisfying, as Fran cis writes in A Time to Talk, what Frost means by form: "proportion of thought and its proportioning in the poem"

If the transcendentalists' essential influence on Frost and Francis was to encourage them to read meaning in natural objects, both poets part company with them in their focus on nature's dark truths. Two such poems whose similar subject matter reflects this focus are Frost's sonnet "The Oven Bird," published in 1916, and Francis's "The Wood Pewee," published in Valhalla and Other Poems. However, this similarity is less significant than the differences that divide Frost from Francis and here concern their tone and imagery. As in Frost's sonnet, Francis translates the song of a New England wood bird into words, hearing in its midsummer tune a portent of autumn's advent. Just as the ovenbird intones "that leaves are old" and "the highway dust is over all", so the wood pewee sings of "the end of summer," the encroachment of fall, and the waning of the year:

In the shade of a tree in the heat of an afternoon
The wood pewee sings its portamento tune
That summer is over-ripe and autumn is soon.
He sings from a twig after flitting to catch a fly.
And whether he sings September or July
He sings of the end of summer and sings goodby.

A harsher quality characterizes Frost's poem, one that is born from scattered images of dryness and diminishment that appear in it. The ovenbird's reminder of the dwindling of flowers from spring to midsummer links nature's diminution to the cycles of birth and death. He says the petals of "pear and cherry bloom" that once fell during brief vernal showers are now overlaid by the "highway dust" that covers "all" ("dust" is itself an intimation of mortality). In the face of seasonal desiccation and the inexorable coming on of autumn, with its withering leaves, the ovenbird knows, unlike "other birds," not to sing a melodious and winsome tune. Or, as Frost puts it, "he knows in singing not to sing".

By contrast, Francis stresses the lyrical beauty of the wood pewee's song, most notably in the shading of vowel sounds in "tree," "heat," and "pewee," and in the choice of the Italian "portamento," which emphasizes the shifting pitch of the bird's lilting tune. Then, Francis plays on short i sounds to accentuate not only the music of the pewee's tune but also the nimbleness of his movement, as the bird "sings from a twig after flitting to catch a fly." Of course, Frost too strings sounds together for a lyrical effect (as in the chiming e sounds of "petal," "pear," and "cherry" in lines 6-7).

It's simply the case that Francis indulges here in a kind of preciousness that tempers the terse and pedagogical conclusion of his poem. Unlike Francis, Frost "knows in singing not to sing." As a result, Francis's poems, generally speaking, do not achieve the bleak axiomatic eloquence that is characteristic of Frost's best lyrics. They rarely rise to the bitter pitch of "The Oven Bird," whose song Frost ultimately "f rames in a "question" ("what to make of a diminished thing"), which is answered by the poem itself (the poem is what he "makes" in the face of diminishment).

But Francis is in his own way as bleak as Frost when he discovers unsettling evidence that implies that the natural world reflects an evil design. This terrifying vision is central to his poem "The Orb Weaver" (1960), which, like Frost's sonnet "Design" (1936), centers on the image of a spider entangling its prey as suggestive of nature's malevolence. Though Frost and Francis show a willingness to probe nature's dark design for evidence of an appalling truth (distinguishing them from Thoreau and from Emerson of the First Series Essays), they maintain a safe distance from the horror they depict.

Each poem starts with a vivid description and is followed by a series of reflections. As a consequence, a musing sensibility is established, which then moves toward horror and proceeds to confront it. Frost and Francis cope with the horror through figures of speech, as well as through the language of opinion and argument. The malefic trinity of spider, moth, and flower is domesticated by its comparison to a kitchen "b roth," the murderous orb weaver by its similitude to "plumping" fruits at harvest. The sestet of "Design" and the last stanza of

"The Orb Weaver" are attempts to comprehend and rationalize the reality each poem describes. The poets thus muster up all their verbal resources to keep their awareness of terror and darkness at bay.

The tide of Frost's sonnet invokes the classical argument of design to prove God's existence, into which the poet introduces the nettlesome problem of natural evil. At the heart of this argument is the question of whether what we respond to as natural evil—the destruction of one species by another—proves either that such predation is random and God does not exist, or that there is a malevolent maker.

In this poem, the terror and darkness derive partly from the central situation and precise description of the white trinity of spider, flower, and moth, and partly from Frost's use of pointed irony, which suggests that a ghastly design in nature lurks behind the spider's and the moth's appearance inside an "innocent heal-all." Frost reinforces the use of white with words in the octave such as "snowdrop," which suggests purity, and "froth," which implies something light and frivolous, heightening the irony and horror that the poem so vividly presents:

I found a dimpled spider, fat and white,
On a white heal-all, holding up a moth
Like a piece of rigid satin cloth—
Assorted characters of death and blight
Mixed ready to begin the morning right,
Like the ingredients of a witches' broth—
A snow-drop spider, a flower like a froth,
And dead wings carried like a paper kite.
What had that flower to do with being white,
The wayside blue and innocent heal-all?
What brought the kindred spider to that height,
Then steered the white moth thither in the night?
What but design of darkness to appall?—
If design govern in a thing so small.

To intensify the horror, Frost summons up a world of black magic as he likens the trinity to "the ingredients of a witches' broth—" a concoction out of a conjurer's cookbook.

In the sestet, he poses the question on which the argument hinges. The verbs "brought" and "steered" suggest that these "assorted characters" are the agents of an inscrutable maker, incapable on their own of voluntary movement. As the sonnet rounds off, the closing couplet offers possibilities. The evidence Frost has presented to prove that the world is governed by a fiendish sorcerer (the "design of darkness to appall"), an argument implicitly supported by the poem's controlled rhyme scheme, is set over against the disquieting possibility that evil in nature results from chance ("If design govern in a thing so small").

The subordinating conjunction complicates the argument that has been built up in the poem to this point

Where Frost's sonnet encompasses both interpretations of the argument from design, Francis's "The Orb Weaver" is unequivocal in its view that a malevolent creator is accountable for the predation that the poem describes. Francis evokes the maker from whom darkness and destruction emanate by means of his description of the spider's physical characteristics, his use of suggestive diction, and his depiction of predation as an emblem of horror (in these respects, the poem is a true heir of Frost's sonnet), all of which is interwoven in four tercets divided into two sections by an isolated seventh line, whose falling rhythms reflect the poem's formal design:

Here is the spinner, the orb weaver,
Devised of jet, embossed with sulphur,
Hanging among the fruits of summer,
Hour after hour serenely sullen,
Ripening as September ripens,
Plumping like a grape or melon.
And in its winding sheet the grasshopper.
The art, the craftsmanship, the cunning,
The patience, the self-control, the waiting,
The sudden dart and the needled poison.
I have no quarrel with the spider
But with the mind or mood that made her
To thrive in nature and in man's nature.

Francis's description implies that the spider is designed

for its environment. The creature's "jet" and "sulphur" tints, the latter of which is "embossed" on its "plumping" body, like an adornment, blend in perfectly "among the fruits of summer." With "jet," Francis associates the spider with evil and emphasizes the sinister quality of its jewel-like beauty, in that the word refers both to a colour and to a type of lustrous coal that was used to fashion personal ornaments. In line 2, the verb "devised" suggests that there is a maker (who is vaguely referred to as a "mind or mood" in the last tercet), which intimates that the spider's presence amid such thriving is the result of design rather than chance. Francis's diction helps create the feeling that a maleficent mover is hovering ominously over this grim tableau of a "sullen" predator "ripening" alongside summer's fruits. "Waiting" is the key hover word here.

A close inspection of the last words in each line reveals that a design is built into the poem's structure. The effect of each line's falling rhythms, as in "weaver," "sulphur," "ripens," and "melon," is twofold. First, it suggests that the poem has a formal design, which supports the argument for an evil design that operates in such small degree in nature (this is also the case in Frost's sonnet). Second, this rhythm sets up expectations so that we come to anticipate a falling off at the end of each line. Francis keeps this rhythm in the isolated line but surprises us with the shocking image of the "grasshopper" wrapped in "a winding sheet."

The closing tercets, which are sunk deep in the language of opinion and argument, stand in striking relationship to the opening section and the isolated line. After the shock of line 7, Francis copes with the intractable through words that reveal his appreciation for the spider's skills: its "art," "craftsmanship," "self-control," and "patience." The tone becomes incantatory, with the nouns accumulating one after another in a kind of verbal hold against horror. But rather than marvel at the spider's natural predatory instincts, adaptability, and survival skills, Francis becomes engaged in a "quarrel" with its maker in the last lines, where he introduces the word "I" for the first time in the poem. He uses language that verges on standard rhetoric, as if to capture his effort to comprehend an appalled sense of reality in which evil flourishes "in nature and in man's nature."

As his "spider" poem shows, Francis, like Frost, incorporates into his poetics a perception of nature that is quite different from the benign view he presents in many of his other poems. Earlier, in discussing Frost, I ventured a brief description of his doubleness as involving contrasting stances toward nature, one of which correlated with his laissez-faire inclination to "let the world come as it would." At this point, I want to consider (in relation to Francis) the other Frost who aggressively asserts his will in resistance to nature, particularly in poems when this stance masks his characteristic wariness at entering into an experiential darkness.

As Richard Poirier defines it, this state of mind expresses itself in Frost's lyrics as "a sense of 'nothingness' or a condition of vacancy," which, according to Poirier, Frost "seems more often to have contrived in order that he may then ostentatiously resist it". "His poems," Poirier goes on, tend again and again to break away from the condition of "bar renness" by means of some abrupt, syntactically and formally signaled change of tone: "They cannot scare me with their empty spaces," or so he says in the last stanza of "Desert Places."

It would appear, then, that Frost evokes this emotional condition not so much to confront it as to shrug it off and flex some poetic muscle. When he takes up this posture, Frost becomes, in Poirier's words, "a performing presence". In contrast, Francis adopts a stance of detached engagement in relation to his "vacancy." Instead of striking a posture of resistance, he explores his condition by becoming simultaneously an observer and the observed, which is to describe a kind of "hovering" between being both subject and object.

As Poirier's comments suggest, Frost's posturing is a calculated maneuver. His remarks are pertinent to what is perhaps Frost's best-known poem. In "Stopping by Woods on a Snowy Evening," Frost's evocation of "barrenness "is a conscious tactic that extends to a strategy of self-idealization, whereby the poet, in shrugging off this condition and asserting his will, disguises his characteristic wariness as tough-minded resistance. At the start, Frost stops his horse in a remote and hauntingly stark landscape on the "darkest evening of the year" between "woods and frozen lake." His experiential condition is represented here by the darkness of the woods that he watches "fill up with snow." The prospect of losing himself in their dense deepness is what he must resist, a prospect that is at once seductive ("lovely") and terrible ("dark"):

The woods are lovely, dark, and deep,
But I have promises to keep,
And miles to go before I sleep,
And miles to go before I sleep. (224-25)

As Poirier notes, Frost's characteristic way of treating self-erasure is to imagine it "as a snowfall which obliterates signs of life"). The poet resists the attraction of losing himself and being swept into oblivion, and thus never enters into the woods. He refuses to submit to nature and, in effect, resists a sort of laissez-faire inclination to go with the natural course of things. Instead, he doggedly asserts that he must get on with living, a realization signaled by the interjection of "But" in the line just before the repetend. The last two lines reinforce that he must be going and attend to the obligations of life.

No less calculating than the posture Frost strikes is the account he related to biographer Lawrance Thompson concerning the poem's composition. As Thompson tells it, Frost had just completed a rough draft of "New Hampshire" at dawn in June 1922. After a short walk outside of his home in Vermont, Frost returned inside, "picked up his pen," began to write a poem, and "seemed to hear the words, as though they were spoken to him, and he wrote them down as best he could, in his fatigue, even though they came so indistinctly at times he was uncertain what he heard". "In a short time," Thompson writes, "and without too much trouble," Frost composed the poem. However, Thompson acknowledges that the poet "was extremely inconsistent in his various accounts of how he wrote 'Stopping By Woods'". Frost often "slipped into the posture of claiming he wrote the èntire poem 'with one stroke of the pen,'" an account that friend and fellow poet John Ciardi reported Frost told him "time and again". At other ti mes, Frost discussed "the difficulties confronted in the writing of it," as he had in 1946 when his comments were published in Preface to Poetry.

But more often than not, as Thompson points out, "thereafter he repeated his idealized version of the event." Frost's preferred account of the poem's composition has a bearing on Poirier's reading of his poems, for, like the tenacious, willful stance that Frost takes up in them, it implies that he consciously cultivated an "idealized version" of himself, which goes beyond the poems to the ficticns he created about how they came into being.

His personal ambition and private grief gave him reasons for cultivating an idealized persona. This image helped shape the public's perception of him as a tough-minded realist, one strikingly at odds with the poet who was insecure about his reputation, and with the troubled man who was emotionally devastated by the calamities that befell his children. Frost's competitive ambition compelled him to guard the reputation he had won for himself when his early books received critical acclaim.

In one instance, as Thompson relates, Frost recruited influential publisher Alfred Harcourt to correct what he felt was Ezra Pound's misleading impression in a critique of North of Boston that he had gone to England because "he felt snubbed by American editors". For a man so very conscious of the public eye, "there was," as Donald Hall writes, "room for only one at the top of the steeple". Frost's idealized self-image also served as a guise to protect him from falling into the abyss of despair and suicide. W hat with the death of his firstborn child from cholera at age three, the institutionalization of the second oldest of his four daughters, the suicide of his son, and the death of his youngest daughter after childbirth, he knew grief and despair. The darkness and the terror in his poems are real. In Hall's words, Robert Frost lived in terror of madness and suicide.When he wrote the poems that told the terror, and that summoned the intelligence to control the terror, he suffered in the writing.

Frost thus created a persona both for the sake of public approval and for warding off deep-seated, even suicidal, fears.

Francis, on the other hand, doesn't resort to self-idealized assertion. If Frost posits "a condition of vacancy" in his poems to ostentatiously resist it, then Francis is perhaps more receptive than Frost to a detached contemplation of this condition. He explores the "vacancy" by appropriating to himself the role of outside observer. Francis's "The Spy," from The Face Against the Glass (1950), presents this condition in terms of a consciousness that is dislocated from itself. The paradoxical situation that the poem describes is that of an unnamed man looking through the window into his "empty house. in the moonlight" after he has left it, "spying," like a Stevensian snowman, "Upon the man who is and is not there":

To leave his empty house yet not to leave it
But make himself a shadow at a window-
Who is this prowler private in the moonlight?
Then at another window and another
His face against the glass and peering in-
What does he think he sees or wants to see?
Soft as milkweed floss the September night
White as milkweed the untroubled moon
Whose face, though far, is also at the window.
Two faces, but the prowler peers in deeper
Spying upon the empty chair, spying
Upon the man who is and is not there. (169)

David Graham suggests that the "man who 'is and is not' present is. the poet". In his autobiography, Francis described the time in his life during which he was writing the poem as a "period of crisis":

I wanted to shrink into my psychic shell,. Night after night, soon after supper, my house became dark and inhospitable. In one sense I was very much at home and in another sense very much not at home. (83)

(Among the crises he faced at this time were a rejection

by Macmillan of The Face against the Glass and the financial burden he incurred when he decided to print the book at his own expense.) The profound isolation that defined his life during this emotionally trying period is imaged in the figure of a "prowler private in the moonlight" and in the "empty" house and chair. The vacant house into which he peers alludes to an emptiness seen from outside, which suggests an inner feeling of isolation.

To this sense of isolation, Francis adds a tinge of anxiety as his description of a picturesque evening lighted by the moon's "untroubled" face invites a comparison with the prowler's spying in at the window. In relation to the face against the glass, the moon's reflection is "far" from the prowler, a distance that intensifies his loneliness. Moreover, the glow of the September night, "soft as milkweed floss," and the pearly colour of the moon, "white as milkweed," illuminate, by contrast, his condition of inward darkness.

As the poem concludes and the moon and the prowler are directly compared, the "prowler peers in deeper" than the moon. "Spying upon the empty chair," he cannot see, ultimately, through his inward darkness.

Instead of demonstrating Frostian self-assertion and resistance to his condition, the speaker remains as he was at the beginning of the poem: dislocated and uncertain, at home and not at home, there and not there, in and out, detached yet paradoxically engaged in the act of watching himself, as if to see how he might appear to the stranger on the other side of the glass. Hovering on the outside looking in, reflecting on his emotional condition, the prowler is not at all the "aged" figure in Frost's "An Old Man's Winter's Night," who responds to the "out-of-doors" that looks "darkly in at him" by making noise, by "clomping" in empty rooms" and "beating on a box", by resisting rather than exploring the darkness. Francis's achievement here of hovering, being both subject and object, being detached from himself yet contemplatively receptive to his "vacancy," defines the way he outgrows Frost's influence.

Francis had made it a project of sorts in his writing to retire from view and detach himself from his poems. "My aim is to get outside myself by means of my poems," he once observed in an interview. "That is, I want to give birth to poems that will detach themselves from me and have a life of their own". In his comments, Francis deemphasizes his presence in favour of the poem itself, a characteristic that Donald Hall noted in writing about Francis's work in "Two Poets Named Robert": "He's invisible—one would not consider him confessional!—yet the imprint of an idiosyncratic vision gives [his] poems their textured particularity". To return to "The Spy" for a moment, where the prowler-poet "make[s] himself a shadow at a window," Francis, in this context, suggests a link between the self-effacement he aims for and the writing of poetry. The English word poet comes from the ancient Greek word for maker. For Francis, writing poetry is closely connected to the aim of detached eng agement implied by this image of the prowler; his "making" is a shadowing of the self rather than an asserting of the will.

It should come as no surprise that Francis found a metaphor for detached engagement in nature. The poem "Cypresses," published in The Orb Weaver (1960) but written in 1957 during the year he spent in Italy as a fellow of the American Academy of Rome, entwines his habit of seeing natural forms as emblems of conduct with the Stoic turning to nature for instruction. In this case, he draws on the symbolic association of cypresses with mourning to emphasize the "dark" lesson they impart; the trees teach "birds. How to be shadows." Like the birds, Francis is detached in darkness but engaged in singing:

At noon they talk of evening and at evening
Of night, but what they say at night
Is a dark secret.
Somebody long ago called them the Trees
Of Death and they have never forgotten.
The name enchants them.
Always an attitude of solitude
To point the paradox of standing
Alone together.
How many years they have been teaching birds

In little schools, by little skills,
How to be shadows.

Francis's choice of birds as the objects of nature's instruction might seem curious at first, but a brief consideration of the source of the poem, as well as the particular context in which he used this image, or had seen it used by Frost, make readily apparent the reason for his choice. His own earlier use of the bird in "The Wood Pewee," which echoed Frost's "The Oven Bird," and the fact that "Cypresses" owes its origins to the visits he paid to the graves of Shelley and Keats, shaded by "the tall cypresses of the Protestant Cemetery" in Rome, are hints that he regarded the bird as an image of the poet. In the context of his aim to detach himself from his poems, the withdrawal of birds into trees to become "shadows" strikes a personal chord for Francis, one that is more resonant perhaps than his homage to poets for whom the birds are surrogates.

This notion of withdrawal accords with Francis's disposition against a poetry of idealized self-assertion. Writing about the poetry of his contemporaries in The Satirical Rogue on Poetry, Francis's reflections on their work reveal his own predilection for detachment: "What I suffer from in other people's poetry is many things, according to poet and poem. But perhaps most of all from the too obtrusive presence of the poet himself".

Later in the same book, he adds, "Much poetry today [1968] gives us the poet himself or herself in massive doses". Coming from a man who took Thoreau literally and withdrew into near seclusion on the outskirts of Amherst, his reflections are consistent with the principles by which he lived. Francis's predilection for detachment, as well as his disinclination to write about himself, explain why he avoids self-promotion in his poetry (in contrast to Frost) and takes up an idiosyncratic perspective as an onlooker of himself. From this perspective, he achieves a distance that allows him to explore, engage, and ultimately accept his "condition of vacancy" even though what is being "accepted" (as in "The Spy") is defeat of a sort.

As I pointed out earlier, it was Frost himself who gave

Francis advice that he later transformed into the stance he takes up in his poems. In A Time to Talk, Francis jotted down what he remembered Frost had said to him during one of their visits in an entry dated April 2, 1933. One remark, in particular, stands out: 'You've got to learn to hover," Frost told him. This remark makes its way into one of the last poems Francis wrote before he died in 1987, "For the Ghost of Robert Frost." The poem is at once a tribute to his mentor and a personal anthem, for out of these words he forges a metaphor for detached engagement, which describes his rigorous way of life and the aim of his writing:

"You've got to learn to hover,"
He said. The way a hummingbird
Hovers over a flower, the way
The flower's fragrance hovers over it.
Not to move on, not to
Keep jumping like a nervous grasshopper
But to hover there until you
Have gathered all that is there
For you or anyone to gather.
"You've got to learn to hover."

Through the image of a hummingbird fluttering over a flower, Francis describes a moment of equipoise. At this point, poise and contemplation are in harmonious balance. As we have seen in Francis's dark-spirited poems, he converts hovering to imaginative activity, detachment to receptivity (rather than resistance), and self-effacement (rather than self-assertion) to engagement. In the end, Francis took Frost's advice more to heart than Frost ever did.

Critical Analysis of " After Apple-Picking" by Experts.

Reuben A. Brower

There is no question here of tones playing against a traditional form; rather, an original rhythmic form grows out of the dramatic setting and the initial commitment in tone. Pre-sleep and sleepy reminiscence of the day condition all that is said, and the speaker's first words show what form his dreamy talk will take. His 'ladder's sticking through a tree'—which is accurate and earthy—but 'through a tree Toward heaven.' As the apple-picker drowses off, narrative of fact about the ice skimmed from the trough gets mixed with dream, and the time references of the tenses become a bit confused:

But I was well
Upon my way to sleep before it fell,
And I could tell
What form my dreaming was about to take.

'Could tell' and 'was about to take' seem to refer both to the morning and to the present state of 'drowsing off.'

Everything said throughout the poem comes to the reader through sentences filled with incantatory repetitions and, rhymes and in waves of sound linked by likeness of pattern. From the opening lines, apparently matter-of-fact talk falls into curious chain-like sentences, rich in end-rhymes and, echoes of many sorts. But although the voice seems to be lapsing into the rhyming fits of insomnia, the fits shape themselves into distinct and subtly varied patterns. Each phase of reminiscence or reflection forms a unit of syntax, all except two without a final stop within the unit; and each unit becomes in effect a stanza marked off by one or two rhyming 'seals.' The last word either introduces a new rhyme that will be picked up in the next stanza:

- Off.
- break.
- it is.

or else it completes a rhyme used earlier and with one exception not used again:

- now.
- take.
- clear.
- in.
- desired.
- worth.
- sleep.

The rhymes of the first type link stanza to stanza. Those of the second type increase the sense of monotonous sameness within each phase, as memories of waking fact and their sleepy distortions become impossible to tell apart. Since the word 'sleep' (10) has already occurred five times, it completes the rhyme and the poem with a special finality of sound and meaning.

The meaning implied by the self-hypnosis and dreamy confusion of rhythm is finely suggested in the image of 'the world of hoary grass,' the blurred seeing of morning that anticipates the night vision. This blurring of experience focuses in the central metaphor of the poem, 'essence of winter sleep.' 'Essence' is both the abstract 'ultimate nature' of sleep and the physical smell, 'the scent of apples'—a metaphysical image in T. S. Eliot's sense of the term. Fragrance and sleep blend, as sight and touch merge in

I cannot rub the strangeness from my sight.

The metaphor is renewed in many other expressions, for example, in 'Magnified apples,' which are apples seen against the sky with daylight accuracy, and also great dream-like spheres. Other similarly precise details are 'blurred through the over-and-over way of recalling and describing them: 'stem end and blossom end,' 'load on load, 'ten thousand thousand.' The closing metaphor of the poem, the woodchuck's 'long sleep,' adds to the strangeness of 'winter sleep' by bringing in the non-human death-like sleep of hibernation. We are finally quite uncertain of what is happening, and that is what the poem is about:

One can see what will trouble
This sleep of mine, whatever sleep it is.

In these two lines tone and rhythm work together beautifully, implying a great deal in relation to Frost's metaphor. The slight elevation of 'One can see' recalls the more mysterious seeing of the morning, just as the almost banal lyricism of 'This sleep of mine' sustains the rhythm of dream-confusion. The rest of the second line, barely iambic, barely rhyming, casual and rough, assures us that the speaker has at least one toe in reality. The contrasts of tone and rhythm, fitting the puzzlement of the sleepers state, look ahead to the woodchuck's sleep and back to the initial balance of tones in 'sticking through a tree Toward heaven still.' The poem is absorbed with 'states-between,' not only of winter sleep, but of all similar areas where real and unreal appear and disappear. 'After Apple-Picking' illustrates exactly Santayana's remark that 'the artist is a person consenting to dream of reality.' The 'consent' in this instance is implied in the perfection of the form.

We have now moved well beyond voices and rhythms to 'the figure a poem makes.' For we should hardly have arrived at the amused confusion of the end of 'After Apple-Picking' unless the poem had carried us on a form that was more than rhythmic, however marvelous. It is characteristic of Frost that the 'sentencing' and the sense are surely controlled, that daylight accuracy and daylight humor are present in statement and tone. It is also characteristic that the figure of sound grows from a metaphorical centre.

John J. Conder

The central problems of the poem are posed in the opening lines of its conclusion with the introduction of the ambiguous word "trouble" and the provocative image of "sleep": "One can see what will trouble This sleep of mine, whatever sleep it is." Although the trouble and the "sleep" are intimately connected in the lines, for purposes of analysis it is best to keep them separate. The speaker himself does so, since he apparently knows what will trouble his sleep but is uncertain about the kind of sleep overtaking him. Arranged in the order most convenient for answering them, two questions emerge in "After Apple-Picking": What is the nature of the sleep? What is the nature of the trouble?

A complex of familiar references points to death as one possible form of sleep. The very situation of the poem, a surcease from picking apples, recalls the Garden of Eden from which, after the apple was picked (and eaten), man was expelled into a world of sin and death. The speaker affirms that he was "well" on his way to sleep even before his morning venture with the sheet of ice. Since life is a process ending in death, the speaker's comment, juxtaposed against the reference to "heaven," promotes the possibility that the speaker may be journeying to an immortal sleep. The season of the year emphasizes nature's death, while the woodchuck's hibernation suggests a pattern of death and resurrection.

Intriguing though these references are, a reader familiar with Frost's playful ways ("I like to fool," he said) knows better than to take them hastily at face value. The most popular reading rejects the possibility of death. Since the speaker's dream, according to this account, represents an ideal rooted in the real world, (his ability to dream about a job well done represents his heaven on earth. His capacity for contemplation sets him apart from the inferior woodchuck, though he does not affirm that man has an immortal soul.

Insofar as this reading rejects death and immortality as one possible form of sleep in "After Apple-Picking," the commentary is consistent with a general opinion that Frost is nonteleological in his thought. Since he neither affirms nor denies that the emergence of mind suggests ultimate meaning in the universe, Frost would necessarily remain neutral in his attitude toward immortality. But if the speaker's dream and sleep exist in life, then to assert that, after his labors, the speaker "is now looking not into the world of effort but the world of dream, of the renewal," is to oversimplify the poem. This view identifies the dream (interpreted as pleasurable) with the sleep (seen as a time for contemplation as well as renewal) and in the process limits both.

Such a reading qualifies the word "trouble" into insignificance (to be troubled by a lovely dream is to be superior to the woodchuck, who cannot dream) and oversimplifies the speaker's attitude toward his experience. Given the feats of association that he makes, given the fact that he speaks in contraries, the speaker's attitude toward his sleep is far more complicated than at first seems clear, and his trouble far more real than might be supposed.

The speaker's attitude toward his sleep is complicated because of the possible kinds of sleep overtaking him. To be sure, this may be a night's sleep from which the speaker will awake, refreshed, ready to turn to those "fresh tasks" mentioned by the puzzled speaker of "The Wood-Pile." This possibility is supported by the reference to "night"; it is at "night" that he is "drowsing off"; the speaker, having completed the last of his labors as best he could, may be about to go to bed.

But the association of night with "essence of winter sleep" gives "night" a metaphoric context and so expands its meaning. Indeed, a simple night's sleep seems an improbable meaning, since the speaker was "well" upon his way to sleep before he dropped the "pane of glass" in the morning. Perhaps, then, his drowsy state may be part of the "essence of winter sleep"; that is, perhaps it is a sleep similar to nature's. Enough correspondences between the human and natural worlds exist to dictate this as one possible kind of sleep. The speaker's apple-picking ceases as the year nears conclusion, and his "drowsing off" is associated with "essence of winter sleep":

Essence of winter sleep is on the night,
The scent of apples: I am drowsing off.

If his sleep is to be like nature's, what then is the point of the reference to the woodchuck? Since the woodchuck surely could not ". say whether it's like his Long sleep, as I describe its coming on, Or just some human sleep," the speaker's avowal to the contrary apparently reduces the conclusion to mere whimsy. Presumably woodchucks do not dream and do not desire great harvests.

Men do. Presumably men do not go into physical hibernation for months. Woodchucks do. But the point of the reference to the woodchuck is not simply to create a contrast between a human and an animal sleep but also to introduce an implied comparison—an inexact analogy between the speaker's sleep and the sleep of nature. If only man has the potential to desire great harvests, his desires may follow a cycle similar to nature's. They may wax and wane like (or with) the seasons; they may emerge, as the woodchuck does in the spring, or lie dormant for months, as the woodchuck does in winter.

For the man who is ". overtired Of the great harvest I myself desired," such an analogy carries with it its own measure of reassurance. Assuming that the desire for harvests and the act of harvesting together are an emblem of man's creative spirit working its will on the world, a reader can see that implicit in this situation is the question: Will my desire, my will, my talents be resurrected, directed toward reaping new harvests? Although he would find it more comforting to think that "just some human sleep" is a single night's sleep which will restore his powers so that he can turn to "fresh tasks," he can be reassured by the analogy between man and, the seasons nonetheless. His desires will lie dormant longer, but they will surely be revived, as nature is.

. The speaker himself is uncertain of the analogy, speculating whether his sleep is like the woodchuck's, ". as I describe its coming on, Or just some human sleep" (italics mine). As he has described that sleep coming on, indeed, the speaker clearly has been speaking contraries. The analogy with nature which his associations establish are, in the process of his speaking, undermined by suggestions that the sleep will be different from nature's.

Those suggestions become explicit in the contrast between the sleep of the woodchuck and "just some human sleep." Precisely because the implied comparison between the speaker's sleep and the woodchuck's is undone by the power of the contrast (men can only have a human sleep), the assurance offered by the comparison with nature is also retracted. The contrast between the two kinds of sleep, furthermore, has been anticipated from the beginning of the poem, thus providing the fullest impact to the concluding line, "Or just some human sleep."

From the outset, nature seems to have become alien to the speaker. The first section concludes with the speaker's commenting that he is no longer interested in picking apples, in appropriating nature to his own uses: "But I am done with apple-picking now." The parallel between his drowsiness and the "essence of winter sleep" is, at best, tenuous, held together by an uncommitted colon in the last line of the statement, "Essence of winter sleep is on the night, The scent of apples: I am drowsing off." The "essence," in short, is more directly associated with "the scent of apples" than with the speaker's sleep. The parallel tenuously established by the colon breaks down in the next section, which describes the strange sight of the winter world through a sheet of ice. Perhaps he does see through this "glass" "the world of hoary grass," but even that is not certain, and no other object in the external world he views is mentioned.

Before he describes the "form" of his dreaming, he significantly lets the pane of ice fall and break, an action in stark contrast to his behaviour during the harvest, when he took special pains to keep the apples from falling. Of course, since the ice is melting, the gesture is perfectly normal. Deliberate mention of the detail, nonetheless, suggests his alienation from nature. Once he could handle it (in the literal and metaphoric senses of that term); now he cannot.

If the speaker is divorced from nature, then what would "just some human sleep" be? One can concede that the speaker is physically and mentally fatigued, his desire for a "great harvest" satiated. In that case it is possible that he is entering the world of renewal, that his sleep will be composed of pleasant dreams, a contemplation of the ideal based on the real; and it is possible that his trouble will be minimal, composed of the physical aftereffects of too much apple-picking: the "ache" and the "pressure" retained by his "instep arch"; the feel of the swaying ladder; the "rumbling sound" of apples. But it is not at all certain that his is the sleep of renewal.

Indeed, to argue with certainty that this is the sleep of renewal, a reader would have to rest his case on the analogy between man's cycle and nature's, an analogy that seems to fail in the poem. Such an analogy, furthermore, would not be consistent with Frost's point of view, one which sharply differentiates man from nature. Both Frost's habit of speaking contraries and his point of view toward nature militate against a simplistic view of sleep and argue for a darker side of "just some human sleep."

That darker side can be discerned by recalling what is lost by the failure of the analogy between man and nature. If nature can renew itself automatically, man, viewed as distinct from nature, cannot be assured of such renewal. Nature has her unknown source of creative revival. What is man's? The source of his creativity is the assumption that his harvest has value, that the activity is worthwhile. If the speaker questions the purpose of his activity, doubts the value of his harvest, then indeed his may be a sleep of the creative powers, one which will last until the doubts are removed.

The speaker makes it eminently clear that he once highly valued his harvest. Simply put, he "desired" a "great harvest," and the desire was sufficiently strong to justify extraordinary discipline and control: "There were ten thousand thousand fruit to touch, Cherish in hand, lift down, and not let fall." The sense of value which he associated with manual contact ("cherish in hand") is confirmed in the lines immediately following:

For all
That struck the earth,
No matter if not bruised or spiked with stubble,
Went surely to the cider-apple heap
As of no worth.

The crucial phrase, "As of no worth," is ambiguous and reflects the speaker's habit of "talking contraries," of retracting "everything. [he] said, nearly. "For to describe the fallen apples as "of no worth" is to imply their worth. It is not possible to tell whether the speaker, now commenting with the advantage of hindsight, would have characterized these apples in the same way during his actual apple-picking. What is clear is that this description of his past activities implies a sense of relative values (fallen apples are inferior to harvested ones), but a highly ambiguous one. Since the speaker has declared that ". I am overtired Of the great harvest I myself desired," he is in a mood to apply the same logic of talking contraries to the harvest itself. If the fallen apples are as "of no worth," then he hints, the harvest itself is as of great worth, a description which implies its opposite. The exhausted speaker, in short, is in doubt about his values.

Doubts related to questions of value are in his mind as he

recounts his apple-picking, so it is not surprising that the dream induced by his venture reflects his confusion. It is by no means certain, of course, whether the "dreaming" is confined to the visual description of the apples or whether it includes all the aftereffects of picking apples. Since this is probably more than a simple night's sleep, it is likely that the dream is much like one experienced when awake, as when a person still feels the rocking of the boat even after he has set foot on firm land.

Assuming that the dream embraces, the full range of sensations, the reader can observe a striking contrast between the visual and the other sensory elements. Only the apples are "magnified"; there is no suggestion that the "ache," the "pressure," the swaying of the ladder and the rumbling of the apples are felt and heard more intensely than during the actual pursuit of the harvest. Not only are the apples larger than life; they are also autonomous, independent of the speaker's control as they appear in the mind's eye: "Magnified apples appear and disappear."

The erratic movement of the apples, certainly, may be quite consistent with the nature of this dream, one experienced when awake. Stare at an object long enough and its impression is retained after the eyes are closed. The eyelids blink shut, and the speaker sees apples. They flick open, and the apples vanish. Quite possibly the image so retained is magnified. But for readers concerned with the depth of the actual in Frost's poetry, such an explanation is hardly sufficient.

Frost no doubt wants to show that the form of the speaker's dreaming is a consequence of the activity which inspired it, since the speaker concludes the dream with the statement, "For I have had too much Of apple-picking: I am overtired" (italics mine), and then describes the apple-picking itself. To settle for a purely naturalistic explanation of the relationship between the two, however, is to limit the poem.

A comparison between the dream and the activity is revealing for what the dream leaves out, and such a comparison must be based on the visual element in the dream, since all the other elements are ascribable to purely natural aftereffects and bear no symbolic relationship to the whole point of picking as many apples as possible: to reap a great harvest.

That sense of discipline associated with value during the apple-picking is not present in the dream. The apples are unrelated to the speaker, moving of their own accord, without his direction, his sense of purpose. Furthermore, they are all magnified; the distinction between those harvested and those lost does not exist. Gone is the speaker's sense of relative values. Associated with the statement ". I am overtired Of the great harvest I myself desired," their magnification and autonomy bring into bold relief the very doubts surfacing toward the end of his description of the actual venture of picking apples. He has literally lost sight of all the values of the harvest. If this is a happy sleep of contemplation, the happiness is highly qualified.

Concerned about his values, the speaker is also concerned about the nature of his sleep, a concern imaged in the contrast between himself and the woodchuck. As part of nature the woodchuck will automatically be renewed. But the speaker may need, for renewal, not simply rest, some period of dormancy, but also some certain knowledge of human values. And where is such knowledge to come from? Recall, this is a poem about what happens after apple-picking. Hardly an allegory either supporting or denouncing Christian doctrine, the work nonetheless relies on overtones of the Fall to enrich its complex meaning.

When man first picked the apple, he was expelled from Eden to labour by the sweat of his brow, a consequence of his newly found knowledge of good and evil. The speaker lives in a fallen world where he has labored and sweated. But he gains no sure knowledge as Adam did. His ladder is pointed toward heaven only, and he has had to descend from it. Man can climb the ladder toward heaven, toward certainty, but when he returns, he discovers how little he has learned with certainty. He cannot even know the nature of his sleep, although the possibilities seem clear.

Perhaps his will be like the woodchuck's sleep, the sleep

of nature, in the limited sense that his creative powers are subject to the same kind of cyclical movement observed in the seasons. At worst, this sleep would be like nature's in its duration, though not in its character (unlike nature, man can dream). Such a sleep, induced by physical and mental fatigue, is not a function of man's uncertain values. His values are certain; his ability to act on them, limited. This is the sleep of renewal.

This meaning of "sleep," though possible in the poem, seems obviated by the apparent failure of the analogy between man and nature. Although Frost allows for its possibility in the reference to the woodchuck, such a sleep seems inconsistent with his larger view of man and nature. A second possible sleep, not far removed from the first, is also ascribable to a straining of the physical and mental powers, a strain just severe enough to confuse the speaker's sense of values and to blur his sense of purpose.

But if he originally possessed a firmly grounded sense of value and purpose, he can be reasonably certain he will awaken from this sleep, from this confusion about values. A good rest, a night's or a month's, will settle the matter. Thereafter, he can turn to "fresh tasks" with no need to investigate his values. Given Frost's larger poetic world, this meaning is the most likely. The will to live and to create provides the ground for man's values.

But in the world of "After Apple-Picking," recovery is not certain. Frost's "feats of association" are so complicated, his performance in hinting so masterful, that the poem suggests the possibility of a third kind of sleep. If the speaker's encounter with the apples has led him to question not just the nature, but the source of his values, then, hi sleep may be longer, even permanent. It is one matter to recover values lost because of fatigue. It is another to be forced to return to their source, particularly if that source is only the "I myself" who "desired." For when desire fails and values falter, what source outside the self can restore desire? In "After Apple-Picking," the ladder only points toward heaven.

What will trouble the speaker's sleep, whatever sleep it

is? He is only falling asleep in this poem, and he does not yet know which sleep his will be. Its duration will determine its nature. It is his uncertainty as to when (or whether) he will awaken which will be carried into his sleep, troubling it. Ironically enough, only when he awakens will he know what sleep it is—or, rather, was.

Bibliography

The Poetry of Robert Frost by *R.A. Brower* (1960)

Robert Frost by *P.L. Gerber* (1966, rev. ed. 1982)

Frost by *E. Jennings* (1966); Robert Frost

The Early Years, 1874-1915 by *L. Thompson* (1966) Robert Frost:

The Years of Triump, 1915-1938 by *L. Thompson* (1970);

Robert Frost by *E. Barry* (1973);

Robert Frost: The Later Years, 1938-1963 by *L. Thompson and R.H. Winnick* (1976);

Robert Frost and New England *by J.C. Kemp* (1979)

Robert Frost Handbook by *J.L. Potter* (1980)

Frost: A Literary Life Reconsidered *W.H. Pritchard* (1984)

Robert Frost Himself by *Stanley Burnshaw* (1986)

A Restless Spirit: The Story of Robert Frost by *N. Bober* (1991)

The Poetry of Robert Frost by *J.R. Doyle Jr.* (1991)

The Poems of Robert Frost by *M. Narcus* (1991)

Robert Frost: A Biography by *Jeffrey Meyers* (1996)

Robert Frost: A Life by *Jay Parini* (1999)

